Appetite

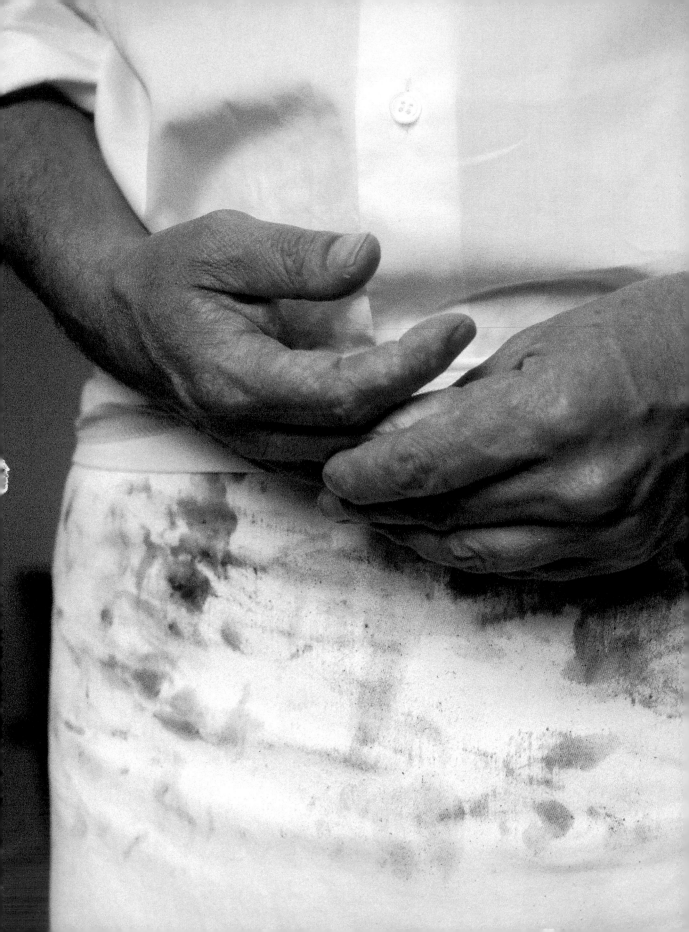

Appetite

so what do you want to eat today?

Nigel Slater

Photographs by Jonathan Lovekin

FOURTH ESTATE • London

For Louise, Jonnie and
Digger, Magrath and Poppy

First published in Great Britain in 2000

by Fourth Estate Limited 6 Salem Road London W2 4BU

www.4thestate.co.uk

Copyright © Nigel Slater 2000

1 3 5 7 9 10 8 6 4 2

The right of Nigel Slater to be identified as the author of this work has been asserted
by them in accordance with the Copyright, Designs and Patents Act 1988.

A catalogue record for this book is available from the British Library.

ISBN 1 84115 288 9

Designed by Vivid Design

Printed in Italy by L.E.G.O S.p.A.

and thanks to . . .

Michael Asare Jonathan Attwood and Bluebird Adrian Barling
Vicky Barnsley and everyone at Fourth Estate Catherine Blyth
Robert Breckman Jane Clarke Chantal Coady Kate Dawkins
Tamasin Day-Lewis Sheryl Garratt Louise Haines Celia Hayley
Kathryn Holliday Allan Jenkins Sybil Kapoor
Nigella Lawson Jonathan Lovekin Lillie Lovekin Patricia Michelson
and everyone at La Fromagerie Jane Middleton Sara Neale
Richard Partin Nung Puinongpho Rosemary Scoular and everyone
at PFD Chris Shamwana and everyone at Vivid Simon Walton
Ruth Watson Frances Whitaker Araminta Whitley and everyone
at LAW Lorna Wing Tracey Winwood Delia and Michael and
everyone at the magazine

. . . for being completely brilliant

Contents

Introduction

I want to tell you about the pleasure, the sheer unbridled joy, of cooking without a recipe. If this sounds scary let me qualify. I want to reveal the delight to be had from making our own decisions about what we eat rather than slavishly following someone else's set of rules, and to suggest that much of our cooking has become too complicated – hence the need to attach ourselves so firmly to recipes – when in truth good eating depends on nothing more than fine ingredients simply cooked.

Think how good a grilled Dover sole is with its drizzle of hazelnut-coloured butter and little slick of creamed spinach. Think of a steak hot from the grill, its edges salty and caught a bit on the pan; or a dish of sizzling greens flavoured with nothing but garlic and oyster sauce. Imagine hot pasta with just a sauce of melting Gorgonzola; purple sprouting and a simple hollandaise; a bowl of steaming noodles in broth with nought but hot garlic and chilli; lamb left to braise with red wine and herbs or a chicken roast golden with butter and lemon. Not one of these is a complex recipe whose every word you must obey. It is good food without pretension. Yet food that you could adapt a little in order to suit your mood or your appetite.

As much as a recipe can help an inexperienced cook produce something to eat, it can also act as a straitjacket, a set of rules that confine and restrict the cook. Recipes are all well and good, and I do not disapprove of them *per se* (I love the way classic recipes are handed down through the years, generation after generation, as part of a country's culture) but what I do feel is that there is a huge difference between following a recipe and learning to cook.

It is worth remembering that in its purest form a recipe was simply a cook's receipt written in a ledger to show where the housekeeping money had gone. At best it was an account of someone's meal, an *aide-mémoire* for the cook who might want to make a successful supper again. To use either as an unshakeable chemical formula is surely missing the point.

I do not intend or wish to put down those lists of amounts and techniques, it is simply that I have come to believe we have become too reliant on the printed recipe and less thoughtful about the ingredient itself, what it wants and what we want from it.

I have for years wondered how it is that some of us get so much satisfaction from making ourselves, our family, our friends and our lovers something to eat while others hate every last second of it. I have come to the conclusion that this could mean we are doing too much, and have been encouraged to make our daily cooking too difficult. I believe there is more pleasure to be had in good ingredients uncontrived. In other words, let the ingredients speak louder than the cook.

If that is the case, and I am pretty sure it is, then it is the recipe, that list of rules and regulations, that is partly to blame. How I look at it is this: if you have something that has been produced or grown with integrity and that you have chosen for its quality of flavour, freshness, or the fact that it is at its point of ultimate ripeness, then it seems pointless (frankly, stupid) to mask its perfection with a mass of other flavours. This does not mean that spices, herbs, aromatics and other ingredients should not be involved, rather that they should be chosen and used carefully and judiciously. Get complicated and we have somehow, surely, lost the point of the main ingredient.

I am convinced that a recipe should not be a set of rules to be followed to the letter for a mind-numbingly uniform result, but when I hear someone praising a recipe because it always works my heart sinks a little. Is that all there is to it? A recipe must work? Surely there is more to it than that. I believe a recipe should be treated as a living thing, something allowed to breathe, to change its nature to suit our ingredients, our mood and our desires.

Have new cooks really come to rely on a set of regimented, foolproof orders that forbid them to use their own gut instincts? To me, there are few greater pleasures than cooking without being glued to a recipe, few more rewarding things than following our own instincts and common sense. Do not ignore those hundreds, thousands, of recipes published every year – there is much fun to be had with them – but I want to suggest, actually to beg, that sometimes we should use them lightly, instead following our own thoughts and hunches.

I want to encourage you to take in the spirit of the recipes that follow but then to deviate according to your ingredients and your feelings. To understand that both our ingredients and our hunger are variables that should not, cannot, be subjected to a set of formulas laid down in tablets of stone. I want to get you to break the rules. I want you to follow your appetite.

why cook?

You don't have to cook. You can send out for a pizza, queue for a hamburger, nuke a ready-made meal in the microwave, or book a table in a restaurant. You can pour water on a pot noodle, stop off for a Chinese takeaway or simply live on toast. I know this because I have done it. If you cook you will only have to trudge round the shops, get your clothes and kitchen dirty, have pots and pans to wash, your hands will smell of onions or fish and then everyone will only eat it anyway. Hours of work for minutes of pleasure. So why bother?

As I said, you don't have to cook. You can get through life perfectly comfortably without lifting so much as a wooden spoon. Fine. Do that. What I want to say is that if you do decide to go through life without cooking you are missing something very, very special. You are losing out on one of the greatest pleasures you can have with your clothes on. Cooking can be as passionate, creative, life-enhancing, uplifting, satisfying and downright exhilarating as anything else you can do with your life. Feeling, sniffing, chopping, sizzling, grilling, frying, roasting, baking, tasting, licking, sucking, biting, savouring and swallowing food are pleasures that would, to put it mildly, be a crime to miss out on. Add to that the buzz, the satisfying tingle that goes down your spine when you watch someone eating something you have made for them, and you have one of the greatest joys known to man.

food talk

Food and cooking have always attracted the worst sort of snobbery. Probably more so than any other subject. The fact is, something is either good to eat or it isn't. Simple as that. Why should it matter whether it is a skewer of chicken we eat on the beach in Bali, an exquisite lunch in a Michelin-starred restaurant in Paris, or a vast bowl of spaghetti we knock up one weekday night at home? There are times when a sausage sandwich made with soft white bread and mustard is quite as delicious as a Thai chicken curry that uses eighteen ingredients. Equally, just because a chef bones

and stuffs, sieves and blends, and reduces his sauces to the consistency of Marmite doesn't mean his food is too showy for its own good, in much the same way as a sandwich can never be too simple. If it rings your bell, then fine. No one should ever think they have the sole right to say what is good or what isn't.

And don't let anyone tell you that the food is the only thing that matters. That's rubbish. Where you eat something, who you eat it with and what you do afterwards is just as important. Eating is a whole package, not just what is on the plate. Food always tastes better in the right place, whether it is fish and chips eaten walking along the seafront or *steak frites* in Paris. Why people feel a delicate, perfectly honed plate of food in a three-star restaurant has the moral high ground over a really good hamburger is beyond me. If both are good to eat, fine examples of their kind, and please you, then fine. Good food is good food.

getting started

So what do we really want to eat? Few of us have the luxury of eating absolutely anything we want to. There are constraints of money, health, availability, and the question of who else we are cooking for. Then I suppose we have to consider our own capabilities. There is also a cultural question. I was brought up to eat meat and two veg. A meal wasn't considered a meal unless there was meat on the plate and a pudding afterwards. It took quite a while for me to realise that the meals I was eating were far from what I actually wanted to eat or how I wanted to eat it. Meals were prepared that way out of habit, without giving a second's thought to the fact that there was an alternative. The idea that sometimes a bowl of soup and some bread would have sufficed would not have been entertained.

As a family, we ate at the table and always with a knife and fork. We never, for instance, ate out of bowls, like the Chinese eat most of their meals and the Italians eat their pasta. We would never have eaten with our hands, save the odd ham sandwich, and even that was cut up into triangles so we could hold it with two fingertips. I didn't hold chopsticks till I was in my twenties. This social conformity stood against everything I felt about food: that eating should be a relaxed affair, eaten in whatever way feels right. The idea of eating at anything other than set times of the day would have been anathema to my parents. My current habit of sitting down to eat at nine o'clock at night would have been unthinkable to them.

The rules have been broken. Most of us now eat more or less what and when we want to. Meals are less rigid, eaten semi-formally at a table, casually from a dish, or in front of television, and I suspect there are few people who would think twice about tucking into something from another culture, be it a bowl of Vietnamese hot and sour soup or a vegetable dosa. To say that we are more adventurous in what we eat is a huge understatement. In one week most of us will get through everything from solitary pasta for one to curry for six, a takeaway pizza to a pub lunch, and from a big bowl of Chinese noodles to a proper family Sunday lunch.

The tyranny of the laid table, the strict adherence to the clock, and the meat-and-two-veg mentality have slowly slipped away, opening doors all along the way. Most of us will try anything at least once and we now have more choice than ever before. We have the confidence to eat whatever we want to, ignoring the rules. Have the possibilities for eating well ever looked rosier?

deciding what to eat

Sometimes we can eat just what we feel like, other times we have to think about what the rest of the household may want. They may be family, they may be flatmates. Taking into account what we fancy and what we know of everyone else's likes and dislikes can turn cooking a meal into a bit of a juggling act, and we cannot realistically hope to get it completely right every time. But I would rather have a bit of hit and miss any day than mindless predictability and missed opportunities.

mood food

What we end up eating for supper often has as much to do with our mood as with our tastebuds. How many times have I come home in the sort of grumpy, fractious mood that can only be soothed by a plate of creamy, cheesy pasta? Whose mood hasn't pushed them into making an out-of-character meal, like grilling a red-blooded steak or throwing together some high-energy snack such as a peanut butter sandwich? Who hasn't sought solace in a bowl of soup? Often these choices are a question of texture and temperature as much as taste. Our body may crave hot, creamy, starchy food because it knows it has a soothing effect, or something green, crisp and fresh because it needs something light and cleansing.

What we choose to eat is not always about the flavours we have in our head ('I feel like something garlicky tonight') but is, more often than not, led by our mood and our need to satisfy a physical or psychological urge. In case you think I have completely lost the plot, I should explain that I am simply suggesting that our temperament, our mood, our state of mind are just as likely to help us decide what we want to eat as anything else. And if our supper is to be truly satisfying, then we need to listen to what it is our mood craves. Otherwise our meal will not quite do the trick.

13

planning a meal

There is neither rhyme nor reason to my own meal planning, nor should there be. I see nothing wrong in satisfying a fancy. This is where I don't understand the weekly shop, the one day each week when the food for the next seven days is piled into a shopping trolley and carted home. I do see the practical need for such a system. After all, if we start work at 9am and get home, knackered, at 7pm, or have spent all day looking after the kids, then just when are we supposed do our shopping? The bit I don't understand is how anyone can predict what they will want to eat next Thursday. How is it possible to predict our mood, or fancies, or the weather five days hence?

In an ideal world we would all be able to shop daily, like in those French films where Madame walks round the market every morning with her basket, choosing something for lunch. Well, for most of us, life just ain't like that. We have to compromise. This is where a small stash of fridge and storecupboard staples helps. They can form the backbone of the meal. The rest – the fresh bits (fish, salad, fruit) that make it exciting – we can hopefully buy daily, especially now the shops are open later, even if it means a quick stop-off on the way home to get whatever takes our eye. It is all very well for foodies to go on about buying everything fresh every day, but in practice our meals are often made up of storecupboard supplies and last-minute whims. No matter how much we try, our meals end up being a bit of a compromise. But that doesn't mean they can't be a delicious compromise.

Who are you cooking for?

for yourself

Good, a night alone. We can please ourselves what we eat. I see no reason why we should go to any less trouble when making ourselves something to eat than when we are cooking for others. So often do we end up putting our own wants aside in order to accommodate the likes and dislikes of our family and friends that a meal alone is a golden opportunity to think of no one but ourselves for once. This may mean curling up in front of the television with a bottle of something nice and waiting for the pizza guy to come, or it could be the chance to cook something that we normally wouldn't – the fish, steak, mussels, curry or whatever it is that our other halves so detest. Now is our opportunity to indulge ourselves because no one is there to tut-tut if we eat an entire family-sized pizza and a tub of cookies-and-cream. Or is this the night on which we can live off a huge bowl of salad because there is no one there to demand meat and two veg? This is the night we suit ourselves.

Cooking for yourself on a regular basis is not as straightforward as a once-a-week feel-good supper. You have to cope with the fact that one is not a particularly practical number to cook for. Even a head of broccoli was made for two. A cake can last a week (or, worse, it ends up as your main source of food for a couple of days). Solo cooking is something you may need to get into the swing of, learning what works for you and what doesn't, though inevitably it is the shopping that is the key, and for which I give some pointers below.

The temptation to live off toast and coffee is irresistible at first, but in my experience it soon wears off. I don't think it works to make large amounts of food that will last for three or four days either. I know it seems like a good idea at the time and lots of others recommend it, but I find that by the third day I never want to see stew/ratatouille/shepherd's pie again as long as I live. Yet making something from scratch night after night just for one can soon wear thin, too.

Having someone to cook for other than yourself is probably the best reason to cook, which can sometimes leave the lone diner asking, 'Why should I bother?' My answer to that, and it is only one of many, is simply because it makes you feel good. Think about it: you have no one to answer to, you can spend as much or as little time as you fancy, you can choose exactly what you want to eat and you can wallow in the sheer unhurried pleasure of pleasing yourself. It also means you can stick a finger up to those well-meaning people who say, 'Are you sure you're eating properly?'

diner à deux

For my money, some of the best times are to be had when you are cooking for just one other, when you can stand and talk as you cook (people love watching others cook, there is something slightly voyeuristic about it). This is the sort of occasion where you can do things like fritters, dropping the battered vegetables into hot fat as you chat, eating each one as it is done, tossing them around in your fingers and blowing on them till they are cool enough to break open and eat. Another sound standing-in-the-kitchen supper are those hot, citrus-scented Thai fishcakes, which you can roll and fry whilst you are talking and drinking, dipping each one into chilli sauce as you go. Don't let your friend join in the cooking. Just let them watch.

Most of us eat in the kitchen nowadays. The up side of this is that you confine your mess to one room, and the meal remains low-key, laid-back. The down side is that you will probably be eating surrounded by the mess you made while cooking, and that you cannot get away with anything. A small price to pay for what is the most precious thing on earth – sharing a meal with someone you love. If that sounds schmaltzy, then so be it. To my mind, there are few better reasons to cook.

Most weekday kitchen suppers for two are one-dish meals, with a few drinks and olives beforehand and probably nothing much to follow. Most days there will be a salad, too, or some cheese, and perhaps, if you are lucky, a pudding. But the crux of the matter will probably be a single dish such as a plate of pasta, some chops or, in winter, a stew of some sort. I tend to cook things like lamb shanks with red wine at the weekend and inevitably there is some left for Monday supper, too. Monday-to-Friday meals shouldn't be too involved; no one wants to eat at ten o'clock if they came in at six.

I do like a little pudding, especially comfort foods such as baked apples with cream in winter (no one can tell me they can't chuck a Bramley with a bit of butter and brown sugar in the oven when they come home), but, failing that, I am happy to go along with a piece of cheese and some fruit. Even a few grapes, washed and thoroughly chilled, or in summer a dish of cherries on crushed ice, with stones to spit out and count.

I am not as keen on formal meals for two. You must know those meals where someone has gone overboard with rich food, schmoozy music and seductive lighting. To my mind there is something pathetically contrived about such times. I am not being cynical, it is just that the formality seems to go against the grain here. The whole point of being friends or lovers is that you don't have to stand on ceremony. Far better is a meal that is as informal as possible. There is nothing more indigestible than a meal where you know the cook has gone to too much trouble.

for the family

No matter how you dress it up, the bare facts are that we have to get a meal on the table for several people virtually every day of the year. Or, to be more accurate, several meals, and snacks, and treats, and parties, and just now and again we might like to have some friends round, too. No matter how much we like cooking and putting food out for others it is still an unstoppable roller-coaster of food, plates, pots and pans – and appetites. One meal finishes and we must start thinking about the next one. And the next, and the next and the next. And there's more. We now need to consider the long-term implications of everything we put in our family's mouths; the likes and dislikes of everyone we are cooking for (a nightmare in itself); and cope with the nagging thought, 'Am I doing enough?'

We alone know our own families, what they want, need, like and love. We know what they will wolf down uncomplainingly and when we may have to resort to what amounts to a softly-softly attempt at force-feeding. We alone know how far we are prepared to go to please them (answer: as far as we have to and further still). If I paint a somewhat bleak picture I don't mean to, I mean only to be practical and to bring balance to the rose-tinted cookie-cutter images of family cooking given elsewhere. One thing I am sure of: every bone in my body believes that you should not try and force a child to eat something he or she does not like. I say this from having been one of those children who was forced to eat what my parents thought was good for me.

Cooking for the family is more, much more than simply getting a meal on the table for ourselves. But it can be ultimately more rewarding (though in truth it rarely feels like it). We can get an even bigger buzz out of it. Yet feeding others on a daily basis is different – we cannot skip supper or open a bottle of wine in lieu. We cannot (quite) put pasta on the table every night.

I offer a few practical points here. You can find the cookie-cutter stuff elsewhere.

♦ It will be easier for everyone if you get the whole family used to expecting the same food as soon as possible. I don't mean inflexibly so (we are surely past that now), but I do think there is much to be said for introducing what are considered 'adult' tastes into children's food as soon as possible. Why grate Cheddar to go on kids' pasta when they are going to have to get used to Parmesan sooner or later? Why introduce them to something that tastes skew-whiff when we are only going to have to right it at some point anyway?

♦ Most of us, I expect, don't even want to imagine a life without pasta, especially those of us with children. Whatever the xenophobic meat-'n'-two-veggists say, pasta is now our national dish. The family no longer unites over a joint of beef. It unites over a bowl of pasta. For the sake of all-round peace and harmony I think it sensible to make the most of this.

♦ If noses are ever turned up at one type of pasta, then try another shape. This may sound simplistic, but I know my heart used to sink when I was presented with macaroni, while penne (those nib-shaped sticks) has always filled me with delight. Noodles are a joy beyond belief (you can make a silly noise whilst slurping them up from the bowl), yet possibly the messiest way there is of feeding a family.

♦ Nothing sticks to the floor quite like spaghetti with tomato sauce and Parmesan.

♦ If the entire family likes pasta you can bet they will also like rice, potato-based meals and even couscous. All are equally beige and becalming. I mean this in the nicest possible way. All provide a bland and satiating base to which you can add other favourite ingredients and can all be served with the same bountiful earth-mother generosity as a giant bowl of pasta pesto.

♦ In winter a huge cauldron of bean and vegetable soup is something that you can dip into and heat up in small quantities any time someone comes in cold and hungry and wanting something 'big' to eat. There is something of the 'feel-good factor' about being the person with the over-flowing ladle.

♦ Introduce your family to your own spaghetti bolognaise before they taste the ready-made stuff. Otherwise they might get a taste for it.

♦ Get kids cooking, or at least helping, as soon as they show the slightest interest in the kitchen – and see the Kids in the Kitchen segment later in this book.

♦ No matter how much time it may save, don't serve up yesterday's leftovers when you come in from work. You will only feel wretched. Better to cook no more than you need of most things, except mash and boiled potatoes, which make great potato cakes and sautéed potatoes that are often better than they were first time round.

♦ Despite the depression that most leftovers bring to the table, I have never found a cold roast has the same effect. There is something quite cheering about finding enough cold meat left on a joint to make a sandwich or a salad. The trick is to bring it to room temperature rather than serve it straight from the fridge, and to add a fresh, pungent sauce and a groovy, knife-sharp salad. Try the piquant sauce on page 170 and some rocket leaves and thinly shaved Manchego cheese.

♦ It is worth remembering those dishes that do improve overnight, like curry, stew and braised lamb. Cook them when you are in the mood and have the time, perhaps at the weekend, then refrigerate them for a night or two, bringing them out for a slow, thorough reheat one evening when you are feeling particularly exhausted. Forty-eight hours in the cool will do wonders for the lamb braise and oxtail stew you will find in these pages.

♦ No one can convince me that children do not like strong flavours. I know I did. Think of the tastes children enjoy: tomato ketchup, flavoured potato crisps, Marmite. They are all incredibly powerful flavours. How can we say that olives are too strong for children when they will happily eat a bag of salt and vinegar crisps? Children who quail at the idea of garlic are often more than happy to tuck into your spaghetti bolognaise. In other words, the idea of garlic is often more frightening than the real thing. We just have to start them early enough. Though we should probably abandon any attempts at getting them to eat capers.

♦ Pudding is not essential and I don't think it is a habit we want to get into every day. Fruit does fine if it is ripe and luscious enough. And if you are very good you can have some ice-cream, too.

♦ I see no reason why we can't resort to a little bribery to get children to try something new. I mean who hasn't occasionally found themselves trading off the odd forkful of something green and healthy for a spoonful of something more appealing? For the record you get one small ball of Ben & Jerry's for six forkfuls of spring greens. But no amount of bribery on earth would get me to like eggs when I was a child and I still dislike them to this day. What I shall never know is whether I might have grown to like them had they not been forced down me by a well-meaning but ultimately foolish parent.

♦ I have always been a lone cook, finding 'help' in the kitchen more trouble than it's worth. OK, so I can't delegate, but I do rope people in to peel the spuds, pull currants from their stalks and top and tail gooseberries. Where I do like company in the kitchen is someone who stands and gossips while I cook, and keeps the glasses topped up. But it is always nice to be asked if you need a hand.

So where do you want to eat?

I love sitting down at a table with a knife and fork – what I suppose you could call proper eating – but I also eat curled up in a squashy chair, plate balanced perilously on my lap; lying on the sofa, propped up by cushions (plate resting on tummy); flat on my stomach while I watch the telly (plate on floor now); and sometimes standing up, plate in one hand, fork in the other. Sometimes I eat at the cooker. It saves washing up and when I am alone no one can see me anyway. I should also admit to eating at the fridge – bits of cheese, a satsuma, a cold sausage, jagged strips of cold roast chicken pulled off the carcass, and, occasionally, an indulgent tub of ice-cream at midnight. But I have never yet had the courage to pull up a chair to it.

at table

My first love is eating at the table. I do this even when I eat alone. There is something self-respecting, slightly decadent perhaps, about a solitary meal eaten at a properly laid table. I used to think it was self indulgent, almost sad, to go to that much trouble just for myself, but I think differently now. I should point out that this is not a daily ritual, but sitting at a table with a linen napkin, a bottle of wine and something to read is the best treat you can give yourself. Better even than retail therapy.

A table will also bring people together. There is an instant intimacy between people sharing food. Think how much more of a buzz there is between a group of friends clustered round a table than at one of those meals where everyone is spread out across the room, balancing plates on their laps. I think this is something you should consider when planning a meal for several people. Even if, like me, you have to drag the garden table into the kitchen to seat them all.

Part of the pleasure of eating at a table is those fleeting moments of anticipation before the meal is ready. Even if you have cooked it yourself and are waiting for it to be ready, there is still a twinge of excitement at things to come, the teasing smell of something almost done. Rather like the time in a restaurant between your order being taken and the food arriving. Moments to savour.

Eaten at the table, even the most insubstantial of snacks becomes an occasion. Breakfast, served like this, with my favourite newspaper to hand, is one of the great joys of living, even if in reality that breakfast consists of nothing more than a yogurt and an espresso. I am not suggesting we do this every day, for every meal, but often.

in the street

Food is a sensuous passion and the lack of a table and chair should not hinder anyone. Eating in the street is not something the British do very well. There's fish and chips, of course, but we are not a nation known for its street food in the way that, say, Thailand is. On foreign soil I am happy to tuck into anything on offer, be it a samosa in the market in Delhi, a skewer of grilled chicken and a plastic bag of chilli dip in Bangkok or a feta and spinach spanakopita on an island in the Aegean. Back home it is more likely to be just a KitKat while waiting for the bus. (Actually that is not quite true; I usually eat peanuts or crisps while waiting for the bus. For some reason KitKats always taste better when you are sitting down.)

Food tastes better out of doors. If there is salt in the air, even more so. Anything eaten in the street as you walk along, sticky-fingered, tonguing stray dribbles from the corners of your mouth, is instantly more delicious, exciting even. It is not just the fresh air that makes what we eat on the hoof taste so good. It is partly the notion that we are doing something slightly forbidden. I cannot be the only person whose parents would have been horrified by the idea of me tucking into a kebab.

As I said, street food is not really part of our culture. Perhaps this is another reason it tastes so good. Is it just me who is happy to stroll around the streets of Istanbul wolfing a salty, cumin-scented kebab, yet would never dream of doing it at home? Or is it that the Turkish kebab stands offer something head and shoulders above anything I can find on my own stamping ground? Have you ever eaten a wing of chicken or a tiny stretched squid from a skewer in Thailand? They have the smokiness from the roadside charcoal brazier over which they are cooked and the sour-sweet hit of a little plastic bag of chilli-vinegar dipping sauce to go with them. That, and the possibility that you are being a little too adventurous, only adds to the excitement. Hot, sour, salty food eaten in the street under deep blue skies is as good as food gets.

in a restaurant

Even the most basic of restaurants gives eating a sense of occasion. Perhaps I cannot let go of the thrill of being taken, in short trousers, to the local steak house, where the fact that I was doing such a grown-up thing as eating out added an unforgettable seasoning to my half-portion of steak, chips and ice-cream. Could it also be connected to the fact that eating in a restaurant was something my parents regarded as a rare treat, or is it just the sheer pleasure of having somebody cook for me? Whatever it was, it is still with me, and I am rarely happier than when unfurling a napkin and perusing a restaurant menu, no matter how cheap and cheerful the place may be.

Eating in restaurants, like phoning for a curry or pizza delivery, is an occasion when we can forget all about cooking. I look forward to days when I don't cook, which is probably a funny thing for a cookery writer to say, but it doesn't mean I find cooking a chore; it just means I appreciate it when someone else does it for me from time to time. Those who insist on chaining themselves to the stove may end up finding cooking less of a pleasure than those of us who balance eating in with regular eating out.

One of the most uplifting things about restaurant eating is that it offers the opportunity to eat things you would not normally make at home. A proper Chinese, Lebanese or Indian meal is made up of several small dishes served at the same time. As anyone who has ever tried it surely knows, this is an exhausting way to cook at home: the cook ends up red-faced and the kitchen resembles a bomb site. Restaurants also enable us to experience cooking techniques that are outside the scope of most home kitchens – tandoori baking, wood-fired roasting, charcoal grilling – and arts that are beyond even the most dextrous of us, such as noodle making or sushi rolling. Perhaps you do these things at home all the time. I know I don't.

Cutting down the work

Cooking is about giving pleasure to ourselves and others. So why do we continually beat ourselves up over it, turning the simplest of suppers into a bit of a palaver? Some of us must, I suppose, get some perverse pleasure from standing over a stove littered with steaming saucepans, and being imprisoned by tottering piles of washing up, but surely the cooking is being used as a scapegoat for some other, more complex scenario. Even so, I do think that we are often guilty of turning dinner, particularly when others are coming round to eat, into a bit of a performance. It could all be so much easier.

I sometimes wonder whether we cook too much, always going to just that little bit too much trouble. I have long suspected that the reason so many of us think of cooking as a chore rather than a pleasure is because we attempt too much. What could be a joy becomes a trial because we have taken on more than we need to, given ourselves a load of hassle and inevitably made too much mess. My theory, and it is not a bad one, is that our national pride is so bruised by the reputation of French and Italian cooks that we feel we have something to prove.

If you watch the French and the Italians, who – and I realise I am generalising here – treat cooking as a pleasure, you will notice that they make less of a fuss than we do about their cooking; they have an ease, a matter of factness about the whole procedure. Yet at the same time they quietly attach more importance to what they eat. We tend to turn a meal into a grand production, especially when we entertain.

The way we put a meal together – starter, main course (with potatoes and several vegetables) and a pudding of some sort – is, I suggest, too much to cope with. And I mean this from the point of view of both cook and eater. No one wants that much food, surely? Aren't two courses enough? And why all those vegetables, and why on earth offer a choice of puddings? If we find ourselves exhausted after cooking a meal or at our wits' end before a dinner party, then could it just be that we are attempting too much? To show off rather than to offer pleasure?

I suggest that instead of cooking in order to give someone a good time we are too often cooking simply to try and impress them. My point is this: should we not be putting all our efforts into finding a superb piece of spanking-fresh fish rather than sweating over a bells-and-whistles sauce to go with a bit of second-rate salmon? Wouldn't it be better all round if our friends found themselves tucking into the best piece of fish (or lamb or steak or whatever) they have had in ages rather than having to compliment us on our elaborate show-off sauce? The complicated recipes, the elaborate table arrangements and the fiddly side dishes are, I think, invariably unnecessary, too often used to distract the diners' attentions from the fact that we have failed to find a truly fine piece of, say, beef. Where I come from, they have a rather quaint way of describing someone as being 'all fur coat and no knickers'. I think you can apply the same saying to meals – especially the dinner-party type.

overachieving

I have never understood the compulsion some people have to make everything themselves. You must have met cooks who insist on making their own spring roll wrappers, noodles, cheese biscuits, grissini, pickles, ketchup and crumpets. Sometimes this is simply because they have nothing else to do and they truly enjoy it but I can't help wondering why they bother. Nine times out of ten the end product isn't as good as ones you can buy in the shops. How many times have you honestly had home-made pasta that was anything like as good as the dried stuff?

If you ask me, these people are either trying to prove something or are living in a world of misinformed romanticism. Like the idea that every Italian mother makes her own pasta every day (she doesn't, she buys it dried just like we do) or that the French housewife wanders round the market each morning with her basket (she queues at the supermarket checkout like the rest of us). And, just for the record, some Indian cooks do use curry powder, they just don't call it that.

I remember once, staying with French friends in Paris, getting up early to get croissants for breakfast. On my return my friend looked amazed. 'Croissants!' she snorted. 'We don't eat croissants for breakfast. Tourists eat croissants. We have cornflakes like the rest of the world.'

What I am saying is that you should not be intimidated into making everything that you put on your table. Charcuterie, bread and olive oil is a good enough start to any meal; shop-bought pâtisserie is a delightful way to end it. No one will give you Brownie points for making your own salt cod, sun-dried tomatoes or Turkish delight. They will just think you are a little bit sad.

refine, edit, simplify ...

♦ Think of what you want to give everyone to eat, then edit it. You may find that one course is entirely expendable, and that the meal would be more enjoyable for everyone concerned if it is simplified.

♦ Go for one top-quality ingredient and do as little to it as possible. That way you will have less to do and less that can go wrong.

♦ Never be ashamed to buy certain parts of the meal from a deli or pastry shop. The French and the Italians think nothing of buying in the dessert from a pâtisserie or the starter from the charcuterie or delicatessen. I suggest we follow their example. What is hidden in the depths of the British cook's psyche that makes us think we need to make our own petits fours?

the first course

It is here, at the start of the meal, that you can cut out much of the work. I almost never offer a starter as such; instead we usually just seem to slide into the main course from the potato crisps that are on the table with drinks. There is nothing wrong with serving a well-made terrine that you have bought from a shop, providing that it is a really good one, that you offer tiny, knobbly gherkins and exquisite olives too, and that you make really excellent toast. For a dinner party (don't you just hate that expression?) you could do what I always do: forget the starter altogether, offering a wooden board with a salami for slicing, some olives, some hummus and some chewy sun-dried tomatoes in olive oil. Offer good bread, too, and a white plate of courgette fritters with wedges of lemon (get a pan of groundnut oil hot, then drop in thin slices of courgette dipped into a thin flour and water batter; when they are crisp and golden, fish the fritters out and put them on kitchen paper to drain). Everyone can sit, pick, nibble and talk while you get on with the main course, scooping more fritters from the hot oil and passing them over as you cook.

If there really must be a starter, then consider the following:

♦ Parma (or San Daniele) ham with either perfectly ripe melon or figs that you have tossed with a little oil, lemon and chopped thyme. Clichés, I know, but if you get sweet, sensationally ripe fruit and truly piquant ham they are difficult to beat.

♦ Olives and salami. I usually have these before dinner, even when I am eating alone, and then add a few other plates such as some grilled aubergine slices with lemon and salt.

♦ Slices of milky buffalo mozzarella, with a few salty olives and extra virgin olive oil to drizzle.

- A mound of hot shell-on prawns for everyone to dig in and peel. Serve with melted butter into which you have squeezed some lemon juice.

- A plate of smoked salmon.

- A bean salad – perhaps warm white haricots with shredded ham, coriander leaf and very finely diced, skinned and seeded tomato.

- A bowl of clear chicken broth, spiked with lemon juice, chopped mint and coriander leaves.

- A plate of salad leaves with crumbled feta and herbs.

- Roast tomatoes, eaten warm with a dressing of wine vinegar and basil leaves.

- Bitter leaves such as frisée with hot lardons, a dressing made from the bacon fat and red wine vinegar.

- The nicest starter in the world is a little plate of shop-bought potted shrimps and some hot, brown toast; and the second is a plate of soft mozzarella, ripe figs and chopped mint.

The essential thing to bear in mind is that the starter should tempt rather than satiate.

the main dish

Don't even think of taking shortcuts here. This is what they have come for. It is rude and lazy to try and palm your friends off with something bought or even semi-bought, such as a Thai curry for which you bought the spice paste ready-made. If you feel that lazy, then don't invite them, or suggest you all go out to a restaurant instead. The main dish needs to be something you have done just for them. This doesn't mean that it cannot be a meal that is cheap to put together or light on effort. A big bowl of pasta with a home-made sauce is fine if it is made with love.

If friends are coming round, then you should assume they are coming for home cooking. What they should not get is some domestic version of a restaurant meal. I hate those sorts of dinners that are cooked from restaurant cookbooks, with little piles of food and twee puddles of sauce around them. If you want that sort of food, then why not go to a restaurant? When some overachieving wannabe presents show-off food at home I always find there is an awkward feeling around the table – what are we supposed to say as Julian presents us with his copy of some visual masterpiece he found in a chef's (ghostwritten) cookery book? What is he trying to prove? Much more fun, I think, is to dump a huge, steaming pie or a vast casserole of fish soup in the middle of the table. It has a deep-rooted, understated generosity about it. Fancy plates of restaurant-style dinner-party cooking just end up looking pretentious.

But even a curry, a gorgeous soup or a roast fish can entail quite a bit of work if you are doing it properly. I always try to choose something that fits in with a relaxed way of eating. One of those recipes where much can be done before everyone arrives. In some cases the entire main dish can be made the day before, if you want. Remember that casseroles and the like always taste better reheated (their flavours conveniently marry and mature overnight), leaving you simply to warm them up when your guests arrive.

You will need to do some last-minute cooking – a rice pilau, spuds of some sort (mash or potato gratin), or a beautiful salad and its dressing, or putting pastry on a tarte Tatin – but who cares if you are doing that when everyone arrives? As we are talking about saving time here, can I suggest that you will find a large oval dish of thinly sliced potatoes baked with stock and onions a much more practical idea than lots of individual potato soufflés? Likewise a bowl of chicory leaves dressed with blue cheese, cream and walnuts is a damn sight less hassle than trying to balance an assortment of paper thin-slices of white radish and grilled scallops in identical towers on side plates. Ideally, I try to get the principal dish made, or at least ready for the oven, so that when everyone finally turns up I am free to be with them too, rather than sweating and scurrying around in front of them. Oh and by the way, don't let any of your guests help. They will ruin everything, then tell everyone they had to bale you out.

pudding

Everyone adores a proper pudding. By which I mean one that contains butter, sugar, flour, cream, fruit or preferably all five. If you have bought other bits rather than made them yourself, then you ought to show willing with a home-made pudding. Otherwise it might look as if you don't care. If the meal has been light you could make a pie or tart, or even a cake. Try old-fashioned recipes that no one else bothers to make nowadays, like bread and butter pudding, rice pudding with gorgeous unusual jam, or how about treacle tart with a bowl of cold, thick cream? Even if some guests may be clucking to themselves that you served bought rillettes or pâté to start with, a home-made trifle, summer pudding or treacle sponge will soon shut them up.

If most of the rest of the meal has been made with your own blood, sweat and tears, then go and buy a fancy cake from a pâtisserie, something blatantly shop-bought rather than the wobbly 'let's-pretend-it's-home-made' variety. Offer it without apology.

A platter of ripe fruit is sometimes more appropriate than a pudding and involves no more effort than tipping a bag of fruit into a colander, rinsing it, then piling it high on a pretty oval platter. But such sloth only works if the fruit is absolutely perfect, extremely ripe, fragrant, and offered in abundance. I cannot emphasise the importance of this enough. Small strawberries, plums, pears and peaches work particularly well. But ripeness and generosity are all. And don't forget to buy several varieties; if nothing else, the jewel colours of a platter of purple, golden and ochre plums will look beautiful in candlelight.

Chocolates, the luxurious sort that cost a fortune, will make everyone's eyes light up. But I go one better. I offer a mixture, on a large dish, of everything from the most expensive hand-made truffles to fingers of KitKat; from broken squares of top-notch dark almond chocolate to chocolate brazils. I have even been known to slice up a cool Mars bar and wedge the pieces in amongst the rose creams and those strips of bitter chocolate-covered orange peel. Something for everyone. And don't forget to add a few After Eights, too.

You never fail with a good-quality storebought ice-cream. If you feel the need to trim it up, then serve it with poached fruits, with a vast, spilling bowl of scarlet berries or with crushed meringues and some raspberry purée made by pushing berries through a sieve and adding a little icing sugar or *eau de vie de framboise*.

Some informal lunches and dinners

spring

♦ A bowl of stew with dumplings and home-made bread; Lancashire cheese and crisp apples.

♦ Steamed fish with chillies and lime leaves; lemon surprise pudding.

♦ Baked ham with mashed potatoes and old-fashioned parsley sauce; almond and apricot cake.

♦ Grilled, marinated chicken with *pommes boulangère* and a fancy-leaf salad; a big bowl of small strawberries.

♦ Fish soup with all the classic accompaniments, including *rouille*, toast and grated cheese; tarte Tatin.

summer

♦ Parma ham; minestrone; Táleggio cheese and figs.

♦ Green olives; baked fish with fennel and lemon; summer pudding.

♦ Chicken curry with rice; fresh mangoes, sliced and served in their juice.

♦ Roast lamb with garlic and rosemary and *pommes dauphinoise*; raspberries.

♦ Roast chicken with tarragon, French beans; chocolate mousse.

autumn

♦ Tiny purple-black olives; roast pork, roast potatoes, frisée salad; ripe pears.

♦ Tomato and basil salad; a big potato-topped fish pie with an accompanying bowl of peas.

♦ Roast vegetables, including late tomatoes, red peppers and pumpkin, with hot chilli sauce on the side; vanilla ice-cream with hot chocolate sauce.

♦ Sausages, including *boudin noir* and proper butcher's bangers, with mountains of mash and onion gravy.

♦ A vast shepherd's pie, runner beans; blackberries.

winter

♦ Moroccan braised lamb shanks and riced potatoes; figs and a bowl of thick yogurt.

♦ Chicory and walnut salad; roast turkey with all the trimmings; coffee and chocolates.

♦ Steak, kidney and mushroom pie (so glorious for a winter's day and no one ever does it anymore), steamed carrots; papaya and passion fruit salad.

The new cook's survival guide

♦ Don't think you have to cook every day.

♦ Don't think you have to cook at all. Good eating is as much about shopping as cooking. Think about cheeses, hams, bread, ready-made fish/vegetable/fruit salads, ready-made meals, shop-bought puddings. They can all fit in somewhere, but preferably not every day. They are ultimately an expensive, unfulfilling way to eat.

♦ You can live on home-made soup and toast.

♦ A diet of home-made soup and toast gets boring after a while.

♦ Take a look at the ready-made meals in the supermarket; they will save you cooking every day. Some of them are not that bad for a once-a-week lazy meal.

♦ Pour yourself a drink before you start cooking.

♦ Some things are worth making in amounts larger than you will need for one meal. Some dishes – casseroles/curries/soups – actually improve overnight in the fridge. It is good to come home to 'something I made earlier'.

♦ Try to cook only as much as you will eat today and tomorrow; come the third day you won't want it, however much that casserole/curry/soup is supposed to improve with keeping.

♦ Remember that there is nothing quite so useful to have around as a cold roast chicken. You can feast off it for the next couple of days.

♦ Overestimate the amount of potatoes and rice you will eat. Anything not eaten today will be fine tomorrow. Think sauté potatoes and fried rice. Think bubble and squeak.

♦ Underestimate the amount of pasta you will eat, there is always a temptation to cook too much and reheated pasta is horrid. Remember there is no such thing as a nice pasta salad, despite what women's magazines would have us believe.

♦ Try to keep at least something in the storecupboard, say olives, pasta, tinned flageolets, olive oil, anchovies, tomato passata, wine, coffee. This way you will never come home to no supper, even if you skip the shops. And check out the emergency storecupboard on page 135.

♦ Pillow packs of ready-prepared salad may seem expensive but the alternative – several types of lettuce in the fridge – will prove more expensive in the long run. What is wrong with a green salad from just one type of lettuce anyway? It's all in the dressing.

♦ Frisée, the mop-haired pale salad leaf, keeps almost as well as an iceberg lettuce and is much more interesting to eat. Try it with bits of hot bacon and a mustard dressing.

♦ Ignore anyone who tells you that you shouldn't drink alone.

♦ A bag of pasta, a lump of Parmesan and a bottle of olive oil are probably the best friends you will ever have. It's another supper for those nights when you cannot be bothered to shop.

♦ Always keep a bag of frozen peas in the house. It will get you out of no end of trouble.

- Poached fruits such as gooseberries, damsons and rhubarb may seem a time-extravagant dessert just for one but remember that they can be eaten the next day for breakfast, too.

- Two cannot live as cheaply as one. It is a myth put about by people trying to justify a decision they have just made.

- Buy one decent lump of cheese instead of three or four different ones. Otherwise you will only end up with lots of little dried-up bits in the fridge. Most food keeps in better condition, for longer, in large pieces. Parmesan, for instance. Buy small whole salamis rather than ready sliced. You can then slice off as much as you need.

- Putting little bits of leftover food on plates is not a good idea. They will only dry up and haunt you every time you open the fridge door. You might as well throw them away in the first place.

- Smoked salmon and champagne is not an indulgence.

- If you halve or quarter a recipe, remember that this may also alter the cooking time. Avoid scaling down recipes that involve gelatine (there are none in this book) or baking powder; it sometimes takes as much to set/rise one portion as four.

- Cultivate recipes that use stale bread or breadcrumbs. Few of us can get through a whole loaf before it goes stale. Dead bread makes very good garlic croûtons when fried in oil till golden and crisp, for scattering willy-nilly over salads and pasta.

- Don't be afraid to make large quantities of your own salad dressings, pesto, tomato sauce. They will keep well enough in a jar in the fridge.

- When you are shopping for supper, remember that as well as steak, chops and liver, poultry and game can also be perfect for one. Think partridge, pigeon and poussin.

- Nothing gives you quite so much confidence as making your own bread. It is one of the easiest things to make and everyone will think you are a genius.

- A bottle of wine is not a challenge. You *can* put a cork in it and keep some for tomorrow.

Food to go

There it is. For all your attempts to eat pure, organically grown, environment-friendly food, you find yourself in a McDonald's or a Burger King. Your teeth sink into that soft, comforting bun and the piquant-sweet sauce squidges up, though there is never quite enough of it. The gherkin smarts on your tongue. A moment of absolute bliss. The doughy bun becomes your best friend. You chase the last bit of sauce around the polystyrene container with a stalk of warm lettuce or a cold French fry and lick the last sweet-salty blob from the corner of your mouth.

There is other stuff, too: slices of lamb cut from a rotating kebab and stuffed into pitta, bought from the sort of shop you have to be seriously drunk even to consider entering; fried chicken in a tub; fish and chips from the paper – if you are lucky, made with fresh fish and fresh potatoes; if not, just a greasy, fishy sop for soaking up vast amounts of alcohol. If the sea is nearby and there

is ozone in the air, then the magic is doubled.

I love this takeaway stuff. The whingeing muzak played in burger restaurants; the smell of the hot paper round your chips; the adrenalin rush of someone drunker than yourself getting lairy in the kebab shop. And I like sugar, too, chocolate eclairs scoffed secretly from the paper bag as you walk or an open box of Smarties in your jacket pocket to dip into as you walk round the shops.

Pizza is another matter. I phone out for one from time to time and it arrives on a bike, hot and thin, its cheese and anchovy topping falling slightly off the crust. I always make sure I have the right change and a bit extra, so the transaction is over quickly and I can get back to the telly with it. It is always difficult to cut and you have to tug at each piece, so that the cheese forms long, teasing stretchy strings. Melted cheese, tomato glop and warm dough. It's a little piece of heaven and probably the reason I don't move to the countryside.

Learning to trust your own taste

You know what you like and what you don't. When shopping for a shirt or a pair of shoes you know immediately when something is right or wrong. You don't even bother to try some things on because you instinctively know that trainers with 4cm-high soles make you look like a giraffe and red always makes you look like a hooker. Other things you dither over ('Does my bum look big in this?') and they end up being rejected. Other times you know, positively, instantly, instinctively that something is right. Well, cooking can be just like that.

At the end of the day a recipe is only telling you about someone else's taste. The writer is not allowing for your own. This is why I get particularly exasperated with the more pedantic branch of the cookery-writing world that insists, 'This is the ultimate recipe for coq au vin/lasagne/chicken tikka and this is how it must be done, otherwise it is just not right.' What they mean is that they have done this recipe over and over again and they think it is just delicious and want you to try it, too. Fair enough. But to assume that their word is law is ridiculous – not to say downright arrogant. Don't be bullied by recipe writers. Listen to what they have to say – they know the pitfalls and also the fun to be had cooking – but trust your own taste, too. If you like the taste of a recipe as it is and the next line says 'add 300ml more cream', then don't be bullied into adding the extra cream. Taste continually as you cook, and trust that taste. The crux of the matter is that it may be their recipe but it is your supper.

the foolproof recipe problem

I have never believed in the foolproof recipe. It simply doesn't exist, despite what people claim. The fact is that no recipe can take into account what I call 'the variables'. How can any recipe tell you to cook a piece of fish for four minutes, then turn it over and cook the other side for two minutes longer? How does the recipe writer know how thick your pan is, the pressure of your gas, your version of moderate or high or simmer or stir? How do they know the accuracy of every oven, the thickness of your every cake tin, the nuances of every pot, pan and cooker? More importantly, how can that recipe assume to know the exact nature of your piece of fish? Telepathy?

The fact is that food varies, and that is what makes it so interesting. Today's piece of cod may be slightly thicker, have larger or finer flakes or thicker skin, than yesterday's. One brand of butter may be different from another. Olive oil changes with every bottle; that is part of its joy. So how can anyone be so pedantic as to give exact timings? Each egg, each steak, each potato is different and will behave in a different way in the pan. That is what cooking is about, and that is why it is essential to understand what you are doing rather than just mindlessly following a recipe.

cooking without a recipe

While some people like the 'certainty' that comes from following an exact recipe, others rarely bother with them. How many times do you hear someone say, 'Oh, I never bother following a recipe, I just throw it all together and it always seems to work out fine'? This does not always mean that they are particularly experienced cooks – it may be more that they have an instinct for what might go with what. A feeling for their food. They may also have read or heard that x is good with y, or vaguely remember something they once ate and enjoyed. Whatever sort of cook you are – or want to be – there is nothing quite so rewarding as following your instincts and finding that they pay off.

why less is more

There is a branch of cookery I called Cluttered Cooking. By this I mean recipes that are so choc-a-bloc full of ingredients, flavourings and seasonings that the main ingredient itself has been lost. I find a lot of so-called Fusion food suffers from this, as does some classical French cookery, where the cook seems to think the more ingredients they throw at something the better the end result will be. What I prefer is the marriage of a few, intelligently chosen ingredients rather than a mishmash of everything in the cupboard.

All the recipes in this book are a result of the pared-down approach. When people say they must have a recipe to follow, I often wonder if it is because they have not grasped the idea of less is more – the approach where just one or two ingredients are added to a piece of fish or meat or a vegetable to which they are perfectly suited.

Whereas I would never attempt or wish to undermine the harmonious mixtures of spices that work to flavour a curry sauce, say, I think we do need to ask WHY we are adding something before we put it in. What will it add and, frankly, what is its point? Anybody who doubts me need only roast a dish of slightly tart, green-speckled tomatoes with a drizzle of olive oil and some salt, whole garlic and black pepper, then compare it with one to which they have added onions, aubergines, peppers, courgettes, tomato sauce and oregano. One taste of the pared-down uncluttered flavour of a roast tomato, its sweet-sharp, thin juices clean and unadulterated, and you will wonder why anyone would ever even consider making ratatouille.

is it done yet?

I am not convinced that 'doneness' can be measured solely by the clock. You know, the instruction to 'bake at 200°C for 25 minutes' or whatever. Timing is one of the most crucial occasions to learn to trust your own judgement. You see, it's about what I call 'the variables' again. The exact nature of your pots, pans and baking tins; the accuracy of your oven; the difference in individual ingredients; and the day itself. Some days everything goes right. Sometimes food simply misbehaves.

smell

Use your nose. At first you can only tell when something is burning. The smell of smoke will alert you to the fact that your supper is probably past the point of perfection. Pretty soon you will find that the smell a dish gives off as it cooks can be a good clue to its progress. Butter will smell nuttier, garlic will smell sweeter when it has softened (but will smell bitter and pungent if it overcooks). Generally speaking, as the juices in vegetables and meat caramelise you will find the food smells sweeter. Think of frying onions – they go from quite pungent when you first put them in the butter to almost sugary and honeyed as they soften.

listen

The sizzle of meat or fish as it fries will tell you if the temperature is correct. When you put food into hot butter, oil or deep fat, the way it sizzles will give a perfect clue as to whether you have got it right. If there is no sound when the food hits the pan, then it is nowhere near hot enough. If it sizzles sweetly without smoking, you are on the right track. When things pop and spit at you it is sometimes a warning that the heat is too high, but it can just as easily mean the food was wet. Some things, such as chicken livers, spit and bang just because they do. There is also a point, and this really only comes with much experience, when you will hear butter or oil go almost silent just before it starts to burn. You will also get to know what a cake sounds like when it is cooked. Which, for the record, is a sort of barely audible hiss and crackle.

touch

Poke it. A gentle prod with your finger will give as good a clue as any that supper is almost done. Sometimes this is quite obvious, such as pastry feeling dry to the fingertips, but sometimes the clues are quite subtle and come only with experience. A steak, for instance, is soft when it is rare, becoming springy when it is medium, and positively firm when well done. The type of print your finger leaves on the surface of a cake is a reliable guide to its progress, but sometimes you have to forget fingers and use your teeth instead; pasta is ready when you bite into it and you like the texture. You can also learn to rely on the point of a knife, particularly to test vegetables – does it slide in without any pressure? And skewers too: do they come out of the cake clean and without any raw cake batter sticking to them? And a coarse-textured pâté is often ready when a skewer inserted into the middle feels warm as you hold it against your bottom lip.

36

look

Very often you will find that something is done when it looks good enough to eat. When meat or fish has formed a golden crust, when broccoli or beans become a deep emerald green, when the edges of a grilled tomato start to char a little. The clue to doneness is nothing more complicated than whether it appeals to you. Whether you want to eat it or not.

and, of course, taste

If you stick your finger in something and it tastes good, it is ready to eat. Try this with chicken stock: take a teaspoon of stock from the pan, blow on it to cool it, then taste it. If it is pale and thin, it is not ready; if its flavour is rich and deep, then it is probably done. I know it sounds simplistic but the truth is that food is often 'done' when you try it and like what you taste.

Oh, and you could keep a vague, but sceptical eye on the time.

The flavour of food, or how to make something taste better

where flavour comes from

The flavour of our food has, to a certain extent, been decreed before we get it into the kitchen. The variety of a vegetable or fruit, the soil in which it has grown, the length of time it takes to get to us and the way it has been stored will affect its flavour every bit as much as our cooking of it. With an animal, the flavour we end up with on our fork is as dependent on the breed of the animal, what it has eaten, the way it has lived, the manner in which it has been slaughtered and butchered as on how we cook it. An inspired cook can turn any old bit of chicken into something worth eating, but how much better that meal would be if the bird had been a good one in the first place.

And this is the point. A meal tastes better if it is made with good ingredients. By good I mean ingredients that are farmed with integrity, whether it be a cabbage that is grown on pesticide-free soil and sold at its peak of lush, squeaking freshness; pork from a traditional breed of pig that has had access to outdoors and eaten good things before being slaughtered with care and butchered by someone who understands; or a peach grown for its flavour rather than its yield, and kept until it reaches its moment of perfect ripeness.

Good ingredients are those that have been produced by somebody who cares about quality rather than someone who is only interested in the money they will bring in – the passionate cheesemaker who fights the bureaucrats and food police to make a deeper-flavoured cheese from unpasteurised milk; the farmer who grows old-fashioned varieties of apples because they taste particularly good, even though he could get a more profitable crop from a tasteless one; the farmer who switches to organic methods because he knows the long-term damage that modern farming can do to the soil.

Good ingredients make for better eating. If you don't believe me, try this. Buy two chickens, one a cheap, plastic-packed pink chook from the bottom of the supermarket freezer and the second an organically produced bird from a quality butcher or, increasingly, from the more enterprising supermarkets. The first one will be very cheap; the second will cost you a small fortune. Rub the frozen bird with margarine, iodised salt and ready-ground pepper; the organic bird with butter, flakes of sea salt and pepper ground from a peppermill. Roast them both till they are golden and tender. Now eat. Can you honestly tell me that the organically reared bird isn't more interesting to eat? Its flesh deeper flavoured, more satisfying in the mouth, its skin more savoury and delectable? Or make stock with the bones. The first will leave you with thin, limpid liquid, the second with rich, golden broth that will set to a firm jelly.

Now tell me this. Wouldn't you rather have the organic, and admittedly expensive, chicken once a fortnight than the cheap, intensively farmed, sad bird twice a week?

how to make something taste better

No matter how carefully we choose our meat, fish, vegetables and fruit, they will emerge from our kitchen much nicer to eat if we have seasoned them thoughtfully. This may mean something as simple as sea salt and black pepper, lemon juice or sugar, or it may be two or three aromatics that work together, such as onions, garlic and ginger. They exaggerate the flavour of the ingredient, making it more interesting to eat. Spices and aromatics add excitement to our food – just think of that sprinkle of chilli and salt you get on street kebabs around the Mediterranean, or the little bowl of soy and vinegar dipping sauce that comes with an order of spring rolls in a Vietnamese restaurant.

The basics are straightforward. Food can taste flat without some sort of seasoning. Salt brings food to life, as do pepper, spices and herbs. It is as easy to add too much as too little, but just the smallest amount of a well-chosen seasoning can make a dish sing. When certain foods are mixed together they bring out the best in one another. Some raw ingredients come to life when seasoned with certain spices and herbs – like salt on steak, a squeeze of passion fruit over a bowl of strawberries or a squirt of lemon juice on a piece of smoky chargrilled lamb. The seasoning accentuates the flavour of the ingredient, whilst making us want to smack our lips.

Before you season anything, it is worth thinking about where the ingredient you are to season has come from, what it ate or where it grew. Does the spice or herb you are about to use come from the same culture, grow in the same place, as the food you are to use it with? Is it a delicately flavoured ingredient that needs equally delicate seasoning, or is it something that begs for loud, in-your-face spicing?

Seasoning is often a matter of instinct. Sometimes you get a hunch, sometimes you just know. No one can tell you what you should season with what; it is just that some things do work rather well – chicken with tarragon, for instance – and it is worth taking note of such traditions. But you must also make up your own mind, I remember a French restaurateur yelling and waving his arms about in horror because I had put mustard on my lamb. I know it is unconventional, it is simply that I happen to like mustard with lamb. The point is that if mustard has been used for hundreds of years as a seasoning for beef, there must be a good reason. You shouldn't let anyone tell you what goes with what but neither should you expect to reinvent the wheel.

what goes with what

Some flavours work together. Others don't. You cannot really argue with the theory that if you like something then it works, but to experiment with marrying flavours in a trial and error situation like a mad scientist will not only take for ever but will probably lead to some really horrid meals. The easy way is to respect a few basic principles about flavours that work especially well together – what belongs with what – which will at least give you the chance of a decent supper. You can then experiment as and when you feel like it. To put it another way, someone has done some of the work for you. Be thankful. You didn't really want to be the one to find out that anchovies are disgusting with bacon, did you?

Some flavours have a natural affinity for each other. In other words, they flatter each other and make for better eating. Much of what is accepted as being a sound partnership makes good

sense but there is also a lot of rubbish talked about what goes with what. I have never agreed, for instance, with the well-known accompaniment for oysters, which some foodies reckon is Tabasco sauce. To my tastebuds this is an abomination. The chilli sauce does nothing for the pure, intense seawater flavour of the shellfish. Yet I am convinced that lemon really brings out the flavour of steak, with which many would just as fiercely disagree. Likewise I put Dijon mustard on my lamb yet fail to be moved by the age-old marriage of cherries with duck.

Yet there are certain combinations of ingredients that seem as if they were made for one another. Think tomato and basil, think sausage and mustard, think Parma ham and melon. There are logical explanations for some of these natural pairings, such as the salt in the ham intensifying the flavour of the melon, but others are beyond analysis. It is simply that there is something intrinsically right about them, and there are some flavours and textures that work together so naturally that they defy the meddlings of any creative cook.

There are flavours and textures that work together in perfect harmony. A roll-call of all that is good about eating: beef and mustard; lamb and garlic; liver and onions; toast and Marmite; steak and béarnaise sauce; duck and five-spice; chicken and tarragon; strawberries and cream. Then there are those successful contrasts of textures that seem like gifts from God – gravy and mashed potato; egg and chips; ripe Brie and crisp white bread; cold vanilla ice-cream and hot chocolate sauce. Some things are simply meant to be.

adding flavour – and taking it away

It seems that some seasonings were made purely for the purpose of flattering and exaggerating the flavour of a particular vegetable, meat, fish or fruit.

You know how a few thyme leaves accentuate the flavour of lamb; how a lemon in the roasting tin adds succulence to a chicken; or the way orange juice lifts the flavour of poached rhubarb. Remember what lemon juice does for fried fish and mint can do for a bowl of peas.

Here is a list of those magic seasonings and the ingredient for which they were, I think, put on this earth (but then of course I could be wrong).

almond: peaches, apricots, dark chocolate, raspberries
anchovy: potatoes, black olives, lamb, garlic
basil: tomatoes
capers: lamb, most fish
cardamom: cream, lamb, milk chocolate
cinnamon: plums, apples, chocolate
coffee: dark chocolate, walnuts
coriander: chicken, lentils
cumin: lamb
dill: salmon, trout,
garlic: lamb, chicken, aubergines, mushrooms, tomatoes (I could go on)

juniper: pork, rabbit, cabbage
lemon: chicken, pork, all fish, peaches
mint: lamb, potatoes, peas
mustard: pork, beef, ham
nutmeg: milk, potatoes
orange: chocolate, strawberries
parsley: cream, white fish
saffron: most fish
soy: pork, greens
star anise: duck, pork
tarragon: chicken
thyme: lamb
vanilla: milk, cream, chocolate

marriages made in heaven

roast pork, crackling, tart apple sauce

cold salmon, new potatoes, mayonnaise

radishes, cold butter and salt

buffalo mozzarella, olive oil and coarsely ground
black pepper

crispy duck, plum sauce, soft, warm pancakes

buttered toast and Marmite

hot sausage and mustard

hot gravy and salad leaves

chicory, Roquefort, walnuts, frisée and strips of
fried bacon

chilli powder, fresh mint and thick yogurt on a
chargrilled lamb kebab

lemon juice and salt on very hot
deep-fried squid

roast grouse, thin gravy, bread sauce

bacon and broad beans

cold roast potatoes with a slick of
hot English mustard

bacon and 'plastic' bread

roast cod, mashed potato

roast cod, earthy lentils

chips, salt and garlic mayonnaise

crisp toast and melted cheese (likewise crisp
pizza and melting mozzarella)

melon and feta cheese

melon and prosciutto

dark chocolate and roasted almonds

cold apple pie and double cream

hot, bitter chocolate sauce poured over cold
vanilla ice-cream

vanilla ice-cream and espresso

purple figs and Roquefort

Measurements − and why you don't really need them

We have been led to believe that measurements must be followed to the letter. Word for word. Gram for gram. Yet it is flexibility that is at the heart of good cooking, not strict adherence to a written formula. It is an understanding of what you are working with, an inkling of what you want to end up with (what you have an appetite for), and the willingness to adapt and respond to your ingredients. A recipe is an idea, a suggestion, an inspiration. A recipe is a general picture, not one of the ten commandments.

Measurements provide a sound starting point for those who need it, but if we are to get more out of cooking than just a 'result', a 'recipe that works', and understand fully the pleasure to be had from making someone something to eat, then we need to trust our instincts. It is this, rather than measuring level, scant or heaped tablespoons of ingredients, that is the soul of good cooking.

If a recipe is to make sense, then I think its measurements must be related to how we buy our food. Standing in front of the vegetable counter at the greengrocer's or rummaging through the fridge at home, I find it impossible to work out what 3 tablespoons of chopped parsley or 250g shredded leeks is in real terms. On the other hand, if someone says a small bunch of parsley, or a large leek, then I can visualise it. That is why most of the ingredients lists in this book use measurements such as 6 tomatoes rather than 425g tomatoes, because it is easier to count than it is to guess the weight of something. And if you argue, 'Well, the tomatoes might be cherry or beefsteak', then you can be sure I will let you know which. Anyone passing a recipe from one to another would do that. Some of the more pernickety amongst us might argue also that one person's small bunch of parsley may be different from another's. Well, yes, it probably is. The point is that in home cooking for friends and family a few parsley leaves either way do not matter. Following a recipe should not exclude us from using our common sense.

As I say, this is home cooking, so the infinite details of grams and millilitres that are essential to haute cuisine don't really apply. Haute cuisine is a different thing altogether because it is so perfectly tuned (that's why it is called haute) that even the smallest amount of something will make a difference. I am not sure that should apply to spag-bol for six. This is the first thing we must understand if we are to grasp something of the joy of cooking by instinct and taste rather than by the ruler. Measurements are simply a guide, giving you a rough idea. The details are up to you and need to alter according to the exact character of the ingredients you have bought and to your whim.

Measurements are sometimes crucial, such as in the base ingredients for a cake or a loaf or when you want to make a classic recipe that has been handed down through generations. Throwing in just what you fancy would risk losing the point, the history and the perfect balance of the dish. Other times, measurements are less crucial, and you can take them with a pinch of salt. I know this is a strange analogy, but you know that wonderful feeling you get when you take off a pair of tight Lycra cycling shorts or a pair of Speedos? Well, that is exactly how your cooking will feel when you stop following recipes gram for gram. Let your cooking loosen up a bit. Let your cooking breathe.

the practicalities

The recipes here do not say, 1 onion, peeled and chopped, 250g chocolate, grated, 1 egg, beaten etc., because that sort of ingredients list encourages us to do all our chopping, grating and slicing before we start and lay it out in little bowls on a tray. This is not a pleasurable way to cook; in fact it makes it all seem like work rather than the pleasure it can so easily be. To do that is an absurd waste of time and a ridiculous use of equipment. The only time-efficient way to cook is to prepare some of the ingredients while the others are cooking.

For instance, while the onions and garlic are softening in olive oil you can chop the tomatoes and bacon or whatever is to go in next. Chop everything beforehand and things dry up and lose their vigour, their freshness. Prepare as you go along, and not before, no matter what any do-it-and-dust-it television cook tells you. That is why the ingredients lists are written the way they are. The exception to this is when you are making a stir-fry. Then you need to get everything chopped before you start cooking because you have to move quickly, bang, bang, bang, otherwise the heat in the pan will drop and it won't live up to its name.

It was a chance comment from a reader that spurred me into writing this book. The comment went along the lines of 'if you don't give exact amounts in a recipe, then how will I know if it is right?' The underlying text stopped me in my tracks. 'How will I know if it is right?' The point being that this reader had so little confidence in their cooking that they didn't even know whether they liked something or not until they were told, 'Yes, that's how it is meant to be.' Whether something is right is neither here nor there. It means nothing in this context. What matters, the only thing that matters, is that we and those we are cooking for like what we have made. Right and wrong doesn't come into it.

Kit

There is a lot of precious twaddle talked about kit: the right pan for this, the correct knife for that. The fact is that if it feels comfortable in your hand and it does the job you need it for, then it is the right pan or the correct knife. After all, you are the one who is going to cook with it. And don't believe that the most expensive is necessarily the best. Yes, of course, you tend to get what you pay for, but if that ninety-nine pence potato peeler feels right, why buy the one that cost ten quid just because some big-shot designer has got his name on it?

If you are going to cook you will need a few pans and a couple of knives, plus odd bits and pieces such as a sieve, a ladle and the like, but don't be persuaded that you need a whole load of fancy stuff. You don't. Really. It will just gather dust. You could, if push came to shove, boil, steam, fry, braise and probably even roast in a single wok, providing you unscrew the wooden handle to put it in the oven. But even I, a confirmed kitchen minimalist, think that is a bit desperate. It is a little like gardening, I guess. You could get away with having nothing more than a spade, but having a fork, a trowel and a rake would make life a lot easier.

What you will need is a couple of deep pans, a frying pan, a roasting tin and some sort of ridged grill pan, and it will be safer and easier if you invest in a couple of well-made knives, but you can cheerfully ignore much of what you see on sale in kitchen shops. A lot of it is there for heavyweight cooks who are into it all in a big, big way, or who simply must have an authentic couscous steamer/paella pan/fish kettle, or who probably have a fetish for kitchen equipment. Oh, and I don't know anyone who has ever used their Moroccan tagine more than twice.

There is enormous pleasure to be had in cooking the same dish year in year out in a favourite pan. I cannot emphasise this enough. A pan that has a history and in which the recipe feels right. I have an old, round-bottomed cooking pot I picked up for pence in India several years ago. As rough as guts, it has now mellowed and developed a certain patina – for which you can read a thick layer of blackened fat. I use it for frying small quantities of food, even though it wobbles about unnervingly – this is not a recommendation – and yet I would miss it so much if it disappeared. Black, tatty and as cheap as chips, it has become part of my kitchen, and therefore my cooking. I might add, though, that it is not worth getting overly attached to your equipment; things break and chip, snap and shatter, and that kind friend who helped peel the potatoes will chuck your favourite knife out with the peelings.

gizmos

I loathe gadgets. My idea of hell is a drawer full of those miraculous, time-saving devices specially designed for cutting pizza/portioning a cake/brushing the soil off mushrooms etc. I know people with kitchens full of gizmos, none of which they ever use. Before you get carried away with one of those gadget catalogues and your credit card, let me warn you that by the time you have played hide and seek with your little diddy that does this or that you could have done the job ten times over.

And yet there are small things that make your cooking more efficient, economical or enjoyable. One of those steel pouring spouts on a cork that fits into the olive oil bottle, for instance, or a potato ricer for making soft mounds of airy mash when you want something lighter than the buttery sort. Or a Chinese bamboo steamer that balances on top of your saucepans. Kit such as this is not essential but it can be a pleasure to use. If you do buy something that doesn't work for you, then you can always take it to the charity shop, where someone else may pick it up for next to nothing and take it home and love it. Just think very, very hard before buying expensive stuff, like an ice-cream machine. Unless you are absolutely convinced you will use it regularly, then back off, or drop lots of hints around your birthday. I should say at this point that I use my (extremely expensive) ice-cream maker all the time. But then I probably eat more ice-cream than most.

serious kit

the griddle

Absolutely essential. I don't know how I ever did without one. A griddle pan is a heavily ribbed frying pan made of cast iron, as heavy as hell but it allows you to get something of that deeply savoury, slightly smoky flavour that meat, fish or vegetables end up with when they are cooked over a charcoal grill. This is achieved by the fact that the food sits on the bars that run diagonally across the pan rather than sitting in the oil or butter of a flat frying pan. A griddle is the same as a griddle pan but rectangular and without a handle. The bonus of this is that it sits over two jets of gas instead of just one, and saves you trying to squeeze in that extra chop.

It has to be said that there will be much smoke. You will need a good extractor fan and, preferably, an open window. Even then you will know about it for a while afterwards. But who cares? The smell of a piece of chicken or lamb cooked on the bars of a griddle is the most appetising there is – even more so when that chicken or lamb is seasoned with thyme or garlic or rosemary. A smell that will really get your juices going.

When you first get a griddle you should wipe it with kitchen paper or a damp cloth after cooking rather than scrubbing it, otherwise it will rust. As it develops a thick patina (which is a rather elegant word for what is actually baked-on fat), it becomes virtually non-stick and can be scrubbed gently with a soft pan scrubber without coming to grief. If you give it a quick rub with vegetable oil after washing, your gorgeous griddle won't rust on you. Except on the bits you miss.

Mine is as old as the hills and much loved. I dread the day I drop it when it is hot and it splits in two. This great hunk of iron could not be easier to use. Put the gas jets on moderately high with the griddle or griddle pan on top, then let it heat slowly (so that it does not crack) until you can just about hold your open palm over it for a few seconds. Rub the food with oil and seasoning and place flat on the griddle, pressing it down with a palette knife as you do so. Leave the food in place until thick, Marmite-coloured lines have appeared on the underside, then turn it over with a pair of tongs and continue, lowering the heat slightly until the meat, fish or vegetables are cooked right through. You may find that you like the look of the brownings left on the griddle after cooking meat. Providing these are not burned, you can make some very intense and seriously savoury juices with them by pouring on a little wine, stock or even water and letting it bubble briefly into a thin pan juice. You will only need a little to drizzle over your steak or chop, as we are talking deeply concentrated meat juices here.

your pans

You'll need some pans, but not half as many as you think. As a general rule, you will get better value from one or two well-chosen, probably rather expensive pans than an entire set you can order for twenty quid from the junk mail that falls out of the Sunday papers. Never has the saying 'quality not quantity' made more sense. Don't even consider those thin, light, non-stick pans with plastic handles and arty enamelling on the outside. They are mostly rubbish. Avoid, too, those mirror-finish so-called professional pans – they spit menacingly when they get hot. I suggest you go for a pan that is heavy for its size and preferably made of stainless steel. Think big. You can't cook fettuccine in a small saucepan.

The pans you end up with should have a heavy, solid base so they don't buckle. It doesn't matter if they are enamelled cast iron or stainless steel, but do make sure they have heatproof handles so they can go in the oven as well as on the hob. Make certain, too, that they will go in the dishwasher. Frankly, I'd sooner part with my television than my dishwasher. And no matter what you have heard elsewhere, don't even think of buying aluminium pans, they send your cooking grey.

At the end of the day, it is down to which pan feels comfortable in your hand and what you can afford. Just rummage through all the pans in the kitchen shop, hold them, feel them and imagine what it will be like to cook with them day in day out. I recommend you buy one and live with it for a while before you go back and buy more. I started out with three pans that cost me almost a month's wages. It was the most extravagant purchase I had ever made, yet I still have them, eighteen years on, and use them every day. For the record, they are Italian, stainless steel, with a layer of copper in the base. Love 'em.

51

a frying pan

You will need a frying pan or two – a small one that can double as an omelette pan and a wider, possibly heavier one for everything else. You will often want to fry a few spices or a little piece of fish and it makes no more sense to fry a tiny quantity in a huge pan (it will burn) than to cram too much into a small one. By shoehorning too much into a small frying pan you end up steaming rather than frying. I have a light, 25cm, French-made, steel frying pan that works brilliantly. It is not without its drawbacks – by which I mean that it rusts if it is left in water or finds its way into the dishwasher. Usually I just rinse it under the tap and wipe it out with kitchen roll, so it has developed its own non-stick surface.

As time goes by, you will soon discover which of your frying pans is best for what. I fry bacon and make omelettes in my thin, French, black-steel pan and use my heavier cast-iron pan for things that benefit from a slower heat, such as sausages or sautéed potatoes. Perversely I never use my sauteuse for sautéed spuds, which just goes to show that no matter what the experts say, your kit – and how you use it – is a rather personal thing. To put it another way, next time someone tells you that you are using the wrong pan for the job, you can just tell them to go away.

a deep-sided frying pan

Known as a sauteuse, this is as invaluable as a piece of kitchen equipment can be. You will probably find that you do everything in it, from frying chicken to poaching fruit. I make risotto in mine, despite what risotti-bores say. You can, of course, fry chicken and chops in a standard, shallow-sided frying pan but you will get splashes of oil all over the show. The deeper sides of a sauteuse also keep some of the heat in, helping things to cook right through to the middle. If you buy one with a lid, and I think you should, you can also braise meat and vegetables in it. Go for one at least 28cm across, with sides about 5cm deep. You could, I suppose, buy a copper one, but I have never really bought into the copper pan doctrine. Yes they look good, but the tin lining wears through, you cannot scrub them, and cleaning them is a pain. That said, some people swear by them, but for my money their downside outweighs their practicality; anyway, good-quality copper cookware costs a small fortune.

a saucepan or two

I suggest you invest in one that is deep and wide, at least 30cm across, for making soup, simmering stock, boiling pasta and anything else that requires the food to circulate in lots of liquid. If you choose one with ovenproof handles it can double as a casserole. When you first see the price of such a pan you may be shocked but I promise you it will be worth it in the long run. Choose one that will look good on the table, which will save transferring your curry or coq au vin to another dish.

A medium-sized, deep pan, about 23–25cm across, will probably be your most useful pan. It is certainly mine. I chose one with two small handles rather than one long one, because long handles cause chaos in the dishwasher and look stupid on the table, whereas you can happily put a pan with neat little ones on the dinner table (unless, of course, you're a bit posh). This pan is the one you will probably use for cooking everything from rice to custard. Make sure it has a lid to it. The smarter pans are sold separately from their lids, but you will need a lid so buy one. You cannot cook decent rice in a pan without a lid. If you plan to do a lot of cooking, I suggest you invest in two such pans.

A small saucepan, by which I mean about 18cm across, is more useful than you might imagine. You will find endless uses for a diddy pan, even though it looks a bit doll's house in the shop. It is great for boiling milk or cooking rice for one, and all those recipes that tell you to melt chocolate/make hollandaise or whatever in a bowl balanced over hot water, but without the bottom of the bowl touching the water, well, this is the pan to use.

a roasting tin

You can roast a chicken in any old tin. If you are considering buying a new one, there's a couple of points to mull over. First, if your roasting tin is too large you run the risk of your roast drying out and even burning. Second, if it is too small you won't be able to cook a loin of pork, a whole sea bass or a hunk of salmon for more than a few people. If ever you intend to roast a leg of lamb for a few friends you will need a good-sized roasting tin, by which I mean 40cm long. And this is the crux of the matter – you need room not just for the lump of meat or fish but for the roast potatoes that go round it. They are almost the best thing about a roast.

Thin roasting tins are cheap and cheerful but they have one major fault, which is that they tend to buckle in the heat. You know what happens when you try to make gravy in a thin pan – it bends and goes 'boing' on the hob. Well, that can lead not only to you burning your precious gravy but also to spilling it all over the cooker. The other point is that any herbs you add to season your roast are more likely to burn to a frazzle in a thin, tinny pan. Go for weight and strength, and for one with a couple of handles.

a casserole

You can make a perfectly fine casserole or stew in your largest pan, be it stainless steel or enamelled cast iron. But you may well need that for cooking the noodles or steamed potatoes to accompany your stew – few things are better than squashing a floury steamed potato into the hot gravy of a thick, deep-brown beef casserole – so you will be glad of another pan. Enamelled cast iron is probably my first choice for a casserole, though I have to say I am not keen on the colours most of them come in. Still, they are classics and with good reason. Their weight, which is considerable, means they retain the heat and cook evenly. They will last you a lifetime. You can chuck them about a bit, too, but they will chip if you drop them.

The other possibility is an earthenware pot. I used to dismiss these as being too romantic, apart from being dangerously fragile, but of late I have rather got into them. Aesthetics sometimes count for a lot and these are delightful to look at and to hold. Food looks gorgeous in them. Once they are broken in, they are amazingly sturdy and ooze character and good living. An earthenware pot will become a friend for life. Or at least until you chip it when you are washing up. You just need to be a bit careful with them, especially on the hob – use a heat diffuser mat under them and a moderate heat. I am not sure what it is about these pans but they seem to work magic with braised meats and especially with bean dishes. Choose a large one about 30cm across, with a lid, then you can cook a vast, robust bean casserole to put on the table when friends come round.

a wok

I love my wok. I bought it years ago in London's Chinatown for a few quid. It is a thin, authentic, Chinese steel job, and was as cheap as they come. Even if you never stir-fry, you may find one useful for steaming and even boiling vegetables. Remember to buy a wok stand too, so that the wok can sit directly over the gas jets and get really, really hot. Don't, please, be tempted by the increasing number of designer woks around. They are usually too heavy to lift or made of the wrong material. For more wokkery, turn to how to do it, page 65.

a cake tin

Now that it has (finally) dawned on me how easy it is to bake a cake, I have had to dig out my cake tins. The ease of extracting the finished cake is the priority here, so I recommend tins with a spring clip on the side or at the very least a removable base. I know they are more expensive but they should last for years. Mine have. Non-stick is a good idea, though I often end up lining them with greaseproof paper anyway. As always, you get what you pay for. Go for broke. Sizewise, I tend to find large ones more useful: a slice cut from a small cake – one less than 20cm – looks a bit stubby and mean, so my cake tins are 23 and 25cm in diameter so you get long, tapering slices.

electric mixers and stuff

When people walk into my kitchen they are often surprised, shocked even, by how basic it is. No gadgets, no copper pans hanging from the ceiling and no state-of-the-art cookware. A place to cook and eat that is devoid of all bells and whistles. That is how I like it, and its utilitarianism suits my style of cooking.

I do, though, recognise something that will make my life easier when I see it. Machines that will beat, whisk, chop, purée and blend for you cut out some of the most mind-numbingly boring bits of cooking and let you get on with the fun side of it. I value my mixer, a great, whirring Kitchen Aid, for beating cake mixtures and meringue, for making crumble, pastry and mayonnaise. I could, I suppose, live without it but I doubt whether you would ever get a cake out of me again.

Whereas an electric mixer can be, if you choose the right one, a thing of beauty, a food processor will always be the ugliest creature in the kitchen. But I am willing to forgive the looks of my shiny plastic whizzer and blitzer in return for its doing almost every kitchen job I hate. Anyone can cook without a machine that will purée soup, make crumble, rub in pastry, chop herbs (though it is not very good at parsley), blitz nuts and dried fruit (though it hates dried apricots) and whiz up spice pastes. But would you want to?

little kit

Small things matter. It is just as important to have the right potato peeler as it is to have the right stove. It is pointless going to all the effort and expense of finding the perfect oven if your can-opener pinches your fingers every time you use it. Comfort, rather than price or design, is the heart of the matter. I find I get quite attached to some small kitchen equipment, particularly peelers and little knives. There is a sentimentality attached to the right paring knife or pastry brush, simply because it works so well and becomes part of your life. Sometimes the cheapest ones work beautifully. Ruthlessly edit what you are offered in shops; it is amazing what you can do without. Clutter is the refuge of an insecure cook.

Sort yourself out a user-friendly example of each of the following, bearing in mind that your first choice may not be quite right. Expect to kiss a few frogs before you find your prince.

♦ **A metal, swivel-bladed vegetable peeler.**

♦ **A Screwpull wine opener.** The most efficent there is, gets the cork out whole every time.

♦ **A cheap bottle opener for beer bottles.** In my (considerable) experience, the worst are the ones attached to fancy corkscrews.

♦ **A couple of wooden spoons.** Try to get at least one with a corner to it for getting into the corners of saucepans.

♦ **A hand-held can opener.**

♦ **A pepper mill.** Avoid the explicitly large ones, however tempting they may be, the tiddlers (obviously) and any designer numbers. Go for a medium-sized one with a lifetime guarantee.

- ◆ **A salt mill.** Similar to a pepper mill but with a plastic mechanism so that it does not corrode. I know you can crumble sea salt flakes between your fingers but sometimes you will find yourself with coarse salt crystals and sometimes you just need really fine salt.

- ◆ **A pestle and mortar.** Strange that all the food processors, spice mills and space-age gadgets have not defeated the good old pestle and mortar. Besides the fact that you can grind spices and mash herbs in them with ease, they are also one of the most pleasing pieces of all to use. As you pound at the spices and herbs with the pestle, the fragrance that comes up is pure aromatherapy. Once you have ground cardamom seeds and pounded basil leaves in a mortar you will understand why I have been banging on about them for so long.

- ◆ **Rubber spatulas.** Invaluable. You can never have too many of these. They will get every last smear of cake mix, every last crumb of crumble and every drop of spice paste from your bowls and pans. The cheap ones tend to be as effective as the dearer ones. Whichever sort you get, they will eventually go soft in the dishwasher and the top will come away from the handle.

- ◆ **Tongs.** Although they have been around for years, a pair of long, strong tongs has become the *de rigueur* kitchen accessory, and with good reason. The joy of them is that you can lift meat, fish and veggies from the grill without poking them with a fork, which would let some of the juices out, and you can get a firm grip on something without squeezing the life out of it. After years of cooking without them, I now find I have three pairs.

- ◆ **Mixing bowls.** Stainless steel or heatproof glass. Big ones about 30cm for bread and pastry making and for marinating; smaller ones for storing bits and pieces in the fridge. The cheap, light ones are really useful. I have found ones with a hook on the side so I can hang them up – useful if, like me, you don't have much cupboard space.

- ◆ **Measuring spoons.** Sometimes, just sometimes, you really do need to measure things. Go for metal rather than plastic, you are less likely to melt them.

- ◆ **A small handheld grater.** I use a tiny one I have had for years, but the Microplane ones with their fat handles are brilliant.

Despite what every kitchen shop might have you believe, you do not need honey dippers, game scissors, pizza wheels, wicker baguette baskets, jelly bags or porridge spurtles. You may want them, and there is no reason why you shouldn't buy them. It is just that you don't need them. Oh, and you do not, and will not, ever need a piping bag.

Whatever kitchen equipment you end up buying, you will probably find that, like me, you assemble a mixture of exquisite design statements and comfy old tat. Rather like my wardrobe. At the end of the day it is not so much a point of adhering to tradition and the right-pan-for-the-right-job correctness, it is simply what feels comfortable, friendly and what works for you.

How to do it

cooking in steam

Have you ever eaten one of those steamed fish, a sea bass perhaps or a trout, cooked the way they do in Thailand or Vietnam? It is brought to the table with juicy, aromatic flesh, lightly flavoured with ginger, lemon grass and coriander. There is something both refreshing and mildly soothing about it – light years away from what comes to mind when we read the words 'steamed fish'.

Steamed food, be it fish or vegetables, used to be something of an anathema to me, lacking, as it does, the deeply savoury, almost caramelised notes of roasting and grilling that I live for. A fish cooked in steam could never make me smack my lips the way one that has caught on the bars of the grill does. It is only recently that I have learned the pleasure that lies in fish or vegetables cooked in a cloud of steam. The point of steaming your supper is that you end up with clean, uncomplicated flavours. This is a peaceful way to cook, which produces gently flavoured results, a pleasant change from the sizzle, crackle and bang of the oven and grill. A fugged-up kitchen on a cold day can be an old-fashioned delight.

You need no special equipment to steam a fish or a pile of greens, although I admit that a steamer of some sort will make life easier. Until I invested in a steamer basket that sits on top of my largest saucepan (eight quid from a Chinese shop) I used a colander, piling it with cauliflower or bok choi, then covering it with a lid. I steamed my fish by wrapping it in kitchen foil and baking it in the oven so that it steamed in the wine and herbs inside the foil. Makeshift, yes, but so what? It worked.

the knack

If you steam a fish, then you will want to retain the cooking juices – it is a waste not to. I do this the Chinese way by putting the fish on a plate or dish of some sort, then sitting the plate in the steamer basket but leaving enough room for the steam to come up through the holes in the basket and circulate round the fish and its seasonings.

Choose a small whole fish, about 500g – such as one of the smaller sea bass that are appearing in fishmonger's nowadays – and ask the fishmonger to clean it. He should leave the head on for the sake of tradition but if the milky, bulging eyes of a cooked fish bother you, then ask the fishmonger to chop it off. When you get your fish home, rinse it well to remove any stray scales or bits of yuk and pat it dry with a paper towel. Now lay the fish, which will be a sparkling steel grey, on a shallow oval dish and tuck something citrus inside its belly – smashed lemon grass, perhaps, lime leaves or just sliced limes – and some shavings of fresh ginger. Place it in the steamer basket and cook for about fifteen minutes, till its flesh is opaque, firm and filled with citrus-scented juice. As understated and elegant as dinner gets. Lift out the fish in its dish and take it to the table. Peel away the skin with a table knife, then gently tease the flesh away from the bones and transfer it to a plate in the largest pieces you can.

Chinese greens, such as bok choi and mustard greens, are vegetables to try in the steamer. They cook in a few minutes and emerge piping hot and full of juice. As you lift them on to a warm plate, pour a little warmed hoisin sauce over them.

Steam potatoes – old floury ones – that you plan to serve with a stew or something with a rich, beefy sauce. Choose big spuds, such as King Edward or Desiree, peeled and cut into quarters. They will fluff untidily around their edges as they steam. There are few things that appeal to me more than mashing a fluffy, white potato into a pool of gravy, or that forkful of pan-fried fish, hollandaise sauce and steamed potato that must be one of the most perfect marriages a kitchen can produce.

a shopping list for steamers

♦   Maris Piper, Desiree or Cara potatoes – peeled and cut into chunks, for stews and casseroles.

♦   Whole sea bass or trout – wrapped in spinach with lemon grass or lime leaves.

♦   Bok choi or other juicy, thick-stalked Chinese greens – eat them piping hot with hoisin sauce.

♦   New or salad potatoes – scrupulously peeled.

♦   The hot, sticky winter pudding on page 416.

on the grill

Cooking meat, fish or vegetables over a grill gives them the most intense, savoury flavour. Yes, of course, there are the food's natural flavours but grilling adds something else: a depth and warmth from the smoke that rises from the hot coals or the bars of the grill, from the herbs and olive oil with which the food is seasoned, and, above all, from the meat juices that caramelise on the grill. The combination, made even more intense with a grinding of sea salt and black pepper, produces the most succulent, salty, savoury food of all.

The cast iron griddle that I mention in the section on kit is the one you want – unless you have an indoor charcoal grill (now you're talking). You heat the heavy, ridged pan gently so it does not crack, then, when it is too hot to hold the palm of your hand over for more than a few seconds, add the oiled and seasoned food. It is best to salt it as it cooks. Steak is an obvious choice but you can grill any flat cut of meat. You will have to be very quick with thin, lean cuts like liver or pork escalopes but a chop is about as fine a thing as you can grill. The outside will catch on the pan's ridges to give a smoky, sweet-salty crust. The inside will, if you keep an eye on it, remain succulent, a pink and juicy contrast to the savoury crust.

the knack of the grill

If your griddle pan is new, you will need to season it. Follow the manufacturer's instructions, as they vary, but what they will probably ask you to do is simply to scrub it well to remove any fragments of iron, then oil it thoroughly – don't miss a centimetre – and warm it slowly over a low heat until it starts to smoke. Turn off the heat and let the pan cool down. I did this two or three times before I used mine. What it does is to bake on an oily film that will eventually stop the food sticking, though you shouldn't expect instant miracles. You may find your first attempts glue themselves to the bars, but before long your griddle will become your best friend. Don't make too thorough a job of washing the grill to start with. Just a good wipe with some kitchen paper will be enough. As the pan ages, you will find that you can wash it, even gently scrub it, without it rusting.

good for grilling

♦ Steak, especially cuts such as rump and sirloin – with béarnaise sauce and chips on the side.

♦ Lamb or pork steaks – marinated in olive oil and lemon.

♦ Aubergines, thinly sliced and then scattered with mint leaves and lemon after grilling.

♦ Prawns in their shell – served with lemon, salt flakes and melted butter for dipping.

♦ Scallops – brushed with melted garlic butter as they brown.

♦ Boned chicken legs and breasts – with salt, lemon and thyme leaves.

♦ Squid – cleaned and scored before cooking, then rolled in coarse salt, chilli and lime afterwards.

in the oven

Oven food is comfort food. A loaf of bread, a baked apple, a Sunday roast, a fish pie, a baked potato, an apple pie, a rice pudding or a fruit cake. Come to think of it, any cake. Few sounds spell comfort as loudly as a joint gently hissing and spitting in the oven, or the smell of a pie wafting through the kitchen and into the rest of the house.

At first glance it may seem that baking or roasting is a big deal. But consider this: you ask your butcher for a chicken, a leg of lamb or a loin of pork, you bring it home, rub it with olive oil, salt, pepper and some crushed thyme or rosemary leaves, you toss in a bay leaf or two and a couple of lemon halves, then put it in a hot oven until it smells good, the meat juicy, the skin golden and crisp. What was the big deal about that?

There are basically two types of roasting: fast and slow. A tender piece of meat (a loin or a fillet, say) can be roasted quickly, while a tougher or bulky piece of meat (ribs of pork or beef, perhaps) will do better roasting at a lower temperature for a longer time. The idea in both cases is to create a crisp, burnished crust or skin while keeping the meat inside juicy and tender.

a few tricks for the perfect roast

♦ Tell your butcher exactly what you are going to do. If he is any good, he will advise you what cut is best. In Italy, France or Spain the butcher would automatically ask what you plan to cook.

♦ Ask the butcher to do anything that seems complicated, like removing bones or tying things up. A lot of people think that this is something everyone should know how to do. Well, they are wrong; it is specialist stuff and best left to experts. A French or Italian cook would never dream of doing stuff like that themselves. That is what the butcher is for.

♦ Do take the meat out of the fridge at least half an hour before roasting to bring it up to room temperature.

♦ Don't forget bits and bobs like lemon, garlic and sprigs of herbs. They make all the difference. Choose woody, oily herbs that can stand the searing heat of the oven. Thick-stemmed, whole sprigs are best – thyme, rosemary, fennel branches and bay, for instance. Tuck them in any cavity and put big bunches of them under the roast, so the meat sits off the roasting tin.

- Lean birds such as pheasant and partridge (particularly simple roasts, these) need a rasher or two of bacon across their breasts to stop them drying out.

- I know it sounds like a fairy tale but leaving the meat to rest for a good ten minutes before carving will make for a better-tasting roast. The science bit is that the juices are reabsorbed into the meat as it relaxes, but what really matters is that resting simply makes the joint or bird easier to carve.

and more

Writing of juices reminds me of the oven's other great triumph – braising. It sounds a major, complex piece of cooking, yet a braise is one of those useful, laughably straightforward dishes you can put in the oven on a low heat and forget about while you get on with other things. In blunt terms you throw meat, vegetables and liquid into a dish and chuck it in a slow oven. But a little more thought and care, adding appropriate herbs and vegetables, will give you something much more memorable.

A braise is about as easy as cooking gets. The meat and vegetables cook all together, and the sauce makes itself. This is hands-off cooking at its most sublime and, because of its gentle cooking temperature, is ideal for those occasions when your guests are the sort who turn up when they feel like it. Timing here is not critical. Half an hour, even longer, either way will not end in tears.

The idea is to bake a large cut of meat, usually a tough cut from a hard-working part of the body, with liquid and aromatic vegetables in a low oven, reducing the meat slowly to tenderness. I often take the cooking so far as to get the meat to the point of collapse, where it falls softly from the bone. The real point, though, is the luxurious pan juices you end up with. The juices from the meat, and the goodness from the bones, fat and cartilage, give body to the sauce. A plate of the tenderest meat with a ladleful of unctuous, velvety sauce to pour over its accompanying potatoes or noodles.

the knack of the braise

- Choose a deep, heavy pot. Don't worry if you have no lid; foil will do.

- I like to brown the meat or poultry and vegetables on top of the stove before adding the liquid and transferring it to the oven, as I think it gives a better flavour. But some people don't bother, saying there is enough flavour anyway.

- You will need a few sweet vegetables, such as onions, celery and carrots, to flavour the gravy.

- Try adding some of the tough-stemmed, robustly flavoured herbs such as thyme, bay and rosemary. Soft-leafed herbs dissolve without trace.

- The liquid, which can be water, light stock or wine, needs to come half way up the meat. It will thicken up with all the goodies from the meat as it cooks.

- If the meat is to tenderise it needs a low heat; 170°C/Gas 3 is as hot as you can take it without risking the meat boiling in its liquid.

- Turn the food once or twice during cooking so that the meat sitting proud of the juices does not dry up.

- Some plain boiled or, better still, riced potatoes will be just great for soaking up the rich juices.

You could use wet polenta, too, or rice or long floppy noodles. A hunk of soft bread, torn from a loaf, is also a good idea, and maybe some fragile salad leaves such as mâche or lettuce to mop up the gravy from your plate.

cooking in a wok

Go to Chinatown, walk into one of the many restaurants where you can see the cooks at work and watch how they use their woks. You will understand more by watching a Chinese cook and his wok in the space of one lunchtime than I can teach you in a thousand words. What will hit you straight away is the intense heat the chefs work with – vast, brutal gas jets spouting from burners as big as a plate. This is the secret behind the best stir-fried food, and is the main reason Chinese meals always taste better in restaurants than they do at home. But that does not mean we shouldn't have a go. Home-cooked Chinese food can be surprisingly good.

I value my wok. I have had so much fun with it, so many good suppers from it. I wouldn't swap it for the world. What you get with a traditional, thin steel wok is a pan that conducts heat efficiently, getting hot enough to cook the food in seconds; so hot, in fact, that you have to shake and toss it continually to prevent the smaller morsels of food, such as chilli and garlic, burning.

Standard domestic cookers do not have the extraordinary power of those in Chinese restaurants. Recently though, some innovative kitchen suppliers have started adding high-power gas jets to their range, but even without this jet-powered addition you can make a stir-fry worth eating.

There are no half measures with using a wok, no wimp's version, no slow lane. A stir-fry stands or falls on the quantity of heat you can summon. Last time I was in Bangkok, I watched a cook and his wok. His one-handled black steel pan never stood still for a second. Even when it did, the food did not. His trick was to get the pan blistering hot and to keep the food moving. The gas roared, the oil crackled, the steam gushed up in sudden clouds as he swirled and tossed the pork and little black beans around in the pan. He sweated but never grimaced, never smiled. Once he had tipped the sizzling contents of his pan on to an oval dish and slung it at the young waiters, he instantly threw his wok back on the heat with more oil and started over again.

Anyone who has tried this at home and ended up with a pallid pile of wet veg may wonder how a stir-fry can ever be really successful in a domestic kitchen. In my experience, and I am someone who uses a wok on a standard domestic gas hob two or three times a week, the answer lies not simply in how hot you can get your wok but what you have in it. Watch a Chinese, Thai or Vietnamese cook stir-frying and you will notice how little food they have in their wok. Everything is in a single layer, the food always touching the pan. Nothing they put in is much bigger than a postage stamp.

The minute you add chopped ingredients to the hot oil the temperature drops dramatically. By the time you have thrown in the vegetables and the odd shake of soy sauce, fish sauce, chicken stock and lemon juice you are well into steaming your supper rather than frying it. The golden rule is to ignore any recipe that says 'serves 4'. Wokkery is for one – two at a push. More than that and you will have too much food in your wok and not enough heat to go round.

Many classic Chinese and Thai recipes start with frying finely chopped chillies, garlic, spring onions and ginger as a flavour base. I should warn those new to the wok that these ingredients cook in seconds, so it is worth making certain that all your other ingredients are to hand, chopped up and ready to chuck in. Getting ready for a stir-fry smacks of some maniacally neat and tidy cook, but this is the one situation where it is worth being prepared, otherwise you are likely to burn your supper.

the law of the wok

◆ Buy a Chinese-made carbon-steel wok.

◆ Avoid heavy, design-led woks.

◆ Get the wok hot before you put in any oil.

◆ Stir-fry only a small amount of food at a time.

◆ Keep the food moving around the pan as it cooks.

◆ Prepare all the ingredients and put them near to the wok before you start cooking; once you start, the cooking will progress very fast.

◆ Everything that is cooked in a wok should be cut into small pieces that can be tossed around the hot pan.

frying in deep oil

Occasionally you might get the urge for a plate of rustling, salty chips, or perhaps a little dish of deep-fried aubergines, hot and grainy with sea salt, to eat before dinner. You may get the odd craving for fish in batter, too, to eat with peas and bread and butter. For me, this is as far as deep-frying goes. I might once in a blue moon do something fancy and fry it, but in my book the deep-fat fryer is really for chips, *frites*, whatever you want to call them. Call me pathetic if you wish, but I don't really like bubbling pans of hot oil in my house. They are dangerous, smelly and put the fear of God into me. Especially when they bubble up, volcano-like, as you lower in the chips.

Yet deep-fried food remains one of the joys of eating. Those crisp, fat chips with their fluffy insides; the untidy mountain of thin *frites* that sits at the side of your steak and softens slightly in the meat juices; feather-light vegetable fritters with their gossamer coating of golden batter, their insides full of hot juice – this is what a big, scary pan of hot oil is for.

fear of frying

◆ Chips need to be fried twice if they are to be really crisp on the outside and fluffy within. The first frying should be at 150°C until they are soft and pale. After draining a while on kitchen paper, they need a second dip at a scary 185–190°C. They are ready when they are as deeply golden as you like. The oil, incidentally, must be deep, but should not come more than half the way up the pan.

◆ Purists insist on beef dripping for chips and I am sure they are right. I tend to use groundnut oil. You can also fry in sunflower or vegetable oil.

◆ I could go on for ever about the dangers of deep-frying. That pan of bubbling oil, carelessly used, could do more harm than any other piece of kitchen equipment. Some cooks make chips for years and never think about the dangers. But I do. I won't make so much as a single fritter without a damp tea towel and a lid at my side to smother the flames. Used with care, and a close watch on the temperature of the oil, a deep-fryer is probably as safe as anything else. I'm just cautious.

♦ Clean oil adds little flavour to whatever you are frying but old oil, with little black bits from previous fryings, will give a nasty taste to anything cooked in it. Old oil is also more likely to burst into flames.

shallow-frying

Shallow-fried food is cooked slowly in butter, olive oil or a bit of both. The food tends to sit proud of the butter, which froths gently around. This is the most pleasing way to cook a whole, white-fleshed fish, such as sole or plaice. The butter bubbles lightly around the edges of the fish, you occasionally splash some of the hot butter over the exposed fillets, and end up with a delicately flavoured, lightly golden fish that tastes of nothing but itself. A spectacular sight on a big, plain white plate with half a lemon and a tumble of green beans at its side.

This is a great way to cook pieces of chicken, too, and you can also pan-fry potatoes, boiled and peeled first; sliced courgettes (dressed with lemon and salt as they emerge crisp and golden from the pan), and big, velvety mushrooms. Pan-fried prawns with lots of chopped garlic; lamb or pork chops; aubergines, drizzled with tahini and lemon; and scallops, sizzled with garlic and chopped pancetta, are other good things I suggest you have a go at. On the sweet side, apples cooked in butter and served with sugar, cream and cinnamon get my vote, as do bananas with brown sugar and ice-cream.

the really important bit

When you pan-fry, you end up with a thin layer of sticky bits on the pan where the food has caught as it cooked. They may form a film over the entire pan or just sit in little nuggets dotted all over the place. However they appear, these are the most precious gems you will come across in all your cooking. They are the caramelised juices of the meat, chicken or vegetables you have just fried and are intensely savoury. They give that deep, sweet-salty flavour to sauces and pan juices. Treasure them. You can incorporate them into your supper by dissolving them in water, wine, stock or juice. Simply remove your food from the pan, turn up the heat, then pour in the liquid and stir until the little flavour deposits have dissolved into the pan juices. They are salty, a bit like superior Marmite (not that Marmite isn't pretty superior as it is), and will add depth and savour to your cooking. Love them; they are worth their weight in gold.

the knack

♦ Pan-frying is all about controlling the temperature of the butter or oil you are cooking in. Get your heat too high and you will find black bits in your butter. Too low and your food will soak up the fat rather than cook in it.

- I often use my non-stick frying pan for this. Others swear by those beautiful, heavy copper sauté pans they used to use in restaurants years ago (a few still do). It is easier to pan-fry in a pan that has a thick base. Thin pans are spiteful and will burn your supper.

- I find it easier to get the empty pan slightly hot first, then slide in the butter or pour in the oil and wait for a minute till it gets hot. It is hot enough when the butter or oil starts to bubble and froth a little. It doesn't have to go wild, but there must be some movement of little bubbles. When you have done this a few times you will probably get to hear when the butter is ready for you to put the food in; the sound changes slightly. That will come with experience. If it has started to smoke, then throw it away and start again, otherwise the butter and oil will be well and truly black by the time your meal is cooked.

- If you move the food around the pan too much it will not have the chance to form a nice golden crust. You will also miss out on those sticky bits I talk about above. When you put the food into the pan, leave it be for a while. This will give it a chance to colour and form a savoury layer, which will keep a lot of the juices in. Despite what some people say, it is essential to get the food sealed in this way, as otherwise the juices just dribble out (some of them do anyway), so it is best not to shove the food around too much. Sometimes things are best left alone to do their magic without interference from us.

- There is more about making sauces from the caramelised juices in the cooking pan on page 178. I think these make the best sauces of all – what you might call integral sauces – but I might mention at this point that it is a good idea not to let the butter and oil brown too much (keep an eye on the heat), as this will affect the flavour of your sauce. Burned pan scrapings will not make a tasty sauce for your chicken. I know this because I have tried it.

cooking in boiling water

You don't need me to tell you how to boil water.

screwing up

All cooks screw up from time to time. If they say they don't, then they are lying. It is very easy to get carried away on the phone with some intriguing morsel of gossip while your supper goes up in smoke (I do it all the time) but it is also quite easy to oversalt, undercook, get slap-happy with the chilli or simply misjudge an idea. When disaster happens, never let it become anything more than it is. Just one bungled meal out of thousands of perfectly edible ones, a hiccup in your culinary life. People who tease you for years about that little embarrassment that happened one Christmas are simply sending out a smokescreen to cover their own insecurities. Just flush it away and get on with something else. Life is too short to cry over burned beans. Who cares? You probably didn't really want beans for supper anyway. Do try to accept others' criticism and encouragement. It will lead to you becoming more confident in the kitchen. But don't stand for too much of other people's 'I think this needs something, darling ...' If they don't like your cooking on a regular basis, then they know what they can do, don't they?

kids in the kitchen

It is never too soon to kindle children's interest in what they eat. We can do this well before they get any thoughts of cooking; simply scrubbing a load of mussels or podding a bag of peas is a good start. I don't agree with forcing anyone to cook but I do think any interest they show is probably best encouraged.

There should be no particular agenda, but the provenance of what a child eats is probably as good a place to start as any. Letting them unpack the shopping is a useful way for them to get the feel of food. But in these days of supermarkets and shrinkwrap it is easy to forget where food really comes from. Unless you are brought up by the sea or in the country, how are you to know that mussels grow on ropes in the sea, that blossom turns into sweet, ripe fruit and piglets grow up into pork chops? I have a strong feeling that the more children learn about their food early on, the more chance they have of growing up to enjoy cooking rather than it becoming a chore. And anyway, children have a right to know that their breakfast came out of a hen's bottom.

If there is any possibility at all of showing children where food comes from, then I suggest you do. Even something as simple as growing cress on (pink) blotter left its mark on me. I can smell those little brown seeds and their long white stems now. First jobs in the kitchen should be fun and memorable. I remember being allowed to peel apples and trying to get the spiral of peel as long as I could before it broke. And trying to peel oranges without the flesh breaking and the juice spurting everywhere. My stepmother would let me put crosses in the bottom of Brussels sprouts and pull black and red currants from their fragile stems. All of this was fun, and are little jobs I still enjoy. (I have since discovered that crossing sprouts is a pointless task. No matter what your mother may say.)

My experience is that kids love, absolutely love, making a mess. We can exploit this. If you think you can stand the cleaning up afterwards, then I suggest you get them started on a pizza. I have yet to find a child who doesn't get a buzz out of making dough from flour, yeast and water. Squidgy, live, floury dough gets the tactile vote. Perhaps it is the warmth, or the feel of the dough rising as you pummel it, or perhaps it is just the fact that they can knock the hell out of something without getting told not to, I don't know, but dough seems to be the place to start. Then there's the fun of decorating the finished dough with tomatoes, cheese, olives and basil. And to top it all, you can eat the result. In fact I think you must. No matter how much it has been fingered and picked up from the floor, no matter how burned or how stuck to the baking sheet. And the strange thing is that it will, I promise you, taste absolutely wonderful.

A cook's guide to shopping

It is the integrity of the ingredient – its freshness, its quality and its provenance – that is the crux of good eating. More so, I think, than any recipe. No matter what magic you work on an ingredient once you get it home, it is the produce itself that holds the key to a good supper. Buy the best-quality ingredients you can find, by which I mean the freshest, purest, most tempting, then do as little to them as possible. Far better, surely, than buying something second grade and trying to tart it up. I don't think this can be emphasised enough.

I don't buy into the old dictum that a good cook should be able to make something delicious from any old ingredients. I don't even see the point. What is the reason for making a classic coq au vin out of a sad, intensively reared bird and a bottle of undrinkable pop? The cook may feel that they have won some minor victory at being able to make supper from a load of old rubbish but it is a hollow victory. Their supper would be much more enjoyable if they had bought a really good chicken in the first place and forgotten about the fancy recipe. Forget the onions, the garlic, the bacon, the mushrooms, the wine, the butter, the parsley and the twee little croûtes. Much better simply to massage the chicken with butter and salt and roast it till the skin is crisp and the flesh rich and tender. The juices in the roasting tin, spiked with black pepper and lemon, will be twice what the fancy-shmancy red wine sauce will ever be. Though I should say at this point that a properly made coq au vin can be a thing of joy when someone takes the time and effort to get it right.

There is no reason for buying something that isn't at its best. That is why I hate shopping lists: you know the scenario, you have pork and spinach on your list but when you get to the shops the pork is too lean and the spinach a bit ropy, so you end up with something to eat that isn't as good as it could have been. This is simply because you decided what you were going to cook before you saw what was on offer. A shopping list is not written in stone. Far better, to my mind, is to let your supper be inspired by what looks best when you get to the shops, by which I mean freshest and most tempting.

But how do we know what we are looking for? How is anyone to know the difference between a good chicken and a bad chicken, or a potato that will be good to eat and one that will be boring? Much depends on experience, recognising what it is that makes something good to eat. Other times it is simply a case of 'once bitten, twice shy'. After a while you start to recognise the signs. But there are many other things we can do until we reach the point where we can tell a good apple just by sniffing it.

specialist shops

Get to know your suppliers. A wise eater makes friends with their local shopkeepers. Specialists such as fishmongers, butchers, greengrocers and the growers selling their produce at farmers' markets are the key to getting something good on your plate. I have got into the habit of asking their advice, picking their brains, flirting with them, and letting them know I am interested in what I eat. They rarely let you down. They want you to enjoy what you buy from them and their advice is usually worth taking seriously – at the end of the day they want you back.

Some people have told me they find specialist shops intimidating. I know what they mean; there are a couple of shops in London I refuse to go in because the staff are so up themselves. But I usually find that, once inside, if you have the courage to admit a certain degree of ignorance even the snottiest of shop assistants will melt a bit (though there will always be one whose sole purpose in life is to make their customers feel small; if you find yourself on the wrong side of someone like this, just tell them to get a life). Rule number one is to remember that we are the ones with the money and they are the ones who want to sell us something.

Once you have made friends with your wine merchant, cheesemonger or deli manager, you are half way to knowing what will be good to eat – because they will tell you. A good greengrocer will tell you which avocado will be ripe for tonight's salad, which mango will be ready in a couple of days and which potatoes are best for baking. Your fishmonger can push you in the direction of fish that is at its peak today. Some shopkeepers and their staff have such passion for what they are selling that they will give you little tasters and tell you about their suppliers.

supermarkets

I suppose we must concede that supermarkets are a cheap and convenient place to shop. Some of the major chains try very hard to source good-quality ingredients and most of them now make an effort to stock locally grown and organic produce. I find them invaluable for boring things such as kitchen foil, paper towels, washing up liquid and all that sort of stuff, but they often have the most stunning range of fresh produce too. Rarely does a greengrocer display such a variety in such tempting condition. Yet they cannot be all things to all men and I must admit that cheese, fish and meat are not their strong points. There is some shopping for which we still need to rely on a specialist.

farmers' markets

Nowhere I have ever shopped displays such fresh and inspiring fruit and vegetables sold with such knowledge and passion as the farmers' markets that are setting up all over the country. The idea is that stallholders can only sell foods they have grown or produced themselves – so no point looking for lemons, bananas and mangoes – and must farm within forty miles or so of the market. The point is that you are buying from people who know and care about what they are selling.

My local farmers' market has produce whose freshness stands head and shoulders above anything I can buy anywhere else. They grow things that are difficult to find elsewhere, such as elderflowers, loganberries and damsons. The cut stems of the vegetables are still wet from being picked that morning and the prices are a steal. I am lucky, of course. Not everyone has a local market. If you do, or you read about one that is due to open, get down there and take a look. I couldn't believe my eyes the first time I saw the quality of the produce. I should point out, though, that not everything you see in farmers' markets is likely to be organically grown, despite its delightfully rustic appearance.

home delivery

Many specialist suppliers (literally thousands) are happy to send food by overnight post. I have bought free-range and organic meat and poultry this way, and cakes, jam, herbs and organically grown fruit and veg. The system works. You simply phone up with your credit card number and your order is packed and sent. It helps if you are at home when it arrives, though most companies ask you where they can leave it if you are not. I have had the odd bottle of fruit juice nicked by passers-by and my vegetables sprayed by a territorial cat once, but most of it has always arrived in one piece. Athough you miss the chance of seeing before you buy, most of the produce is extremely fine, though you should not expect bargain-basement prices. This is top-quality produce bought either by phone or over the internet and, frankly, we must be prepared to pay for that sort of service.

One system I have used for several years now is the organic box scheme, a weekly delivery of organically grown fruit and vegetables that turns up rain or shine on my doorstep. The contents are a mystery until I dig down into the bag, but they are always seasonal, and as locally grown as possible. I recommend such schemes to anyone who hasn't tried them, though it must be said that some are better than others. I use it as a blueprint for the week's eating, moulding my cooking around what comes out of the bag. It is rather like going to market, but where someone else has done the difficult bit deciding what to buy and how to get it home. The downside can be that if you don't like, say, pumpkins or beetroot you are stuck with them just because they happen to be in season. If your family is a bit picky, you may find this system doesn't work for you.

What emerges from this is that shoppers have more ways than ever of finding something good to cook. What country dwellers lack in supermarkets they gain in farm shops. What urban shoppers miss in being able to get eggs from the farm they gain in having a choice of ethnic shops on their doorsteps. And anyone with a telephone and a credit card can access good food, too.

One way or another, there is now a vast array of good food out there for us to cook with, the really important point being that anyone with sound ingredients in their shopping basket is more than half way to a good supper.

Salt, pepper and other seasonings

salt

The best salt is that which you can lick from a wet finger and be reminded instantly of the sea. There should be no hint of bitterness, no aftertaste. Just a temptation to dip your finger in again.

Food without salt can be dull and flat tasting but even a little will bring out the flavour of most foods, especially meat, pasta and vegetables. I have tried adding little or no salt to food on endless occasions – sometimes it is a case of 'I just clean forgot' – but it is invariably a horrid mistake, ending in a deeply disappointing meal. That doesn't mean we should add it willy-nilly. It does, though, mean that we need to look closely at how much we use. For instance, I rarely come across many of us who put enough salt in the water in which we are to cook pasta (try doubling up the amount you use some time and see how much more interesting your pasta becomes) but, by the same token, I do find that many a vegetable has been ruined by overzealousness.

The amount of salt you add to your food is entirely up to you. Some people like more, some less. Which is why some of us like to add more at the table. And some foods are more in need of it than others. Steak without salt is hardly worth eating, chips taste flat, pasta almost impossible to swallow.

Much is made of when to add salt. The idea that adding it to raw meat before cooking makes the juices leach out has much truth in it. When I am roasting a chicken, duck, guinea fowl or joint of meat, I salt and pepper it rather generously but only just before it goes in the oven. If I am cooking something on the grill, I don't add salt until it is actually cooking, usually as I turn over the chop or steak. Almost without question, I salt again after cooking.

I have cooked with every imaginable type and brand. Several have been so bitter that I have finished the packet off by using it to melt the ice on the garden path, or for murdering the slugs that munch their way through my lupins. Others have been too expensive to use in quantities large enough to season the pasta water. The one I use by choice is Maldon sea salt, a mild salt without any bitter aftertaste. What I especially like about it is the ease with which you can crumble the icy, pyramid-shaped flakes over your food. A rather pleasing feeling between the fingers, and something that only adds to the anticipation of what is to come.

pepper

Black pepper will add warm, aromatic notes to your cooking, both during the cooking process and as a last-minute seasoning. It is the early seasoning that gives depth and warmth to food, the last-minute one that carries a fresh, slightly hot, and (very) faintly citrus aroma. This is the point of pepper, the extremely volatile oils that you catch shortly after grinding. I sometimes detect a slight lemony edge to freshly ground pepper but it is the subtle warmth we are really after.

Pepper's aromatic oils survive well inside the peppercorns' hard, wrinkled outer coating. Peppercorns I have stored for a couple of years are just as fragrant as sun-dried ones I have picked up from the ground in pepper gardens in southern India (imagine rolling hillsides of tea bushes, dotted with tall trees with pepper vines winding their way up the trunks). But once the pepper is milled, the precious oil that carries the aroma doesn't hang around. This is why it is essential to grind pepper only as you need it. If you don't believe me, grind half-a-dozen black peppercorns with a pestle and mortar and inhale deeply; now sniff a pot of ready-ground pepper. So if you find a little drum of ready-ground pepper in someone's kitchen, hurl it in the bin. A good hard pitch from about six feet away should make the point, especially if you can get it in in one.

I don't use much white pepper. I find it hot and lacking the fragrance of the black. I often read that it is used by chefs who don't want little specks of black pepper in their sauces. It sounds precious, I know, but they are talking about very refined 'high cooking'. We are talking about supper. Where it really does make a difference is in the classic French recipe for *steak au poivre* – where a fillet or sirloin steak is seasoned with a thin crust of crushed black and white peppercorns, then fried gently in butter, and a sauce is made from the pan juices and usually a little brandy. Sometimes the heat of the white pepper is softened by the addition of cream, though not in my kitchen. The two types of peppercorns – one hot, the other tantalisingly aromatic – both play their part in the recipe.

Nothing I can tell you about what freshly ground pepper can add to your supper could be as helpful as making your own *steak au poivre*:

steak au poivre. Start by roughly crushing black and white peppercorns with a pestle and mortar. You will need about twice as much aromatic black as hot white; reckon on about a tablespoon of mixed peppercorns for each finger-thick steak. They will burn if you crush them too finely. You can use any cut of steak but rump has the best flavour. Press the steaks down on to the crushed peppercorns so they stick firmly, then grind over a little salt and fry them in butter and a very little oil (to stop the butter burning). You will need a thick slice of butter for each steak, gently frothing in a frying pan over a moderate heat. Turn the steaks after three or four minutes, spooning the bubbling butter over them from time to time. What you are aiming for is meat with a pink, juicy interior and a buttery, hot and aromatic crust. Lift out the steaks on to hot plates, tip away most of the fat from the pan and pour in a couple of glugs from the brandy bottle. Let it bubble and froth, then add another, thicker slice of butter, scraping at the pan to dissolve any crusty bits. Tip the foaming brandy/meat-juice/butter sauce over the steaks.

A few sautéed potatoes on the side would be good. You can develop the recipe further by trying a thin cut of pork instead of the steak; adding a little cream to the pan after the brandy; swapping the brandy for Marsala or Madeira (the alcohol needs to be sweet to balance the heat of the pepper); or substituting milder soft green peppercorns for the white. Anything, in fact, that will give you a balance of heat, sweetness and buttery, juicy, aromatic meat.

Green peppercorns, soft and a little salty from their brine, are one of my favourite spices. They have a pleasing piquancy and an inner heat that sneaks up on you slowly as you eat. Warm rather than hot, they are simply fresh peppercorns that have been pulled from the vine and stored in salt water. They come in bottles and tins. I am not impressed with the dried variety. Rinse them thoroughly before use to rid them of some of their saltiness, then use them whole as a seasoning for pan-fried pork chops or liver, crushed and stirred into butter for steak, or add them to the butter when you bake whole giant mushrooms. You can throw them into chicken liver pâté or into the hollows of a stoned avocado. The ballbearing-sized, frog-green berries are at their piquant, peppery best dropped into the pan juices of a fried pork chop, the sticky gunge from the bottom of the pan loosened with a little wine and cream. The brine from the tin, which is seriously hot and salty, can be added in very small amounts to sauces that need a bit of oomph. If you intend to keep any back for this, transfer it from the tin to a glass jar. You will probably forget it is in the fridge but its effect can be astonishing for enlivening a cream sauce for, say, roast cod.

garlic

Garlic can be whatever you want it to be – sweet and subtle or loud and proud. What it adds to your supper will depend on its age, how you cut it and how you cook it. Young garlic is more gently flavoured than old; sliced is subtler than chopped; and slow-cooked garlic is softer in flavour and smell than garlic fried at a high temperature. The youngest, freshest and juiciest garlic is mild enough to eat raw; just don't expect anyone to want to snog you afterwards.

When it is roasted to a honeyed gold, it will add a warm, discreet, garlicky note to your cooking and your kitchen will smell like an old French bistro at lunchtime. When it is crushed to a pulp and gently fried, the pungency will be a little stronger, as if someone was making garlic bread in the next room. Chopped into little nibs and fried to a nutty brown, it will fill the air with the unmistakable, hunger-inducing smell of a good Chinese restaurant.

To see just how sweet garlic can be, cut a young, mild clove in half and rub it around the inside of an ovenproof earthenware dish, then fill it almost to the rim with thinly sliced potatoes and double cream. After cooking it for an hour in a moderately hot oven, the kitchen will be full of the sweet smell of baking garlic, and the potatoes and cream will have a deeply embedded but softly warming flavour of garlic. To experience the more upfront face of garlic, chop it finely and fry it at a high temperature in a wok until it is a deep caramel colour. The result will be exciting, pungent and in your face. Long, slow cooking softens the bulb's flavour. A blast of high heat will make it shout.

Young garlic, in the shops throughout the summer, has a light, gentle smell and plump, brilliant-white cloves, and is faint enough to eat raw – in a salad, say – provided it is sliced so finely you can see through it. As garlic gets older, the supple white skin dries to the colour of parchment and becomes brittle and flaky, but more important to the cook is that the flavour becomes harsher and more pungent. Once little green shoots have started to appear, the garlic is past its best.

New garlic's state of health is easy to assess. It should be plump and firm, with a delicate, appetising smell, its white skin and stalk bendy and flushed with green or mauve. As it matures you have to be a bit more circumspect, prodding and squeezing each head of garlic before you part with your money. Pass on any that have hollow skin, missing or exposed cloves or are sporting little green shoots. Go for heads whose cloves are hard and plump, with an unblemished skin. Store them in a cool, dry place. They are better in a cupboard than in the fridge.

The green shoots inside older cloves are highly indigestible for most people, so when chopping the garlic, poke out the green bit with the point of a small knife and get rid of it. It is best not to use any garlic that is dark in colour or a bit withered; besides giving everyone stomach ache, your supper will have an acrid, pungent note to it rather than a subtle appetising whiff.

To taste garlic at its most discreet and romantic, have a go at the *pommes dauphinoise* on page 262. To get the unforgettable message of garlic at its pushiest, try this.

garlic prawns. Toss as many raw prawns as you can afford (you'll need about eight each) in olive oil and crushed garlic (one or two really fat, juicy cloves per person). Get the overhead grill hot, put the prawns on a grill pan and cook them until their skins have turned brilliant orange-pink. While they are cooking, melt a little butter in a pan. At the table, let everyone peel away their own shells, dipping the prawns into the warm butter and a little dish of salt as they go.

olive oil

Olive oil, the unctuous green liquor made from crushing ripe olives in a heavy press, is both a fragrant liquid to pour over your salad and a cooking medium. You can use it as a gently flavoured, enriching medium in which to soften onions, garlic and other aromatics over heat to form the flavour base of a more complex dish, such as a soup, a casserole or a braise; as a lubricant and seasoning to rub on to meat before it is grilled (tastes good and stops the meat sticking to the bars); to fry chicken, potatoes, meat or fish in a shallow pan (adds flavour and stops the food from burning on the pan); and as something in which to preserve little goat's cheeses, sardines and olives (keeps the air off them and seasons them with the appropriate flavours of a sunnier climate). Olive oil is as essential as salt or pepper in a modern kitchen. You could almost say, no olive oil, no supper.

Olive oil comes principally from Mediterranean countries, where it has long been the blood in the veins of the local cooking. Over the last twenty years or so, the British have taken it into their kitchens, keeping their traditional solid fats such as butter and lard for baking and for where the grassy, peppery flavour of olive oil would be inappropriate – in cakes, a bacon sandwich or (to my taste) mashed potato.

More pretentious claptrap is talked about olive oil than almost anything else in the kitchen. So here are a few points that will interest the new cook or those new to olive oil.

♦ Take no notice of anyone who says you need to pay a fortune to get good olive oil. You don't.

♦ Olive oil varies in flavour, colour and viscosity according to the variety of olive, the country the olives grew in and the way the oil was made. Some are distinctly peppery, others grassy or fruity. Some are mild and light, while some fall from the bottle in slow, heavy glugs. No single oil is necessarily better than another. It is simply a matter of taste and what you intend to use it for. So choose one that suits you.

♦ Supermarket olive oils are not to be sneered at. Some of them have a good flavour and excellent price.

♦ I find a medium-weight olive oil, with a fairly light, fruity flavour, best for everyday cooking. Others might prefer something heavier. I think it is best to avoid the very strongly flavoured oils for everyday cooking; their peppery taste can overpower, their unctuousness can pall on the palate. Save the very rich, green oil, possibly from a single estate rather than a blend, for using undiluted by other ingredients. For pouring over crisp, hot toast, for instance.

- Take no notice of those who pour scorn on the habit of dunking snippets of chewy, crusty bread into a little dish of emerald-green new season's oil as a precursor to a meal. If the oil is fresh and fruity, it will spike your appetite for what is to come.

- I don't really buy into the habit of having several olive oils open at once. Certainly I think you need a good medium-weight oil for general cooking and perhaps a bigger-flavoured oil for drizzling over pasta and vegetables and for dunking your bread in, but that is it. Anyone who juggles half-a-dozen bottles of oil is just being pretentious. Or shall I put it another way? It is not something you would ever see done in homes where olive oil is made.

other oils and fats

Most cultures have a cheap, relatively bland oil for general cooking. They use it for deep-frying and for recipes where a stronger-flavoured oil such as olive would be inappropriate. I don't really want my chips to taste of olive oil. In France and China, they tend to use groundnut oil, in India palm or coconut oil and in America corn or vegetable oil. Flavourless oils such as groundnut are also useful for mixing with olive oil in salad dressings and mayonnaise, where using olive oil alone would give too strong a taste. If you are a purist, you will probably demand coconut oil for your authentic Keralan curry. Truth told, cooks there are converting to groundnut, which is deemed healthier. As I don't like the smell of sunflower and corn oil when they get hot, I tend to use a standard supermarket groundnut oil, made from peanuts and virtually tasteless. Purists would insist on beef dripping or even horse fat for frying their chips. I am with them on the beef dripping.

There are some fancy oils about, too, made from walnuts, hazelnuts, pumpkin seeds and even pistachios. They are all quite delicious in their own way, and I certainly think worth trying at some point, but they do not keep well, so if you do buy a bottle, then get ready for an entire month of salads dressed with hazelnut oil. The only one I use regularly is a French walnut oil, which makes a very good dressing with lemon juice, salt and pepper for a plain green salad. Even then, I often mix it with a little olive or groundnut oil, as some brands can be too much of a good thing.

butter

Glorious stuff. I use it in pastry and cakes, for shallow-frying fish and, of course, for toast. Ignore the alternatives – to my mind they are all filthy. No matter what the hype says, nothing can ever taste as good as butter. I prefer pale, sweet, unsalted butter for cooking and on bread, and generally buy French or Italian. Salted butter is what you want, in obscene, heart-stopping amounts, on thick, hot toast or crumpets. If ever you are tempted to stray to the 'let's-pretend-it's-butter' type of fats, then it is worth remembering that margarine is a chemically treated hydrogenated vegetable oil with added colourings and flavourings. Butter is purely churned cream. I suggest you buy it in small amounts (especially as we are cooking with less of it nowadays) and keep it very cold and very well wrapped. Butter has a nasty habit of absorbing every flavour in your fridge.

81

lardo, lard, pancetta and bacon

Sitting in a restaurant way up in the Italian Alps, snow falling and the fire roaring in the grate, I fell in love with lardo, the snow-white, herb-scented pork fat that they serve in paper-thin slices at the start of a meal. There it was presented on a plate with sea salt, black pepper and a bottle of olive oil for us to help ourselves to. This fragrant fat is becoming more popular in Britain now, but you need to look to your nearest Italian deli for it. Chopped into small dice, it is an unctuous medium in which to cook onions and garlic to start a winter soup or braise.

Lard, the blocks of soft white fat traditionally used for making pastry for pork pies and for frying chips, features rarely in my cooking nowadays. I am no health missionary, yet even I balk at using this particular fat in large amounts, and not simply because of its cloying feel in the mouth. But I still think you cannot beat a fruit pie pastry crust made with half butter and half lard. The lard makes the pastry light and crumbly, the butter gives it flavour.

Pancetta, the sweet, delicately piquant, mountain-cured pork from Italy, is often sold in thin slices like Parma ham, yet I find it more useful bought in the piece so that it can be diced and used to start a soup or sauce, or to fry until crisp and scatter over salads. If you fry pancetta quickly over a high heat, you will get golden cubes of aromatic pork. If you cook it slowly in a heavy-based pan, the fat will melt without colouring, providing a rich oil in which to fry the onions and herbs to start a sauce or braise. Ignore the plastic-wrapped, ready-cut slices in the supermarket; they seem to have little of the mild, herbal aroma of pancetta bought in the lump from an Italian deli. Along with mineral water, a wedge of Parmesan and a bottle of olive oil, this is a must to keep in the fridge.

To get the true joy of pancetta, I recommend you eat it with something bland and starchy. It is especially good with pasta and broad beans. Try small cubes of pancetta, slowly fried with similarly diced potatoes until the spuds have soaked up the pancetta's fragrant fat. Let them crisp and crumble a little as they slowly cook, then toss in a little salt and chopped parsley.

baked mozzarella with pancetta. Halve a ball of buffalo mozzarella, roll it in a little black pepper, crushed garlic and chopped thyme leaves, then wrap it in a couple of thin slices of pancetta. Colour it lightly golden in a little oil in a frying pan, then transfer to a hot oven until the pancetta is starting to crisp and the cheese is beginning to melt and ooze.

Rashers of smoked bacon are absurdly useful in the kitchen. Grill them till curled, crisp and salty, then snip them into a salad, scatter them over a thick winter soup or eat with grilled tomatoes and buttery mushrooms for a weekend breakfast. I am sure the world is divided into those who like their bacon streaky (cut from the belly) and those who like it cut from the leaner back. I am a streaky bacon fan, because I like the fat as much as I like the lean, and I don't think anything else is right for a bacon sandwich. It has to be said that bacon is not gently aromatic in the way pancetta is but it still makes the world's greatest sandwich. Buy loose bacon from a butcher, cheesemonger or grocer's shop rather than the wet stuff sold in sweaty plastic pouches in the supermarket. Look for bacon that is slightly dry to the touch, a dark pinky-maroon and with a sweet, cool smell. The best I have ever eaten, and which I recommend to you, was from a Gloucester Old Spot, mildly smoked, rich with creamy white fat and a smell from heaven. But doesn't all bacon smell pretty good?

83

goose fat

Silky and obscenely rich, goose fat is a rare and expensive treat. Buy it in tins or glass jars, or save it from the roasting tin for roasting potatoes. Sublime; as sexy as it gets.

> **potatoes roasted in goose fat.** Bring peeled and quartered potatoes, or halved and thoroughly scrubbed new potatoes, to the boil in salted water, then let them cook at a low bubble until just tender. Drain them and drop into a frying pan in which you have melted enough goose fat to form a thick layer on the bottom of the pan. Tuck in a few unpeeled but lightly squashed garlic cloves and shake in some thyme leaves, then leave to cook over a low heat. Shake the pan from time to time, unsticking any stubborn potatoes with a palette knife. After half an hour or so, their outsides should have developed a delectable, sticky, golden crust. The insides should be sodden with velvety goose fat and have taken up something of the perfume of the garlic and thyme. Salt them liberally.

Sour and salty things

limes

The lime is the lemon of the tropics, hardy enough to withstand Asia's searing heat and serving much the same purpose in the kitchens of Thailand, Vietnam and India that the lemon does in kitchens around the Med. But there is more to it than that. The lime is subtly more aromatic, and has, to my nose anyway, more effervescence. Appropriately there is something that feels right about using lime with tropical fruit – it is especially suited to papaya and mango but it seems most at home with small, viciously hot chillies. The tiny, wrinkled fruit known as kaffir or Thai limes have no juice but the most mystical citrus notes. Scratch one and see.

lime leaves and lemon grass

I have read a thousand times or more that lemons and limes are suitable substitutes for stalks of lemon grass and the leaves of the lime tree that appear in much Southeast Asian cooking. I disagree. Neither lime juice nor lemon zest has quite the same sparkle or aromatic quality. They are both easier to find now, though we are not exactly talking about the corner shop. Try a big-name supermarket or, of course, Chinatown. I have had much luck freezing lime leaves with only a little loss of their citrus zest. Dried leaves, on the other hand, are fragrant enough but seem to lose much of their magic once reconstituted. Either is essential in Thai fishcakes and green curries, adding something that the fruit and its juice cannot quite replicate. I sometimes think a cracked lime leaf is probably one of my favourite smells.

lemons

The juice of a lemon gives a knife-sharp vibrancy to our food, cutting through cloying richness and making its flavours sing. The grated zest, taken with care from directly above the white pith, will lend tart freshness to mousses, fools and cakes. In my book, the lemon reaches its zenith when it meets the lightly salted, caramelised edges of grilled lamb or chicken. Never could a mouthful of food be so tantalisingly savoury. So essential is this fruit's tart kick that in my kitchen lemons rank alongside salt, garlic and pepper.

Buying them is less straightforward than it seems. You would think, wouldn't you, that a lemon – being less fragile than, say, a peach – would be very much like any other lemon. In fact, they are as different as you can imagine. The thin-skinned ones seem to have more juice, the thicker ones seem more fragrant. Then, of course, there are the huge Italian ones that ooze juice so sweet you could almost drink it.

One thing is for sure: you will get more juice from a lemon that is warm, so leave them somewhere warm for a while before you squeeze them. I keep mine on the kitchen windowsill.

vinegar

Sourness in the kitchen is underrated. It took me years to realise this. A bite of sharpness in a sauce or a salad dressing can bring food to life, making it sing in the mouth. It's not just in salad dressings that a snap of acidity is good news but in sauces, too – particularly cream-based sauces which tend to cloy – and in the pan juices of Sunday roasts and grilled meat. What is especially useful is vinegar's ability to help adjust the seasoning of something that is too rich, too sweet or too cloying. This alone makes it an essential kitchen ingredient.

Vinegar can be made from wine, cider or sherry. Malt vinegar is strictly for pickling – onions, red cabbage and the like – and for shaking over chips from the chippy. Even though it is sour, good vinegar will have a rounded feel, and no harshness. You should be able to taste it from a teaspoon without a shudder. I have been tempted by all manner of vinegars in the past, many of which lurked in the cupboard for months (or, more truthfully, years) but you don't need a cupboard full. The most useful is a medium-priced red wine vinegar. The cheap ones tend to be a bit sharp, the most expensive being almost too mild to call vinegar. I sprinkle a few drops into the pan juices for liver or lamb chops, or shake it with olive oil to make a simple salad dressing.

White wine vinegar is a bit sharper than red and is good for buttery hollandaise and béarnaise sauces but I find I use much less than red, and could, at a push, do without it. What I do find really useful is tarragon vinegar – white wine in which tarragon stems and leaves have been macerated. I use this (incorrectly) in hollandaise and no one has ever said anything. It makes a clean-tasting salad dressing and I would personally choose it over plain white wine vinegar.

It probably sounds as if I am encouraging you to splurge on the unnecessary but I really do recommend you buy some sherry vinegar. It has a warm, nutty, autumnal flavour and gives a rich, round sour-sweetness to a green salad. I use it all the time, certainly more than white or tarragon vinegar. Get an old one if you can. If you think you need an excuse, try the following:

lamb steaks with sherry vinegar. Pour enough olive oil into a shallow pan to cover the bottom, let it get hot over a moderate heat, then put in a couple of salted, peppered and thymed lamb chump chops. Let them fry for three minutes, then turn them, cover with a lid and continue to cook until they are golden brown on both sides, the insides a ruby pink. Transfer the chops to a warm plate, tip the oil out of the pan, then pour in four good big glugs of sherry vinegar. It will seem an awful lot, but it will boil down to a thin, shiny juice as you scrape at the pan, stirring in the small layer of goo the lamb has left behind. Just as it is starting to look as if it will disappear, whisk in a thick slice of cold butter and you will see the juices become what you could loosely call a sauce. Grind in salt and black pepper, then pour the hot and bubbling, sweet-sharp juices over the chops. There will be just enough to wet them. Some sautéed potatoes would be nice to mop up the juices.

Balsamic vinegar is as mellow as vinegar gets. This thick, black-brown vinegar from Modena in northern Italy is made by allowing white grape juice to evaporate slowly in wooden barrels over a period of years until it is glossy, sticky, sweet, nutty, rich and velvety. I cannot pretend it is essential to our cooking in the way red wine vinegar is, and if I had to choose between this and sherry vinegar I would probably plump for the latter, but it is something that every cook might like to buy as a treat:

to enrich salad dressings and, I think even more importantly, to give depth to roasting juices and for shaking over grilled beef and lamb. It is not quite as versatile as some cooks would have you believe (like sun-dried tomatoes, balsamic vinegar can end up in the daftest places), but once you start using it you may find you cannot do without it.

You can pay the earth for a bottle of Aceto Balsamico Tradizionale di Modena. In some really smart food shops and Italian delis there can be as many as six different kinds of balsamic vinegar, with prices ranging from a couple of pounds to somewhere in the high two-figures. What they are asking you to pay for is scarcity (there are only about thirty families producing a total of less than 10,000 litres a year) and maturity: some balsamic vinegar can be aged for as long as fifty years (by which time it looks like treacle). To avoid a cheap, thin version, buy one that boasts the word tradizionale on its label. To get a clue to the sort of mellowness balsamic vinegar can add to your cooking, try this recipe:

> **baked field mushrooms with balsamic vinegar.** You will need one huge or two smaller mushrooms per person and a big roasting tin or baking sheet. Fit the mushrooms in snugly, then add butter in generous dollops, along with salt, black pepper, a little crushed garlic (no more than half a clove per 'shroom) and some balsamic vinegar. I usually just slosh it into the cups of the mushrooms, but it must be about half a tablespoon or so per large field mushroom. Bake at 200°C/Gas 6 until the fungi are soft and very, very tender – a matter of twenty to twenty-five minutes. Squeeze a lemon over at the table.

nam pla

Also known as Thai or Vietnamese fish sauce. Try to ignore that it is made from fermented anchovies (you wouldn't believe the smell of the factories) and concentrate on the fact that this thin brown liquid will add a warm, savoury depth to your soups, noodle dishes and stir-fries.

soy sauce

Dark is sweeter than light and Japanese shoyu is less salty than either. As a rough guide use light soy during cooking and dark as a table seasoning, but as always it is up to you.

Hot stuff

mustard

How I love mustard. Apart from a Mr Whippy-style dollop next to a steak, it is a major flavouring for everything from pasta to pork chops. I stand accused of overusing this particular ingredient, for which my enthusiasm never seems to dim.

Mustard adds a deep, aromatic pungency to your cooking, milder than the other 'bringers of heat', such as chillies and horseradish, and with more savoury depth. There are several types, from the searing heat of vivid yellow English to the mild, sweet flavour of dark, smooth German mustard. All mustards are interesting to the cook, and it is worth trying the whole range until you find one that suits you and your cooking.

There are several ways of getting mustard's spicy heat into your food; the most obvious is to spread it straight from the jar. The second is to add it to a sauce during cooking. The immediate hit of most of the mustard oil will evaporate, slowly softening into the general savour of the casserole or braise. This means that you will lose the instant fierceness but retain the deeper, herbal notes. The third way is to add it at the end of cooking – say, to the meat juices or cream. Here you will get the initial exciting flash of heat, too.

My first love is smooth, pale French Dijon. It is hot, clean and deeply savoury. I use it in salad dressings, on the side of the plate with steak, lamb and chicken, on ham sandwiches and stirred into any sauce or casserole that asks simply for 'mustard'. Cooking without Dijon mustard would be flat – the thought of a thin, crusty ham baguette without a slathering of Dijon fills me with gloom. This mustard really shines in the kitchen, stirred into gravy or a sauce for chops or to add a warming depth to a sauce for a pork casserole.

Moutarde de Meaux, the grainy, slightly milder mustard with many of the seeds left in, is, I think, the best for a classic cream and mustard sauce for pork chops.

The ultra-hot English mustard is the one most people swear by for smearing on roast beef but its extra heat also tempers pleasingly with slow cooking, offering a deep-rooted quality to a rich casserole. Use more than the merest smear and your eyes will water and your nose will run. I buy the old-fashioned powder, which is a pain to mix up every time you use it but is better than having an ageing jar of ready-made taking up fridge space (I have a pathological hatred of jars and tubes that go crusty round the top).

fresh chillies

Add a tiny red birdseye, a crisp green Serrano or a plump Scotch Bonnet to your cooking and your food comes alive, your eyes sparkle, your nose runs. A fresh chilli might lack the smoky depth of the dried versions, but they add excitment and a clean biting tingle that becomes addictive. The legend is the smaller the chilli, the hotter it is. This is a good rule of thumb but I have often come across a rogue that either disappoints or blows my mind. Slice them finely and remove the seeds to soften some of the effect. An ingredient to excite and awaken the senses.

dried chillies

It's amazing the difference a little dried chilli can make to your cooking. I am not talking purely in terms of heat here but of flavour, too. It takes a while to suss out the different characteristics of various types of chilli and to realise that they have more to offer than just a blast of heat. Unlike the mouth-tingling sparkle of fresh chillies, dried ones offer a much richer warmth, especially when cooked slowly in stews and curries.

Dried chillies, mostly the deepest garnet red, are available whole, crushed or powdered. In some dishes you may find it easiest to use whole chillies rather than crushed. You have greater control over the heat they give to your food. Rather than adhering to the quantities in a recipe, you can control the heat yourself by 'walking the chilli', which means using a whole dried chilli pepper and removing it when the sauce is hot enough. Organised cooks tie a piece of string to the stalk; I just chuck it in, then fish around with a spoon when it has done its bit.

Over the years I have decided that crushed dried chillies are more useful to me than whole or powdered ones. I use whole chillies in stews but I suspect that too many end their days hanging beside the cooker in a string gathering dust. Ideally you might have all three types in your kitchen, and if you are a chilli aficionado then probably several different varieties – you can even get a range of ground chillies now – all of whose heat, sweetness and flavour will differ. The strength you enjoy is purely personal and I am afraid the only way to find out is by trial and error. I spent years being too timid with my use of chillies. But that was before I knew that if you add too much chilli to something, its heat can be softened by the addition of cream, yogurt or coconut milk.

So scatter a pinch on your pasta, a little more in your tomato sauce and more still in a curry. See what happens, remembering to give each addition time to develop its flavour within the sauce.

chilli sauces

Very useful, especially for those who eat lots of noodles. There are several available, from the classic Vietnamese brand in the red bottle, through Thai and Chinese and, of course, the famous one from Louisiana that is an essential component of a bloody Mary. They all differ slightly in consistency and heat and I am afraid you will just have to try several until you find the one you like best. Unlike dried chillies, chilli sauce is good for last-minute adjustments to your cooking, even as late as at the table. I once had a Vietnamese flatmate who shook his precious sauce on everything he put in his mouth. Even his chewing gum.

chilli prawns. Sticky, garlicky finger food as hot as you like. In a wok or thin pan set over a high heat, fry a couple of cloves of crushed or very finely chopped garlic in a little oil until pale nut brown. Then throw in a handful of raw prawns, shell on, and toss them around in the heat till they turn salmon red. We are talking only a couple of minutes here. Toss in a few shakes of chilli sauce – I recommend a Thai or Chinese one for this but for no other reason than that it seems appropriate – then a flick of crushed sea salt. Roughly chopped coriander leaves and a squeeze of lime would be great here, too. Tear the hot, sticky prawns apart with your fingers, adding more chilli, salt and lime as you want.

Some useful spices

You don't need a cupboard full of spices, a little glass army of ground dust losing its magic and passing its sell-by date. Why not keep just a small amount of each of your favourites, bought whole so that they keep their precious fragrance till you need them? Most of us will get more joy from a few common spices in good condition than a show-off array of pots of ready-ground powder. The mystery, and point, of spices fades rapidly once their seeds, roots or stems have been ground. I know others will tell you differently but, believe me, once you have ground some spices and their essential oils have been released, their sweet, musky, citrus or peppery fragrances don't hang around for long.

cumin seeds

Earthy, musty, mysterious. If you are planning to cook Indian recipes, and I hope you are, then you will need some cumin seeds – they are the backbone of many traditional masalas, or spice mixes. To me, ground cumin sometimes has a whiff of armpits to it.

ground turmeric

A stunning shade of ochre, similar to the vivid yellow-orange of monks' robes that you see in Thailand, this spice will add serious colour to your curry. And also to your hands and clothes. And to your tea towels, fingernails and hair. So take care. To my nose, there is something ancient and dusty about the smell of turmeric, reminding me of ginger, old houses and old-fashioned chalky emulsion paint. In your cooking it adds a very slight bitterness, a distinct yet pleasing muskiness and a vibrant yellow hue.

cardamom pods

My favourite spice, heavily perfumed, lemony and camphoric. I find something magical about the black seeds inside cardamom's pale green pods. As I bash away at the seeds with a pestle and mortar, the heavenly scent that wafts up reminds me of the little spice-dealing shops in the back streets of Cochin in Kerala.

Cardamom is as happy in sweets and pastries as it is in a garam masala, the mild, sweet Indian spice mix. I always throw several cardamom pods into a rice pilau. They make the most mysteriously scented ice-cream, especially when you add a little rosewater. I sometimes put a cardamom pod in an espresso, just as the Arabs do. I rarely use the white or dark brown ones, which I feel lack much of the magic of the green. Buying ready-ground cardamom is utterly pointless. I think there is no more elusive spice.

cinnamon sticks

Not to be confused with the similar-looking cassia, which is thicker and less delicate. These add a warming note to poached fruits, curries and pilaus. A stick of cinnamon lends as much sweet, woody warmth to a dish of rice pudding as it does to a chicken curry. I have seen quills of cinnamon, made from the bark of the cinnamon tree, being rolled in huts in the forest in Sri Lanka, where the local farmers insist that the finest are thin and unblemished. Fat sticks are usually padded with loose bits of bark and tend to lose some of their stuffing in the cooking. I suggest you keep a bundle of sticks around; they are surprisingly useful and you can grind them in a coffee grinder. If you end up not using them, you can always tie them to the Christmas tree.

coriander seeds

If you crush a handful of oval, honey-coloured Indian coriander seeds (the round ones are from Morocco) in a pestle and mortar, the smell that greets you is warm and faintly tinged with orange. I find the tiny ridged seeds can be ground most successfully in a coffee mill. They add a layer of warmth to a curry and are often used alongside smaller amounts of cumin. What I don't like is when people leave them in their sauces and you have to fish them out methodically.

fennel seeds

Aniseed flavourings are useful to the cook, be they in the form of fresh chervil or tarragon leaves; a dried spice such as anise, fennel seed or star anise (for Chinese roast duck); fresh fennel bulbs and fronds; or even a bottle of Pernod or Ricard. Fennel seeds are one of the most useful dried spices, sitting as comfortably in Mediterranean cooking as they do in Indian. Pale green and ridged, they make a flattering seasoning for roast pork. Try scattering a few over a pork loin before it goes in the oven.

and more

I also suggest you might like to have a nutmeg or two in the house for grating its sweet, ephemeral warmth into fruit cakes and white sauces; some blue-black gin-and-tonic-scented juniper berries for crushing and dropping into pork casseroles or grinding on to pan-fried pork chops; and a little box of saffron stamens for giving a golden earthiness to fish soup and rice.

Herbs

dried herbs

It is fashionable to dismiss all dried herbs with a wave of the hand. And, to be honest, most of them are a waste of space. No dried herb can compare with a fresh one. Dried sage is musty, coriander is pointless, thyme tastes flat and parsley is a joke. But hang on. There are one or two dried herbs that I think are worth having around. Tarragon is surprisingly good in a chicken pie. Dried mint – though nothing like the fresh – adds interest to a yogurt marinade for grilled chicken and is used extensively in the Middle East, despite the fresh herb being cheap and plentiful. And dried oregano is used on every pizza from Florence to Sicily. In fact, I actually prefer dried oregano to fresh. So let's not be too dismissive.

The best of the lot is herbes de Provence, an aromatic, slightly sweet mixture of thyme, lavender, savory and fennel seeds. Sometimes you will find other herbs in there, too. I throw this seasoning around with gay abandon, especially on chicken before grilling and on lamb before it goes in the oven. When the smoke rises from the grill, the smell reminds me of holidays in the South of France. If you refuse to use any other dried herb (and well you might), then at least try this.

fresh herbs

Herbs can form part of the backbone of a recipe – for example, when thyme and bay are cooked slowly with onions, garlic and celery to create an aromatic base for a soup, stew or braise. Or they can be the point of a recipe, such as when basil is pounded with garlic, Parmesan and olive oil to make a pesto sauce for pasta. Either way, herbs will add untold fragrance and flavour to your cooking.

The herbs to add at the start of cooking are usually those with woody stems and tough leaves, which tend to give up their flavour gradually. I am thinking here of robust herbs whose taste is not dispelled by cooking, such as thyme, rosemary, bay and sage. They work best in the cooking juices of meat and vegetables, and will even stand up to the relentless heat of the barbecue (try scattering rosemary needles on lamb chops). They are true pot herbs, and though aficionados may happily add raw thyme leaves or young rosemary to their salads, this is not for most of us.

The more ephemeral herbs, whose essential oils are at their best when the herbs are warmed rather than cooked, are mostly tender and floppy-leafed. Think of dill, basil, coriander, parsley leaves (the stalks are fine for slow cooking) and mint. These are better used raw, and do not take kindly to long cooking. Stew basil, mint or tarragon and you will have nothing to show at the end.

I buy my herbs in small bunches rather than in those silly little cellophane packets, rinsing them under cold water, then putting them, still damp, into a plastic click-top box in the fridge. That way they seem to keep for days in good condition and I can pick at them as and when I need them. When they start to wilt, I chuck them into soup.

There are hundreds of herbs, most of which are of interest to the cook. Do try the lemon thymes and the Thai basils if you come across them. Here are a few of the most popular and available herbs, and the ones I have found to be the most useful.

thyme

Coarse-leafed, warm and earthy thyme grows on hillsides around the Mediterranean and will feel at home in any recipe involving (as you might expect) lamb, garlic, olives, sweet onions and tomatoes. An onion tart, perhaps, a dish of roasted garlic or a rich meat stew. Think of the bold-tasting food of the Med: the smoky grills of lamb and pork, the robust fish and rabbit casseroles, the tomato sauces and the salty sheep's and goat's milk cheeses. Add small whole branches of thyme to a lamb braise or rabbit stew so that you can lift them out when they have done their work. Use chopped leaves in soups or coarse pâtés, or as a rub for a shoulder or leg of lamb. Add them to minced lamb or pork with chilli flakes and lemon zest to make meatballs. If you are the sort of person who makes a stuffing for your Sunday roast chicken, then this is your herb, too. Use the smallest, tenderest leaves of thyme in a feta and spinach salad.

If you are wondering why thyme often lacks the clout of the thyme that you smell by the sea, it is probably something to do with the soil in which it is grown. Rich soil seems to soften its pungency. The fancy thymes, with their hints of aniseed and orange, are worth trying. But it is the everyday garden thyme that is probably the most useful – just crushing its tiny leaves in the palm of your hand is instantly redolent of those long climbs up Greek hillsides, when every footstep releases the smell of herbs. Perhaps this is the reason I think of thyme as the quintessential grilling herb. Its flavour will stand up to the searing heat, and it seems so right with the charred edges of grilled pork and lamb. Choose small leaves and moisten them with olive oil, crushed garlic cloves, black pepper and lemon juice, then massage over lamb steaks or chops an hour or more before grilling.

bay

Bay sits quietly in the background, sending out mild, savoury notes that you can barely put your finger on. It needs moisture and long, gentle cooking to work its magic. Bay leaves are particularly worth using in any slow-cooked recipe that includes meat, red wine, garlic and onions. They are often what is missing when a stock or white sauce tastes flat. Their effect is subtle and, though it sounds strange, is actually more noticeable by its absence.

To experience the discreet yet important difference bay makes to a recipe, try this:

pommes boulangère. Slice four or five potatoes thinly and jumble them in a shallow baking dish with salt and pepper, four crushed garlic cloves, a thinly sliced onion and four bay leaves. Pour over enough vegetable or chicken stock (from a cube or tub) to come level with the top layer, then bake in an oven preheated to 180°C/Gas 4 for an hour or so, till they are knife-point tender and starting to collapse into the stock.

rosemary

Used sparingly – a branch or two tucked under a pork roast; a few needles scattered over lamb or sardines destined for the grill; a twig submerged in a lamb casserole – rosemary will add the pine and camphor aroma of the Mediterranean to your cooking. Use any one of the many varieties in a lamb, chicken or rabbit marinade, where it will provide a gently resinous background flavour.

sage

Medicinal, musty and camphoric. Use with caution (unless you actually like the taste of mothballs). A couple of leaves added to liver as it fries will give a pleasing warmth. I have to say that it works better in the garden than it does in the kitchen.

tarragon

I am hopelessly in love with the aniseed notes of tarragon and would happily admit that a classic chicken tarragon is one of my favourite things to eat. Though tender in the extreme, tarragon is a herb that needs cooking, the heat softening its assertive flavour. Used raw – say, in a salad – it is too much of a good thing and can overpower the other ingredients. The raw leaves can work if you chop them very finely and leave them to sit in a mixture of olive oil and vinegar for a while before using it to dress a salad. Even then it can be pushy.

Tarragon was born for chicken. Whether you poke a handful into a free-ranger before roasting, or sauté some chicken thighs and make a sauce with the pan scrapings dislodged with white wine and thickened with cream, you will end up with a sublime supper. Rabbit, too.

A béarnaise sauce, the egg and butter emulsion spiked with wine vinegar and shallot, needs a sprig of tarragon, too. Make a liquid seasoning with the tarragon, shallot, a few peppercorns and a few glugs of vinegar, adding it to the egg yolks before you whisk in the butter. A handful of chopped tarragon can be stirred in once the sauce has thickened.

98

You can use this herb with olive oil but it much prefers dairy produce. I often add a scattering of leaves to mushrooms that I am frying in butter and which will end up on thick, soft toast. Don't worry if the leaves go a bit floppy in the fridge; there is still plenty of flavour in them yet.

coriander

The world's most popular herb. At first cautious of its in-your-face, like-it-or-loathe-it reputation, I now buy this frilly-leafed herb by the large bunch, using its almost addictive flavour in salads, vegetables and stir-fries and in great handfuls in Thai curries.

Coriander is one to add at the end of your cooking as a last-minute seasoning rather than at the start when you are making a flavour base with onions and garlic – as you might with thyme or bay. The flavour disappears on cooking. Be warned, though. People who dislike it tend to do so with a vengeance. It is worth shouting, 'Is there anyone who doesn't like coriander?' before you chuck it over everyone's supper.

Coriander – cilantro to Americans – usually works in dishes in which you have already used soy sauce and garlic, seafood, chicken, lime juice or chillies. Chillies and coriander (one hot, the other cool) is a match made in heaven.

Bunches of coriander seem to keep best rolled in damp newspaper and tucked into the salad drawer of the fridge (the stems go slimy in water). Choose perky bunches, if possible with their roots on. Not simply because they keep better that way but because the roots can be scrubbed and added to Thai curry paste.

It may not be love at first bite. Those new to this herb, originally from southern Europe and now grown everywhere from South America to China, may find it takes a while to understand the appeal. Then bang. One day you wake up and find yourself a junkie.

parsley

A peaceful, grounding herb that soothes rather than excites. Think roast cod and creamy parsley sauce. Think boiled gammon, broad beans and parsley sauce. Like coriander, it's a herb for adding towards the end of cooking, though the stalks sheared of their leaves can and should be added early on to stocks and soups. The freshness of the leaves becomes cabbagy with long cooking.

Either the flat Mediterranean variety or the mossy, curly British will lend an earthy greenness to your cooking. Its flavour does much for fish. Hence the pairing of parsley sauce and parsley butter with cod and haddock. I dislike the way some cooks throw it willy-nilly over everything. Parsley should be used only when it suits the flavour of the dish.

The most vivid use for flat-leafed parsley is in tabbouleh, the Lebanese cracked wheat salad. The herb freshens and adds lushness to the bland, chewy grain. Try it:

tabbouleh. Take equal amounts of bulgur wheat and bright and bushy flat-leaf parsley. Rinse the wheat in a sieve and then soak it for twenty minutes in cold water. It should plump up a little. Chop the parsley, then toss it with the drained grain, enough extra virgin olive oil to moisten and enough lemon juice to make your lips smart. Eat as is with grilled fish or chicken, or toss in some crumbled feta, chopped tomatoes and chopped mint and eat it as a main-course salad with hunks of bread.

basil

Basil's soft, tender leaves with their hint of pepper and clove are inextricably linked to the cooking, and particularly the salads and pasta, of the Mediterranean. Bright sun intensifies basil's perfume, which is partly why the tomato salad we make at home with supermarket basil tastes less interesting than the ones we have eaten on the terrace of a trattoria in southern Italy.

I buy basil plants ad nauseam, with the promise that I shall definitely keep this one alive. I never do. I forget to water their thin compost, even when I keep the plant perched behind the sink. The basil I have grown myself from seed has been stronger stemmed and more intensely flavoured, though it has a habit of suddenly expiring on me. Buying a couple of stocky, bushy plants from a garden centre will work for you if you are the sort of person who needs just a few leaves for salad and can manage to pick only the tips of the plant and the occasional large leaf so that the plant is with you all summer. If you make lots of pesto, then it is probably best to forget plants altogether. Buy great, bushy bunches from an Italian grocer's or a supermarket.

Basil loves being warm but loathes being cooked, which is why Italian cooks allow the heat of the just-drained pasta to warm their pesto rather than heating it separately. The warm pasta releases the basil's fragrance; too much heat kills it. I sometimes tuck some basil leaves inside tomatoes that I am baking or grilling but the effect is even more successful if I simply add the torn-up leaves with a dousing of olive oil at the end of cooking .

dill

Another of the aniseed flavours, but this time with the merest hint of lemon. I am more fond of dill than most cooks, adding it to salmon steaks that I am wrapping in foil (with a splash of white wine) and baking. I sometimes stir the chopped fronds into hollandaise for salmon, though its primary use is in vast quantities to coat gravad lax, the herb-cured Scandinavian salmon. Try tossing hot new potatoes in melted butter and finely chopped dill for a change.

chives

Despite my love of the other members of the allium family – onions, leeks and garlic – I rarely use chives. Perhaps it is overkill from the chive-flavoured cream cheeses so popular in my childhood, or simply that I prefer my onions cooked. I find the flavour of raw onion lingers longer than I would like. Yet chives are an undeniably popular herb, giving mild onion notes to salads and omelettes.

mint

The freshest, cleanest-tasting of all culinary herbs. Which is presumably why it is used in toothpaste. Try it the English way, dropped into the water for boiling new potatoes or chopped finely and moistened with vinegar and a little sugar to accompany roast lamb (food snobs will tell you that mint sauce should never be served with roast lamb but I disagree). Better still, use the tenderest leaves – the older ones tend to be on the hairy side – finely chopped in lentil salads, with bulgur wheat, parsley and lemon juice (lots, please) or left whole and stuffed into Vietnamese rice paper rolls. I like to hide whole mint leaves in warm pitta bread stuffed with charcoal-grilled lamb, yogurt and garlic. Mint is one of the few herbs that keeps better in a jug of water than in the fridge.

growing your own

I have not (yet) been bitten by the grow-your-own-food bug – that rosy ideal where you have tended every carrot in your stew and every apple in your pie. Yet I do grow a few vegetables and herbs. I must admit that the tomatoes I pick from my own straggly plants and even the basil from my own replanted supermarket bush seem to have a more intense flavour than those from the shops, though nothing I grow tastes better than anything I buy from the farmers' market. I am certainly more careful with my own produce than with things I buy in the shops, and have a certain reverence for the thyme, coriander, rhubarb and courgettes I grow. There is a certain ceremony attached to eating them. Which, in its own way, adds to the pleasure. I think I have more respect for them.

I am not going to wave my arms around and suggest that you dig up your roses for rows of swedes and Brussels sprouts, but I cannot pretend that eating food you have tended yourself doesn't carry with it something special. Freshness – the speed with which food ends up in the market (and therefore in your kitchen) – is probably the most important factor in determining food quality, and as important as whether it is grown organically or not, so the whole grow-your-own thing starts to make sense. Something picked or dug from the garden moments before you cook and eat it is a thing of almost immeasurable pleasure.

Vegetables and fruit – how to get the best

I make no attempt to cover every vegetable here. Just to offer a few hints where I think it might help.

greens

spinach

Whether you are buying young, heart-shaped leaves for a salad (try them with crumbled feta and olive oil) or the larger, deeply veined cooking spinach to steam and serve with butter, both should be perky, lush and deep emerald green. The big leaves should squeak as you rummage through the box. Check the packs of ready-washed baby leaves in the supermarket for any hint of wetness or slimy edges. Such fragility is quick to turn. British garden-grown spinach appears throughout the summer, then it's imports from the Med. Both sorts need a thorough washing, though you will have to be tender with the younger leaves. They store well for a couple of days sprayed with water and squeezed into a plastic bag. Two favourite ways: a salad of young leaves with snippets of crisp bacon and juicy grapes (you need not peel but you must pip); and the older, larger leaves washed, steamed or briefly boiled, then roughly chopped and reheated in butter. A dusting of nutmeg is good here too, as is a spoonful of cream. Dairy produce mellows the oxalic acid in the leaves – that's the stuff that makes your teeth feel fuzzy. It is worth buying about three times as much spinach as you think you will need. No matter how briefly you cook them, even the perkiest of leaves wither to a fraction of their original selves.

cabbage and spring greens

Don't even think of getting fancy with cabbage. Nothing beats a quick blanching in boiling, salted water, a good squeeze and then a slathering of melted butter. Do this at the last minute, making certain to squeeze out the excess water, and be generous with the butter. Whether you are using the hard white cabbage, the deep blue-green Savoy or a gorgeous bunch of spring greens, just go for the ones that look most exciting – by which I mean lots of crisp-stemmed, beautiful leaves dotted with dew and begging you to buy. Oh, and throw out any recipe you may have for stuffed cabbage, even mine. They are all disgusting.

kale

Not for wimps. Earthy, pungent and very good for you (fibre, iron, potassium etc). Choose the smallest leaves and discard the coarsest stems, then steam or boil briefly in salted water. Loves butter, so be generous with it.

cauliflower

Look for creamy heads of cauliflower with hard, tightly packed florets, still with their fringe of pale-green leaves. Pass by any that are bruised or soft or that have been over-trimmed – a sure sign of age and the greengrocer being desperate to get them out of the shop. Passé it may be, but there are few more suitable ends for a cauliflower than to find itself boiled, drained and coated in a properly made cheese sauce. Resist the temptation to undercook. The *raison d'être* of a cauli is to end its days as a soft and gentle supper to soothe the frazzled and overworked.

broccoli

Locally grown broccoli is available throughout spring, summer and autumn, though it tastes like a winter veg to me. Just the thing for those times when your body tells you it wants something green, healthy and vitamin rich. Sold in tempting shrink-wrapped posies in the supermarket (so easy to pick up) or in loose bunches at the greengrocer's, broccoli lasts better than most other green vegetables. It is the iceberg lettuce of the cabbage family. As a healthy green vegetable it is unbeatable, but I can't help thinking of it as boring. And why does it go cold so quickly? Even more so when it is fashionably undercooked. Where it becomes interesting is when it is briefly steamed, then stir-fried Chinese-style with lots of garlic and soy.

purple sprouting broccoli

One of the glories of spring. Long, slender stalks of broccoli with a purple head. Love it. Cooked with a careful eye on the clock, those tender stems can be as good to eat as asparagus. Especially if you can be bothered to make a bowl of hollandaise to dip them in. Don't strip off the leaves; they are good to eat, too.

brussels sprouts

Why are you even thinking of buying a bag of pungent, watery little balls that give you wind?

chinese greens

Why anyone would choose to eat Brussels sprouts when they can buy Chinese greens is anyone's guess. The most accessible of these are:

Bok choi – thick, short, white stems that are crisp and full of juice, with small, tender, dark-green leaves. Sold in plump bunches (the stems are the shape of those little white Chinese soup spoons), great for steaming and stir-frying.

Gaai choi – thin, bright-green stems with floppy leaves and tiny yellow flowers. Best just as the buds open. Hot, mustard flavour. Great with pork or chicken.

To taste them at their best, lay Chinese greens in a steamer basket or colander and cook over boiling water till tender. When the stems are soft to the point of a knife, lift them out and dress while hot with oyster sauce and a shake or two of dark soy sauce.

roots and other earthy vegetables

carrots

This vivid orange root is at its sweetest in spring. Left in the ground till winter, it develops an earthiness, too. Either way, carrots are at their best eaten crisp and raw from the bag, still dripping from a quick scrub under an ice-cold tap while you unpack the rest of the shopping. I never serve them as a vegetable, preferring the dramatic raw crunch of the uncooked. Diced and fried slowly in oil, bacon fat or butter with onions and other aromatics, they add a deep sweetness to a braise, soup or stew. Store in the bottom of the fridge or in a brown paper bag somewhere cool and dry.

parsnips

With the underlying sweetness common to all root vegetables, the parsnip is at its best roasted till amber coloured and sticky, its flesh fluffy, its toasted edges deep brown and chewy. A sensation alongside rare roast beef. Boiled and mashed with hot milk and butter, it makes a blissful mound of soothing starch for you to scoop on to your fork with roast pork or baked ham. And there's more. The parsnip takes spices better than almost any other vegetable. Try stirring garam masala and cream into parsnip mash, or a spoonful of grain mustard, or crushed chilli flakes and mint into parsnip soup. Choose heavy specimens (they go spongy as they get older), avoiding both the giant woody ones and the tasteless mini-versions that some supermarkets try to sell us.

beetroot

The beets you want are about as big as golf balls, with a frilly plume of ruby-red and emerald leaves. (The ones you don't want are ready cooked, vinegared and wrapped in plastic.) They will be small and very sweet. Try baking them in foil till knife-point tender – their flavour will deepen – then peel and split them and dunk them into thick soured cream. Baby beets, barely bigger than a gobstopper, can be boiled to tenderness in fifteen minutes. A sweet treat with a bit of boiled ham. Store raw beetroot in the fridge, where it will keep in fine nick for several weeks.

jerusalem artichokes

I am enormously fond of Jerusalem artichokes, especially when their warm earthiness is exploited in a soup. Even without the help of a dairy tub, they produce a velvety soup. Like carrots, they make a watery mash but will roast as sweet as a nut, going gooey at the edges like a parsnip. Choose plump, hard tubers. The smoother ones are easier to peel, though there is no need to be particularly fussy; the odd bit of ivory skin won't hurt. If you have never tried Jerusalem artichokes, please let me tempt you. Throw a few around the roast for a start, then have a go at some soup – it is the most voluptuous, soothing and delicate of all. Oh, and by the way, I almost forgot. They make you fart.

sweet potatoes

Ignore all those recipes for pie, cheesecake and God knows what. The only way to enjoy the golden, caramel flesh of a sweet potato is to cook it like a baked potato. It is ready when you see sticky beads of nectar bubbling from its skin and perfect when it feels soft and squashy and near a state of collapse. Split the soft skin with a knife, then mash butter into its frothy, orange-gold flesh, beating it gently with a fork till it will take no more. Eat it immediately, skin and all, while the butter is still running in rivulets. And don't even think of making sweet potato pie.

swedes

Peel, boil, drain thoroughly, then mash with lots of butter and black pepper for a mild, silky accompaniment to roast lamb or pork. Any other recipe is probably a waste of time.

potatoes

The texture of a potato is as important as its flavour. I think I would say even more so. There are two main types: the small, waxy ones and the crumbly, floury ones. You need dry-fleshed, floury spuds – the thick-skinned, pale-fleshed King Edward, Maris Piper and Wilja varieties – for any recipe where you want a dry, fluffy, open texture that also crisps up well on the outside – say, for chips or sautéed or roast potatoes and, of course, for baked potatoes and mash. When you want something firm and buttery, which will soak up stock, cream, oil or butter without collapsing, such as for a salad, a creamy gratin or for eating *au naturel*, then I suggest a fudgy, yellow-fleshed variety such as Charlotte, La Ratte or the pink-skinned Fir Apple. If you have bought your spuds at a supermarket rather than the greengrocer's or market, take them out of their plastic bag as soon as you get home and store them in a cool, dark, dry place. Use the fridge only if there is nowhere else. Look out for unusual varieties, too, like the aptly named Purple Congo or the Salad Red; they are fun. In May and June, seek out the tiny, kidney-shaped Jerseys. In spring and high summer it is worth sucking up to friends who grow their own new potatoes. Pulled from the ground just before you cook them (in salted water with a little mint, like your mother used to), they are an unbeatable treat.

celery

A bit of a cook's vegetable, this one. I mean, few people would buy it to eat as a vegetable in its own right, though it would certainly get my vote. Try laying the separated sticks in a shallow baking dish, covering them with stock or water, then braising them in a low oven. Few vegetables turn out as juicy. I think celery reaches its zenith when served as a vegetable alongside a roast accompanied with gravy. Braised celery and gravy from a roast is a splendid thing. Its principal use, though, is as an aromatic with onion and carrot, giving body to soup and stock and forming the base for a braise. Celery's mild bitterness lends a clean note to chicken stock. What is more, the stems give crunch and body to a salad, make a gentle, consoling soup, and, eaten raw and cold from the fridge, provide a feel-smug alternative to eating yet another potato crisp. Look for unblemished heads – peer down past the turret of leaves to check that the stems are good looking all through. British-grown celery is available throughout the autumn and winter. The green stuff is juicier but milder tasting; white celery has a deeper flavour. Take your pick.

leeks

Think of the leek as a sweet, silky, user-friendly onion. Locally grown leeks are available in some form or another all year round, though I suggest you avoid the real whoppers, which can be a bit woody in the middle. The pencil-thin ones are a delicacy. Try them steamed and dressed with a mustardy

vinaigrette and snippets of chopped, crisply fried bacon. Leeks can get you out of loads of trouble: you can cut them thick and fry them as a sweet, buttery accompaniment to grilled meat or fish; you can simmer them in stock and blitz them into a cleansing, nourishing soup; cook them slowly in butter and oil as the principal filling for a quiche (they marry perfectly with the creamy wibble-wobble custard filling); or you can add them to a braise, stew or soup instead of or as well as onions. Leeks really shine in a thin stew with fatty lamb, eaten with bacon or pancetta, or with potatoes in the ultimate cold-weather soup.

onions

Onions are the heart and soul of much of our cooking, a savoury base on which to build up flavour and body. Yes, but I like them as a vegetable too, cooked very slowly in butter so that they end up soft, glossy and golden, their flesh slithery and melting, their edges tinged with sweet, brown caramel. You need patience to let them cook to that stage, and you can never cook enough. Especially when the rest of the family smells them cooking, and they are served with gravy and fluffy mashed potato. As I said, though, they are the heart and soul of our casseroles and braises, our stews and pies, our curries and gravies. They are as much a part of the kitchen basics as salt, pepper, garlic and lemon. They will make you cry, or at least the volatile substance, allicin, in them will. The tears dry up once the sweet smell of frying onions fills the kitchen.

Shop for onions that are firm and tight, with thick skins. Locally grown ones are available from early autumn to late spring. Which is, of course, just when we are most likely to need them. And have you ever tried them peeled, briefly boiled and baked in butter? Soft, golden globes of sugar to flatter your roast beef and mustard.

shallots

Graceful, oval, tapered onions, their golden skin flushed with pink. Look out for them from November to March, giving them a squeeze before you buy; they should be firm and smooth. Chop them as fine as tea leaves for buttery sauces, or roast them whole like a baked potato, then slip the silky flesh from its skin and smear with soft butter and crumbled farmhouse cheese.

other good things

sweetcorn

A late-summer and autumn treat. Pick them up and fondle them before you commit yourself. The husk should be pale green and the silky threads underneath soft and fresh. The cob itself should be hard and crisp, with no blemishes or missing kernels. Do nothing clever with them, just get them to the pot as quickly as possible. Simply boil them in lots of water, then eat with melted butter and salt, letting the sweet, buttery juices dribble down your chin.

asparagus

The British season is from the middle of May till the end of June. A delicacy not to be missed. There is imported stuff for the rest of the year but it rarely comes up to scratch. Check the ends of each bundle, avoiding any that are cracked and dry or appear woody. You need them fresh and damp. Like sweetcorn, time is crucial here, and the clock is ticking from the moment the spears are cut. Hurry them to a pot of boiling water – ignoring all that twaddle about tying up the bundle with string or, most laughably, standing them proud in the water by surrounding them with new potatoes. They will come to no harm if you allow them to move about in the water. They are cooked when the spears will bend gently and a knifepoint goes into the thick end of the stalk with ease. If you can bear not to eat them with hollandaise sauce, remember you can roast them too, wrapped in foil with a spoonful of water and a slice of butter tucked inside.

chicory

Look for firm heads with no bruising, the whiter the better. When you come across any of the ravishingly beautiful red-tipped variety that open like parrot tulips, snap them up. Eat them as a scrunchy winter salad with crumbled Roquefort and a drizzle of walnut oil or blanch them in boiling water, then drain and bake under a cheese sauce – for perfection, wrapped in bacon.

avocados

Tricky. Often sold underripe so that you can get them home in one piece. Some supermarkets are now packing ripe ones in stiff plastic so you can eat them the day you buy but most of the time we have to take pot luck. Treat them with care when choosing. I hate to watch shoppers digging their thumbs in, then throwing them around. A gentle squeeze in the palm of your hand should indicate one that is nearly ripe. Just avoid any with black marks; they will be black and bitter inside. This is one vegetable (actually it's a fruit) that we need to bring to ripeness at home rather than trust a shopkeeper. They have enough to think about. My favourite, for both flavour and practicality, is the Hass variety, the ones with the thick, dark alligator skin. Their flesh is nutty and buttery and their hard skins offer some protection on the way home from the shops. If you want to get fancy with them I suggest serving them with warm, streaky bacon with its fat used as the dressing. Soft green peppercorns work well here, too. A little lemon juice will bring out their flavour and stop their gentle green flesh turning brown. To accelerate their ripening, you can put a ripe banana amongst them; the gasses it gives off will speed up the avocado's progress.

111

mushrooms

An autumn shopper in an Italian or French market is likely to be greeted with an array of mushrooms that would terrify the average British cook. So many flavours, colour and shapes. Aren't some of these supposed to be poisonous? You need do no more than fry any of them in butter with a little garlic and parsley or roast them with thyme and bacon, turning them over in the butter so that they soften and caramelise. In the UK, things have been looking up lately, with the supermarkets offering apricot-coloured chanterelles, shaggy chestnut mushrooms and thin enoki that look like nothing more than cotton buds. The top end of the deli market may also have a fat, toadstool-shaped porcini or two, though it will cost you a fortune. Try anything you can find. My favourites are still the huge field mushrooms, with their velvety undercarriage of brown gills. I know they lack the designer foodie cachet of the wild ones but I love their beefsteak-like texture. I roast them with garlic and butter until they are tender and full of savoury juice. And I love the way their salty juice soaks through buttered toast as the finest 'something-on-toast' supper in the world.

Most people tell you not to wash mushrooms, but how else are you supposed to get rid of the grit and growing medium? Go over each one with a make-up brush? Ignore them all and dunk your fungi very briefly into a bowl of cold water, giving them no time to sponge it up. Let them dry on kitchen paper before cooking them. And dry them you must – a soggy champignon will not brown.

Mushrooms will keep for a few days in a brown paper bag at the bottom of the fridge. In plastic they go slimy and black, which is fine if you take your fungi woodsy and autumnal.

beans

Fresh green beans snap crisply, exuding little beads of juice. They will smell like childhood summers. The imported haricot beans, lean and green, are great with fish, especially if you avoid the modern trend of undercooking them. They have the best flavour when they are boiled till slightly limp. But runner beans, which appear from midsummer throughout the autumn, have a deeper flavour and charming pink and purple mottled beans inside, and beg for a splash of melted butter. Fancy Italian borlotti are becoming a little easier to find now and are the fresh version of the dried beans we use in winter. Some of them are pink and cream and as beautiful as a vegetable can get. Boil them in lots of rolling, salted water and serve them with a drizzle of very fruity, emerald-green olive oil.

broad beans

Mealy, buttery, early summer beans that you either love or hate. Choose them when they are small; they toughen with age. The trick is not just to remove them from their pods but also to remove their grey skins when they are cooked. Apart from tossing the little things in hot bacon fat before you eat them, you really should try them with a clean-tasting sheep's milk cheese or ricotta.

peas

I am a fan of the frozen pea, grateful for its sweetness and convenience. Yet the fresh peas that appear in our shops in June and July offer something more – the delight of popping them from their pods and the childlike pleasure of eating them raw. Try them in a salad with sharp feta cheese.

aubergines

The most elegant of all vegetables, ranging from the diminutive green pea aubergine of the Thai kitchen through every shade of mauve, purple and cream. Recipes will instruct you to salt them but I recommend you take no notice – that habit belongs to the days before the bitterness was bred out of them. What salting does do is soften them so that they soak up less oil in the frying pan. A useful vegetable to have around; even one alone can be supper if you slice and flour it, then fry it till it is crisp and meltingly tender and dollop a little pesto, garlic mayonnaise or tomato sauce on the side. Look out for the charming cream and mauve aubergines that appear from time to time.

fruit

mangoes

Fewer fruits promise as much as a ripe mango, its tender skin the colour of sunset, its soft flesh heavy with juice. Ripeness, and your judgement of it, is crucial. There will be a heavy fragrance, and maybe the odd black dot. Hold a fruit you suspect of ripeness as tenderly as you might hold a breast, and squeeze it gently. If the fruit gives a little all round and you fear a firmer squeeze will do damage, then it is more than likely ready. The smaller, saffron-yellow Alphonse that appears in late spring has perhaps the most fragrant flesh of all. Ignore all recipes except possibly mango fool (fold the puréed flesh into softly, softly whipped cream and chill) and eat the ripe fruit as if you were eating a … no, I had better not.

papaya

Pear-shaped, golden fruit with deep orange-pink flesh holding hundreds of pearl-like black seeds in its middle. Discard them and rub a cut lime around the cut halves of the fruit, then eat its jelly-textured flesh with a teaspoon. They are scented at the stalk end when ripe and sometimes show the start of pock marks. Don't even think of cooking with them. One of my very favourite fruit (the others being melons, raspberries, peaches and figs) and one in which I indulge at breakfast, winter and summer. I can only suggest you do the same.

passion fruit

These golf-ball-sized, purple-black fruit are only ripe when wizened, but they should still be heavy. Light ones may have dried out. Cut your fruit in half, taking care the seeds don't squirt out, then suck out the sweetly tart juice and the scrunchy seeds. Prudes will use a teaspoon. Those who spit out the seeds may be missing the point. Squirt them over pavlova or vanilla ice-cream or make a fool with their juice and just a very few of their seeds. They add depth of flavour to strawberries, blackberries and pineapple.

pineapple

Not one for the cook, a pineapple is at its juicy best peeled and cut into thick slices for breakfast or dessert. Ripe ones are heavily, almost overpoweringly, fragrant and their flesh will yield when squeezed. The old trick of testing ripeness by tugging out a leaf is unreliable. Go by the smell.

melon

Perfection is a melon that drips with juice as you cut it and scoop out the seeds. The pale-green, almost blue Charentais has deep salmon-orange flesh and makes a fine sorbet. You simply mash the flesh of two large, very ripe fruit with a thin sugar syrup (made by dissolving 100g caster sugar in 100ml warm water), then freeze it in a plastic box, whisking it every hour till it is virtually frozen.

Salt will bring out the flavour of all melons, including the green-fleshed Ogen and the scarlet watermelon. Or try them with prosciutto, or a chunk of feta cheese marinated in olive oil and chopped mint, as a first course or light lunch.

peaches

A fruit for the hand rather than the kitchen. The white peach, with its tints of rose, has the heaviest scent and is my favourite, especially in a salad with raspberries. Others will prefer the classic golden-fleshed peach with its deep, almost claret-coloured skin. Don't cook with any of them, but check their progress towards ripeness daily with a sniff and a firm, loving squeeze.

nectarines

At its best this vermilion fruit offers sweet juice and a stone that comes away with ease. But it lacks the sexy fuzz of the peach, though no doubt there are those who find that a plus. Firmer fleshed than the peach, though with similar flavour, it is good for slicing into a richly coloured salad with blackberries and mild and milky buffalo mozzarella.

oranges

Look for fruit whose skin is not shiny with wax and that seem heavy for their size. They will be full of juice. Great for breakfast but also for their zest, which, if removed without any of the white pith underneath, is deeply aromatic, like the fruit's blossom. The juice adds depth to berries of all sorts, while the zest adds a warm, almost Eastern flavour to sponge cakes.

blood oranges

The juice is the thing. Serve it by the long glassful with ice and perhaps just the tiniest drop-splash of orange flower water. Good for soaking sponges, for making sorbets and for adding to the icing of a summer cake. In spring, when they first appear, I meticulously peel them, then slice their flesh into a watercress salad to go with roast duck or baked mackerel.

grapefruit

I use the tartness of this fruit to add some razzmatazz to morning orange juice but also in a salad with fennel to accompany baked fish or dressed crab.

figs

I rarely cook a fig, preferring to offer them piled on a dish with slices of prosciutto or goat's cheese, or simply to bite gently into them and suck at their crunchy seeds. Ripeness is everything, but rarely do I find a fig not worth eating. Put them on a sunny windowledge before you indulge; the warmth will make them even more delectable. Green, blush and purple figs can all be good. I like them pulled apart rather than sliced, and eaten with milky buffalo mozzarella or crème fraîche. A salad of purple figs and blackberries is staggeringly beautiful.

berries and currants

raspberries

The most intensely flavoured raspberries are those that appear late season, so look out for deep claret-red fruit in late summer and early autumn. Pile them into a bowl and serve with a jug of cream. When you have had your fill of eating them as they are, try them with very softly whipped cream and melted bitter chocolate, the latter setting to a crisp as you drizzle it over the piles of cold cream.

blackberries

Tart-sweet clusters of tiny berries in the wild; fatter, juicier and (sadly) sweeter when cultivated. Keep an eye out for them during August and September. Make the best old-fashioned pie of all with tart apples and good under a crumble, too. Try them in a salad with green-fleshed melon. The winter imports aren't at all bad and will liven up your muesli.

black currants

Sprinkle a little sugar and a tablespoon of water over the picked fruit and bring them to the boil. As the fruit bursts and the sugar melts you get an intensely flavoured, purple-black compote to pour over ice cream or poached pears. Or use them in a crumble and give everyone purple teeth. I like to float a little puddle of black currant compote over the top of a pot of chocolate mousse. Strange, but a gorgeously sensuous combination.

red currants

Tiny, tart little jewels. Use them in summer pudding (it ain't a summer pudding without them) and in a compote with black currants and raspberries or throw a handful into your breakfast muesli. I strip them of their stalks then toss them into a bowl of raspberries for dessert.

and more

From time to time less usual berries appear in the shops – loganberries, tay berries, golden raspberries, pink currants, and as an especially rare treat, mulberries. Buy them whenever you see them – providing, of course, that they are in good condition. I rarely do anything fancy with such finds myself, invariably wolfing them from the punnet even before I get them home.

Cheese

Choosing a cheese is the one bit of shopping I enjoy above all others. Should it be a melting Saint Félicien, a snow-white button of English goat's cheese, a smelly, honey-coloured Banon in its chestnut leaf and rafia parcel, or a tiny, coin-shaped Cabécou? And if I do choose a Cabécou, should it be a new one with its week-old, fragile crust or something six times as old and pungent? Perhaps it should be a wedge instead, cut from a large, muslin-wrapped Cheddar, or something from the Dales, or an obscenely creamy Gorgonzola.

I do recommend that we cook with cheese but even more that we eat it for its own sake, with good bread. This is when cheese becomes a meal rather than an ingredient. A whole cheese placed in the centre of the table and eaten in all its glory with bread, tiny gherkins and a few olives is a cheese to celebrate. A long, thin wedge of Brie de Meaux in spring, perhaps; an undulating square of Pont-l'Evêque; a thick triangle cut from a mature Taleggio; and, in the winter months, an oozing Vacherin spooned like soup from its wooden box. These, along with Gouda so heavily matured it becomes the colour of beeswax, a sharp and grainy Parmesan to eat with a Comice pear, or a moist and crumbly Cotherstone, are cheeses that are worth travelling to a specialist for, or visiting their website and ordering by mail.

Supermarket cheeses, no matter what anyone tries to tell us, are simply not the same. Even when you get the same farm sending the same cheese to a major supermarket as to a specialist shop, the supermarket cheese is somehow never quite as good. God knows what they do to it. Like meat and fish, we must be prepared to go further than down the aisle of a supermarket if we want to experience just how good a cheese can be.

If we are going to cook with the stuff (and why not?), then it is worth thinking of it as the principal ingredient rather than a seasoning or savoury crust to something else. The most gorgeous supper of all is the one where I bake a whole, melting goat's cheese or Camembert in a layer of puff pastry. Rolling the pastry thinly will ensure it stays crisp. Sealing the edges tightly will keep the insides from leaking out. As the pastry cooks, the cheese inside starts to melt. When you take the baked parcel from the oven and cut it, the golden pastry flakes and crumbles and the cheese comes flowing out like liquid velvet.

Fish and other pleasures

There are few things I would rather cook than a fish. Take a spanking-fresh plaice or lemon sole, for instance: I love gently flicking sizzling butter over it in the pan as it makes its short journey from raw to cooked. I have been cooking fish since I was a kid and yet still marvel at the way the flesh so quickly loses its transparency and sets to a clean pearly white. On the plate it is the inherent lightness that appeals – fish is always a gentle meal. I suspect I also set much store by the immediacy with which a fish supper can be ready.

I say an almost daily thank-you that I have a decent fishmonger close by. It is not an exaggeration to say that his location had a part to play in where I chose to live. Supermarket fish is all right, by which I mean it is a perfectly reasonable place to buy your fish, but there is something more interesting about the sight and fresh sea smell of a fishmonger's slab, not to mention the promise of consulting someone who knows his trade. Especially if you arrive with an open mind and without a shopping list.

I have said before that the less you do to fish, the better it tastes, and I stand firm by this. This does not mean that a shake of spice or a bubbled-down sauce of wine and cream won't be good, but it does mean that you may find much pleasure in a fine fish simply cooked.

going fishing (or as near as most of us get to it)

You know what to look for in the shop: bright, sparkling eyes that say 'buy me, buy me' and a skin that twinkles iridescently on the ice. The only dull fish worth considering is hake, which has a great deal of flavour but has never been much of a looker. Every fish is different but they do fall fairly neatly into categories which, while being important to the academic, are even more so to someone in search of supper.

oily-fleshed fish

Think of these as long, sleek, torpedo-shaped fish whose skin is shimmering blue and silver – like oil on a puddle – and whose flesh is pink, brown or beige rather than white. I am talking here of mackerel, salmon, trout, herring, sardines and tuna, the strongly flavoured fish that smell so enticing when their flesh catches and crisps here and there under the grill. Having enough oil in them already, they respond especially well to the dry heat of the grill or oven rather than a panful of butter, and need something tart with them such as tomato, lemon or white wine vinegar rather than copious butter or cream.

flat fish for cooking whole

Luxuriously proportioned pearl-white fish such as sole, plaice, the delightful lemon sole, brill and the phenomenally expensive turbot. Elegant, graceful fish that need nothing more than a large pan of fresh, sweet butter and maybe a few soft herbs.

small fish for baking whole

Pretty pink mullet, small sea bass, small red bream and those rather lovely-looking fish from tropical waters. The stunning beauty of these fish begs us, surely, to leave them whole for all to see their loveliness. Bake them with a little wine and a few strong-tasting herbs such as thyme and bay, then bring them to the table in their baking dish.

big, round-bodied fish

Meaty fish with fat, chalk-white flakes to eat as a thick chunk of fillet or a juicy steak cut across the body. Think haddock, hake, cod, whiting – fish that are so large you rarely see them whole. These are the guys whose firm flesh will take a bit of rough and tumble such as being mashed for fishcakes or cooked under a potato crust in a pie. I would add the exquisite sea bass to this bunch, too, though you are more likely to want to bake its prime flesh whole and its price will forbid you making a fishcake of it.

crab, mussels, clams and prawns

I cannot help thinking of crab and prawns as summer fare and keeping mussels and clams for winter, when in fact they are all available in good nick for much of the year. I buy both whole cooked crabs to pull apart for a summer lunch and dressed crab with which to make fishcakes, soup, and watercress sandwiches. Look out for live (grey) prawns; they provide the juiciest eating, especially when grilled and dipped into melted butter and salt. Mussels need nothing more than a thorough clean. The notion that they should shut when tapped firmly on the side of the sink is an unreliable check for freshness. What you should do is push each mussel hard between your fingers and thumb, squeezing the two shells tightly together. They should not give too much, as if they are fighting to keep together. You will feel their strength. If the shells part easily with little pressure, then you know they are dead or dying. Go for small, sweet, clean-shelled mussels and avoid at all costs those fat and flabby green-lipped mussels that have become so popular. You want your mussels tight and sweet.

getting your fish ready for the stove

I see no point in doing the dirty work ourselves. Ask the fishmonger to gut and fillet, scale and slice. This is not an imposition and you shouldn't (mustn't) feel guilty about asking; it is part of his job and he will probably take great pride in it. Anyway, we have enough to do when we get home. As much respect as I have for fish and fishermen, I really don't want to smell like one.

When you get your fish home it is worth unwrapping it, giving it a good rinse in cold running water and putting it on a plate with a few ice cubes and a cover of some sort before popping it into the coldest part of the fridge (that's the top shelf) until you are ready to get out the pan, the butter, the parsley and the lemon.

Chicken

A golden chicken, plainly roasted with butter and tarragon, is, for me, the ultimate lunch. Rather than have chicken as part of a thrown-together after-work supper, it is something over which I make a bit of fuss, as one might Christmas lunch. So that the bird, with its glistening skin and herby, garlicky juice, becomes something of an occasion.

choosing your chicken

I know everyone tells you to look for a plump bird but I think there is more to it than that. Some of the tastiest chicken I have ever eaten has come from birds that were positively scrawny. The point is not simply how big a breast your chicken has but what breed it is, what sort of food it has been eating and how much exercise it got. Even the way it was slaughtered will affect the taste and tenderness. So you can cheerfully ignore all that stuff about plump breasts.

It must be free range and preferably organically fed. I say 'must' because there seems to me to be no point in eating anything less either in terms of interest of flavour or, just as importantly, in terms of quality of life for the bird. I do think you want a chicken that has been allowed to forage for at least some of its food, and I hate, too, the idea of eating something that lived without ever seeing daylight. When meat of any sort is cheap it is invariably the animal who pays. Quality of life, even when we cut that life short to feed ourselves (or, more truthfully, because we just happen to fancy a bit of roast chicken) has much effect on eating quality. Fancy sauces can hide a stringy old bird but, as I have said before, this book is about dressing food down not dressing it up, so you need to start with a fine fowl.

A good chicken is not difficult to find. Most butchers and supermarkets now have a range of birds whose top end will include some that seem to cost a fortune but will, in the end, be better value (partly because you can use their strong bones for soup). Sometimes our suppliers even let us know which farm they are from (my local butcher is very good at this). If we are to enjoy, I mean really enjoy, our roast chicken, such things matter.

cooking your chicken

When you get your shopping home I suggest you remove any wrapping, rinse the chicken and put it in the fridge. This will encourage the skin to dry out a bit before you cook it, giving you delectably crisp skin (wet meat of any sort never seems to crisp nicely and, if you are cooking it in a shallow pan on the hob, will spit and bang at you).

You can judge a chicken's doneness by its juice. The juices that spurt out as you cut should be clear and pale gold with no sign of blood. The most sure-fire way is to insert a thin metal skewer – the sort you might use for kebabs or to gauge the readiness of a fruit cake – into the deepest, thickest part of the bird, which is where the legs sit tight against the breast. If the juice that runs out is clear, then your supper is probably ready.

Duck, game and some other possibilities

Game birds (I use the word lightly here, they are pretty much all farmed now) can also make great eating. They are probably the quintessential autumn meat. Pheasant, partridge and grouse are my favourite. Lean, deeply flavoured flesh and great bones to gnaw. I cook them all at a high temperature. You can expect a pheasant to take about forty-five minutes at 190°C/Gas 5, a partridge thirty to forty-five minutes at the same, whilst a glorious grouse will take just thirty-five minutes. Keep them moist with a bit of streaky bacon while they roast (they have no natural fat and are inclined to dryness) but you should remove the bacon ten minutes before they are due out, just to colour the breast. Make a bit of gravy with a glass of Madeira and the scrapings from the pan, whisking in a little butter at the end, if you wish. You only really need a puddle of bread sauce with them and a couple of crisp and fluffy roast potatoes.

I must put in a few words for the duck and the guinea fowl. The latter can be treated pretty much as chicken, though you should expect darker and deeper-tasting meat. Duck, having all that fat to keep it afloat, needs a little care if it is not to be greasy. Tear out the lumps of soft white fat from inside the carcass and prick the duck's skin all over so that some of the fat escapes during roasting, then rub the skin with salt before you put it in the oven. There are a million ways to ensure that the fat does not become a problem, some rather more contrived than others, but I have to say that I have never really found it to be quite as bad as some people make out. The trick is to get the wrapping off as soon as you can, leave the bird in the fridge, uncovered, overnight to dry out the skin and then give it a good rub with salt. As the duck roasts (it will take about an hour to roast a 2kg duck and it will be an absolute feast for two), tip off much of the fat that has collected in the roasting tin. Save every drop of it for roasting some potatoes another day.

Pork

Sweet meat, jelly-textured fat, crisp crackling.

The glory of pork is its juicy, sweet meat, lashings of wobbly fat and crisp skin that puffs up into crackling. Anyone who suggests that pork should be lean is missing the whole point. The fat bastes the meat as it cooks, adding flavour and succulence. In fact, if you choose the right cut and cook it on the bone you won't come across a juicier meat.

Pork makes a gorgeous, tantalising roast. The smell of a joint of pork crackling and spitting in the oven is one of the great pleasures of cooking. But it can also be grilled or braised slowly. A pork braise is a joyous supper with thick, savoury juices. Cold-weather cooking at its best.

what are you looking for?

Presumably you intend to eat pork for supper – or Sunday lunch – because you have a fancy for a piece of meat that is succulent, sweet and warming. For juicy meat you will need to buy a piece on the bone; with plenty of fat attached it will warm and comfort, too. If you are looking for a deep, rich flavour, you need meat from a traditional, old-fashioned breed of pig that has been allowed to grow slowly, giving its flavour time to develop. If you want crackling, too, then you will need meat from an animal that has a strong, tough skin, one that has lived some of its life in the open air.

where to get it

Butcher's shops are often better hunting grounds for good pork than supermarkets. They seem to understand the reasons we want to eat pork. I have trouble getting supermarket pork to crackle properly. This is down to the breeds of pig they specify their farmers should raise, the unnatural life they lead and the fact that their meat is sold cocooned in plastic and therefore wet to the touch. Wet pork will not puff and crackle. It will just sit in the oven and sulk. Even if you get your bits of pig from the butcher I suggest you unwrap it as soon as you get home and chill it thoroughly overnight. Dry skin roasts to a golden crisp, especially if you rub some salt into it.

If you get the chance to shop in Chinatown, this is the place to buy your pork – the butchers there understand this meat more than anyone. Their own cuisine revolves around it. A lot of small farms that specialise in producing organically reared pigs will send their meat by post; all you need is a telephone and a credit card.

getting the best

Meat from a farmer who breeds old-fashioned varieties of pig is more pleasing to eat than meat from the mass-produced pig of commerce. It stands to sense that an animal who has lived partly out of doors and been allowed to snuffle out something interesting to eat will itself be more interesting to eat than one that has never seem the light of day and has been fed purely on factory-made pellets. But it is also partly a question of time. Traditional breeds such as Gloucester Old Spot and Tamworth are slow-growing animals that don't take kindly to modern intensive farming techniques. Flavour takes time to develop in an animal (which is why veal and spring lamb taste of so little). Modern farming is all about saving time and money, hence the abundance of cheap, flabby pork. Meat from a small, specialist producer will cost you more, because the turnaround is slower. Few of us would want the life of a hands-on farmer. But what you get for your money is deep-flavoured meat from an animal that has developed a good strong hide for our crackling, and possibly even had a name rather than a number. We need to eat less meat but of better quality. Happy pigs taste better.

a bit of a pig – but which bit?

So, you know why you want pork for supper and how to get hold of it. Now what do you want to do with it? If you roast it you will have an easy-peasy meal suitable for a crowd and some left for cold, to eat in thin slices with salt and pickles. If you grill it you will have a quick, convenient supper for one or two.

For roasting, you could buy a piece of leg, shoulder, loin or belly. These are big bits, some of which are funny shapes and tricky to carve. Frankly, too much fuss is made about carving. All you really want is some juicy chunks of meat on your plate, so who cares if they get there by being hacked about a bit? Just ask the butcher to saw through any really difficult bits for you. If you fancy that masterly rolled and tied leg or loin in the butcher's window, then fine, go for it, but do ask him for the bones (or at least some bones) to stick in the roasting tin. They will do their magic and flavour

127

the gravy. The size you need depends on how many you are feeding. A 2kg piece on the bone will feed six and leave a bit for cold later. Off the bone, you will need about 1.8kg. It is worth buying more than you need. Cold roast pork is a Good Thing to have in your fridge.

If you are looking for a meal for one or two, you have the choice of a loin or spare rib chop. The loin chop is the one with a strip of fat along its edge and, if you are lucky, a slice of kidney attached; the spare rib chop has the fat marbled though the flesh. Both are good but the spare rib chop is less likely to dry up as you cook it.

how do you want to season it?

Your pork should taste wonderful even if your only seasoning is sea salt and black pepper. Just rub it all over, flesh and fat, with a generous hand, poking it into every nook and cranny. It will go on more evenly if you rub it in with a glug of olive oil. Massage it in as if you were putting suntan oil on your lover. Roast or grill it, then serve with half a lemon to freshen up its flat sweetness.

There are other simple flavours that flatter pork too. As you might expect these are things that contrast with a sweet and fatty meat. Lemon, tart apples, ginger and mustard are surely enough (some people would add plums, oranges, apricots and the like, but I think that's getting a bit fancy). It is a strong meat, so you can add the more robust herbs to the list, such as thyme and sage. Also anything with aniseed – fennel bulb or fennel seeds, star anise or Pernod (add the merest drop to the cooking juices) – oh, and juniper berries because of their fragrant, pine-like bitterness.

the crackling

You will come across as many suggestions for how to get crunchy crackling as there are cooks. The truth is that it is down to the breed of animal and its lifestyle. It will help if you make sure the skin is dry before roasting, if it is scored in thin lines across the skin with a razor-sharp knife (I use a Stanley knife if the butcher hasn't done it for me) and if you have rubbed it meaningfully with sea salt just before sticking it in the oven.

the meat

Just as roast beef tastes better when carved thinly, so pork seems juicier when hacked off in thick lumps. Ideally, everyone gets a strip of crackling that is crisp on top and fatty and velvety underneath. And remember that the bones, particularly if caught in the heat of the grill or oven, are particularly sweet to suck. Gnawing at a grilled chop bone is almost the point of the thing.

the juices

When pork roasts, its juices caramelise to a sticky goo in the bottom of the roasting tin. There is bags of rich, bitter-sweet flavour there. Release that flavour by letting the goo down with liquid – it can be white wine, cider (apples again) or simply water. When you lift out the roast to rest before carving, put the roasting tin on the heat and dissolve the sticky bits in your chosen liquid. Bring it to the boil, taste it for salt and pepper and use it to moisten the meat once it is on the plate. Juicy meat, luscious fat, crisp crackling and deep gold, savoury juices.

Lamb

If pork is the quintessential winter meat, full of wobbly fat to keep us warm, then lamb is the meat for summer Sunday lunches, roasted with herbs and eaten with salad and copious amounts of chilled red wine. The thing is to keep it pink.

a garlicky crust with juicy pink meat within

Notice I say pink and not red. The difference is subtle but crucial. I do not belong to the band who are happy to eat a slice of roast lamb as rare as if it were a piece of beef. It may be fashionable to eat it that way but no one ever seems to mention the small point that it is also stone cold. If I must err on one side or the other (no cook gets it perfect every time), I would rather have my lamb on the brown side than the bloody. I say a roast is easy, too, and it is, but you must keep an eye on it so you get the meat at its most juicy. And this is the trick: you cook it at a high heat for a short time, so the fat crisps up and the meat is in no danger of drying out. And frankly there isn't much else to it.

what are you looking for?

Spring lamb from young, jelly-legged animals barely old enough to leave their mother is much prized and is written about with awe. The flesh is so pale and tender it cuts like butter. As you might expect, meat this young (we are talking infanticide here) roasts in minutes. But I stand apart from the cognoscenti on this (and many other matters, too) and I really cannot join in their chorus. To me, the flavour is just the wrong side of mild; the texture as interesting as marshmallow. I prefer lamb that comes from an older animal, one that has eaten more than milk and built up a bit of muscle.

I recommend you look for lamb that is red rather than pink and whose fat is crisp and creamy. Your butcher will help. This will only come from an animal that has been fed on grass for a few months and has had some sort of a life. If you can call having your head down in the grass for six months a life. The best lamb I have ever eaten was in Greece, from a scrawny old sheep, one that spent its days desperately rummaging for grass amongst the rocks and taking in a bit of wild thyme and garlic shoots on the way. It was overcooked but the flavour was deep and herbal, and it still had some clear juice to its brown flesh.

to the slaughter

Lamb is not an easy meat to carve unless you take its bones away, and therefore its soul. In my book you have no alternative but to hack away the best you can. Lamb is not worth cooking unless it still has a bone attached. The poncy noisette, a slice of boned loin tied up with string, says it all. Its meat is tender but flaccid (though oh, so easy to carve). Lamb chops, which sound so unimaginative as your voice wavers across the butcher's counter, can be the best lamb meal of all, as their flesh singes on the grill, flecked with olive oil, garlic and thyme. And don't forget there is a bone to chew.

A summer roast can be a leg or a shoulder. You must carve the meat from the bone but don't worry if it comes away in tatters. The flavour will still be fine. Save every drop of juice, it is all the lubricant you need. A thickened gravy will flood this meat.

in the oven

On many occasions I have thrown a leg of lamb in the oven seasoned with nothing but salt and pepper and it came out tender, sweet and melting. I will happily argue that anything more interesting could be considered an intrusion, yet there are one or two flavours that add interest and depth of savour, by which I mean garlic, garlic and garlic. Thyme and rosemary, too, and, strangely, anchovy (which does not taste even remotely fishy in this instance). But these ingredients apart, anything else is added simply because we like it rather than because it is doing much for the lamb.

On the grill, which I insist is the best place for a lamb to end its days, you need little more than the charring (in other words the caramelised meat juices) caused by the grill bars and a crumbling of sea salt to get the most out of it. On the other hand, if you have had the temerity to let your chump chops, cutlets or steaks rest for an hour in a bowl of peppery olive oil, garlic and thyme, you may get an even more stimulating result. A Middle Eastern spicing of cumin, ground chilli and lemon works well, as does chopped fresh mint.

A roast shoulder or leg can be sublime with sliced cloves of garlic and the odd anchovy fillet stuck into holes pierced over the skin, or rubbed all over with a mash of oil, rosemary, oregano and garlic before it goes in the oven. And while we are cooking our lamb on the bone, I must mention the shanks that have recently become so popular again. The good thing is that you get your own little bone all to yourself to carve and chip away at. This is the only time, with the possible exception of a heart-warming Irish stew, that I will countenance brown meat. A long, slow braise with wine and onions and a herb or two renders this awkwardly shaped cut some of the most tender meat you can have. The bone somehow enriches the meat as it cooks. I think of it as the bone virtually basting the meat from within.

131

Beef

A Sunday plate of roast beef, its flesh rudely pink and as soft as butter, is a meal entrenched in my memory. That rare and exquisite forkful where velvety beef meets hot gravy, roast potato and the merest dab of mustard is glorious. The gravy-sodden Yorkshire pudding (I belong to the soggy camp rather than the crisp and airy one), the buttered cabbage and the horseradish all combine to make this one of the greatest dinners on earth.

the blood is the thing

If I am to eat beef at all, then it must, absolutely must, be pink going on red. Its fat must be crisp on top and quivering below and it must be on the table no more often than once every blue moon. Brown beef, and I include everything from *paupiette de boeuf* to *boeuf bourguignon* here, is an anathema to me. I can extract no pleasure from beef that has no hint of pink to it.

Regular readers have probably searched in vain for beef recipes in my books. There was a hamburger in *Real Fast Food*, a steak in *Real Cooking* and a braised oxtail recipe (my only nod to brown beef) in my weekly *Observer* column, but that has been the sum of it. I make no apologies for this. I can only enthuse about things I actually like and think worth encouraging, reminding of or

passing on to others. And where I would honestly put *steak frites* with sauce béarnaise as one of my three or four favourite dishes, I refuse to lie in order to make a collection of recipes appear more balanced or encyclopaedic.

The only occasion I do get excited about beef that is far from pink is when you braise an oxtail till it is almost black, its skin jammy and as sticky as treacle.

the all-important marbling

Fat should run through the flesh of a piece of beef like a road map. It is this marbling of fat that makes or breaks a piece of beef. Check carefully before you buy. Great wodges of the stuff will result in beef that cooks unevenly and falls apart when you carve. What you are looking for is a visible and even veining of fat, so that the meat will be, in effect, moistened as it cooks. I think of the fat melting into the meat as it roasts. Lean meat is less sumptuous than meat with a reasonable level of fat. So you can safely ignore those so-called healthy-eating writers who recommend 'lean meat'. I argue that it is better to eat a decent piece of beef once a month than something lean and lacking once a week.

the Sunday joint

I think a rib gives the juiciest roast, the bone being the crucial point. Of course, we are talking big money here, especially if you are feeding family and friends and are buying well-hung meat from a first-class supply. Magnificent, but the very devil to carve. A boned rib, rolled and tied with string, is what most people seem to go for; it has much of the flavour and tenderness but is immeasurably easier to slice. The choice is yours. I would rather go for bone-in and hope that someone round the table is more dextrous at carving than I am. For six people I suggest a piece about 2kg in weight. I know this sounds a lot, but believe me it isn't (except in money). You want something left for cold. Ask the butcher to chine the joint, which simply means that he will loosen the meat away from the backbone to make carving easier. Even then it is a bit of a struggle.

133

Do bring your meat to room temperature before you put it in the oven. Beef on the bone needs half an hour per kilo at 220°C/Gas 7. Couldn't be easier to remember. Fifteen minutes per 500g works for calculating the cooking time of smaller family joints. For a boned joint, aim for twenty-five minutes per kilo. This will give you rare meat, though the ends will be better done. I have read recipes that tinker around with the temperature. One actually altered the setting four times. I am not sure any of this is strictly necessary, though it must have worked for them.

The real trick is to switch off the oven once the joint is ready and leave it be, resting quietly, for at least fifteen minutes. Half an hour won't hurt that much. Otherwise all the juices will pour out and you will be left with dry meat. Resting the meat before you carve it should ensure that sublime thing: thin slices of rare, melting beef with deeply savoury fat and gloriously pink and bloody flesh.

the bits and pieces

The horseradishsaucemustardyorkshirepuddingandroastpotatoes are part and parcel of a Sunday roast beef lunch. Don't even try to do anything else, your guests will hate you. The gravy recipe you are looking for is on page 176.

Storecupboard – a shortlist to save your life

I feel so inadequate, such a fraud, when I read most cook's lists of essential storecupboard items. They bear little or no resemblance to what I have in my cupboards, most of them sounding more like an inventory of Harrod's food hall than a list of useful things to have around. And why do they always seem to include porcini, those rare and costly little packets of dried mushrooms?

There is, though, a handful of things I feel uncomfortable without – coffee, a loaf, olive oil, a lemon or two, a lump of Parmesan and a packet of pasta. In the fridge I would make sure there is also mineral water, a couple of bottles of cold beer and a bottle of wine. I know that at least I can make myself a piece of toast, perk myself up with an espresso, and knock up a bowl of pasta for supper – with olive oil, lemon, breadcrumbs and Parmesan. I know that I can put my feet up with a cold beer. I would feel very twitchy knowing that there was no wine in the house. It would be like knowing there was no hot water in the pipes. Having said that, I have lost count of how many times I have opened my fridge to find only a lump of rock-hard Parmesan, a bottle of Champagne and half a carton of milk on-the-turn.

So what about that bowl of freshly made chicken stock that real cooks are supposed to have smugly tucked away in their fridge? Well yes, I do try to (smugly) make stock from the bones of every chicken I roast, and usually remember to buy a few chicken wings to add to the pan as well, but it is a bonus rather than a basic. It just so happens that it is a bonus, though in practice not that much more useful than a tub of good-quality stock powder. It is simply that the texture of something like a risotto is so much more sensual made with real, lightly jellied chicken stock. But as I said, it is a bonus rather than something we should feel guilty about not achieving.

The list of basics that follows is a seriously edited blueprint of what you might find useful to have in your cupboards and fridge. I haven't included anything for the deep-freeze because I don't have one. These are not necessarily things you may need to follow the recipes in this book, they are simply a few bits and pieces that I have found tend to make my life easier and more pleasurable if I have them to hand.

135

salt. Coarse, flat flakes of Maldon sea salt. Easy to crush between your fingers or in a mill.

pepper. Whole black, in a mill.

garlic. A head or two for garlic bread or pasta.

lemons. A cook is lost without a lemon, so is anyone trying to make a gin and tonic.

olive oil. Nothing fancy, just a fruity olive oil, cheap enough to cook with.

pasta. Dried, Italian-made fettuccine, penne or orecchiette.

noodles. Dried, Chinese or Japanese for soup.

rice. Arborio for risotto, basmati for a pilau.

olives. Tiny black ones from Italy or Provence.

cheese. For this basic list I will just suggest a lump of Parmesan for grating into your pasta or risotto (we are talking emergency here).

soy sauce. Chinese or the less salty Japanese shoyu for perking up a bowl of noodles.

stock. I have used Marigold vegetable bouillon for years without apology and it's fine for a bowl of noodles (add *nam pla*, soy, garlic and lemon, too).

spices. A very basic list might read crushed dried chillies, whole green cardamoms, cumin seeds and nutmeg, all of which turn a bowl of rice into a jolly fine pilau. You can throw the chillies into a tomato sauce for pasta or soup, too.

Smarties. I have never known anyone refuse a Smartie.

sauces. *Nam pla* (Thai fish sauce) for noodle soup, chilli sauce and Worcestershire sauce – if only for a Bloody Mary on a Sunday morning.

tomato juice. Bottled or canned, for Bloody Marys and because a big glass of it can fill a hole when you are very hungry or on the way out somewhere.

Marmite. For spreading on soldiers.

tomatoes. Tins of, for emergency pasta sauce.

baked beans. Canned, for any time.

pancetta. Keep a small block rather than thin slices in the fridge for pasta, leafy salads and posh bacon sandwiches.

and really good ground coffee. Because you never know when someone just might come back for it and, of course, some wine, some mineral water and some cold beers.

Eating for the season

There is a point in the year at which fruit and vegetables are at their best. By which I mean their most luscious, fragrant and flavoursome. Ideally that is when we want to eat them, to catch them at that moment of full, bursting, uninhibited ripeness. There are few edible pleasures more satisfying than a perfect piece of fruit. Think of that blackberry oozing with purple juice picked from the hedgerow in September or the smell of a freshly picked runner bean in July, snapped in half, its little mauve beans tucked inside. Anyone who fails to take advantage of such things is missing out on something very special.

But the seasons are short. The English asparagus season, for instance, is a matter of only six weeks during May and June, so greengrocers and supermarkets extend the seasons by importing produce from other countries. So we get French strawberries a few weeks before ours, and Italian asparagus a few weeks after. I think we should probably be grateful for this. But there is also now a system where we can buy almost anything at any time of the year. This means we can eat Malaysian sweetcorn in February (ours appears in August and September), African mangetout in January and Spanish raspberries in March. I will not knock this. Sometimes it makes a pleasant change to eat green beans in the depths of winter, but I do think that eating locally grown produce in its natural season is something we should make the most of. The argument that English tomatoes or strawberries picked at the height of summer *always* taste better than those flown in from elsewhere is, frankly, something of a myth. The truth of the matter is that they very often do taste better, and it would be silly not to take advantage of that.

I think there is another thing a little more intangible: there is something that just feels right about eating food in its natural season, something intrinsically comfortable about eating English strawberries in June, Scottish raspberries in September and locally grown runner beans in August.

The blame or congratulations for blurring the seasons must go fairly and squarely to the supermarkets. They cannot duck this one. They tell us that shoppers demand strawberries, asparagus and runner beans fifty-two weeks a year. I do not believe this. I have never believed this. Have you ever complained to a supermarket that you cannot buy runner beans at Christmas? No, of course, you haven't and neither have I. What the supermarkets mean is that they want to sell us asparagus and strawberries fifty-two weeks a year.

Having extolled the virtues of eating the right food at the right time, I don't take this to extremes. If we did not import vegetables in the winter months we would have to live on a never-ending diet of cabbage, roots and spinach. I love mashed swede and parsnips with butter and black pepper and I am obsessively fond of crisp, dark-green cabbages, but do I really want them all winter long? The answer is no. The result is that I make the most of local foods sold in their natural season, and suggest you do too, but I then cherry-pick from the imports, cheering myself up with the odd punnet of strawberries or a packet of neatly trimmed green beans in February, if I feel like it.

January

Detox month, and it is as if nature knows. Suddenly the broccoli seems a deeper green, the purple sprouting more perky, the oranges juicier. Despite the cold and the wet, our greengrocer's shops look the picture of health.

Forced rhubarb, pale pink and as tempting as a marshmallow, beckons in its long box; tight-skinned clementines and baggy satsumas beg our attention (so easy to peel and even easier to eat) and boxes of pink-shelled lychees offer soft juice and heavenly fragrance. Everything that is good for us suddenly looks good too. Don't bother with the apricots that appear from heaven knows where. They are cotton wool with a stone inside. Go instead for pineapples, bananas and sticky Tunisian dates.

The stars of the month must be the brassicas; the pointed spring cabbages, the crinkle-leaved Savoys as big as your hat and the long, thin black-green leaves of cavolo nero. If we are lucky we will see sprout tops, as well, still with their pea-sized Brussels attached. I tear them all up and add them to chick pea or lentil soups. There is a crispness to our root vegetables, too, and even celeriac, the knobbliest of them all, tempts with its hard, creamy-white flesh. Try it grated and mixed with mustardy mayonnaise or mashed half and half with potatoes (put the celeriac on ten minutes before the tatties).

This is also when we want some proper winter food – shepherd's pie, Irish stew and braised oxtail the colour of treacle. We can bash amber-fleshed swedes with black pepper and butter and make bowls of absurdly hot, sweet onion soup. We could even steam a pudding. Use up the marmalade to top a sponge pudding or have a go at jam roly-poly, even if simply for the nostalgic smell of steaming muslin.

Meal of the month must be something of the meal-in-a-bowl variety ladled into warm dishes by a generous hand. Try a gammon joint braised with winter roots, white beans and stock. The fat from the ham will warm you through and turn that old bag of haricots from the back of the cupboard into a velvety, consoling treat for a cold and bitter night.

February

It may seem a touch puritanical, not to mention xenophobic, but I think of this month as another one in which to make the most of locally grown root vegetables and greens. Those less under the thrall of roast parsnips, mashed celeriac and buttered dark-green cabbage may like to cheer themselves up with a bag of neat, green *haricots verts* from a warmer climate. They will sit more comfortably with the baked cod that is usually so firm and juicy at this time of year.

This month's top-notch veg is purple sprouting broccoli, arriving at the local farmers' markets and greengrocer's by the crateful. I can barely get enough of it, and will even go to the trouble of making hollandaise sauce to dunk it in when everyone else is out. In fact, I cannot help thinking that this, rather than absurdly expensive and tasteless imported asparagus, is what we should be eating

on February 14th as we gaze pathetically into one another's eyes. Few vegetables are as beautiful to look at or as toothsome to eat.

Knobbly, farty Jerusalem artichokes make the most velvety of soups. Note that cream is a necessity in this one rather than a luxury. Some bacon, added with the onions before you put in the artichokes and stock, will give depth and smoky savour.

Game has all but finished but I still think it worth picking up a couple of pigeons to stew with onions, bacon, mushrooms, garlic and red wine. Put them in a low oven and forget about them for an hour or two, then have them and their thin gravy with plenty of mashed swede or potato and celeriac. This is the month to try the oxtail stew on page 364. You need to pick a bone-shiveringly cold day for it.

The fishermen have an even harder time than usual in this cold and often stormy month, but they still come in with cod, mackerel, whiting and sole in fine fettle. My old, scribbled shopping lists all mention lemon sole as being something that I find in perfect health at this time of year. It just needs grilling, with some of that purple sprouting and hollandaise on the side.

Pineapples, lychees and all manner of oranges are the fruits to look out for. I sometimes dump a bag of perfumed lychees on the table after supper in lieu of pudding. So scented and juicy are they that no one ever complains. Citrus fruits of all kinds are at their peak. We should wallow in their sweet juice.

March

The low point of the cook's year, and I could almost scream at the mundaneness of it all. Tired roots, apples that have been in store since autumn, and stinky old sprouts don't exactly help. Even the rhubarb has lost its naughty pinkness. This is the month I splash out on golden fruits from tropical climates – the mangoes, papaya and passion fruit that we can use to bring some sunshine to the table. It is their juices I crave, sweet, tart and full of promise. Suck the saffron-coloured juice and crunchy seeds from a passion fruit and tell me you don't feel better.

The farmers' markets and organic bags suffer too at this time of the year, but we should continue to use them. It is unfair to be a fair-weather friend when the farmers are knee-deep in mud trying to find something to interest us. Spirits lift a little at the sight of a crate of purple sprouting – entertain nothing that is limp, and risk making some hollandaise for it. Such a supper, the lush purple greens and unctuous, canary-coloured sauce, is standard March fare in my house, usually eaten with a heart-warming baked Maris Piper with some Gorgonzola or Cashel blue to mash into it.

Seafood ain't bad this month. Mussels are fat and juicy (I chuck them at a wet pan, slam on the lid and let them steam till their shells open, then prise off the occupied shell, filling it with a blob of garlic butter and some fresh breadcrumbs. A minute under the grill and the kitchen will smell like the South of France on a summer's day). Then there are native oysters to tip down our throats and some sparkling mackerel to roast.

I might make the last truly winter casserole some time this month. Something light and stewy, like braised lamb with carrots, awash in their golden broth. A roast will cheer us up, with all the sticky bits – roast parsnips and potatoes and a jug of boozy gravy. Madeira, usually too sweet for me, adds a glow to the pan juices of any roast; just whisk a glass of it in and stir in all the pan goodies. A feast. Even so, this is not much of a month for the greedy, or anyone evenly remotely interested in their tummy.

April

April can be winter or spring depending on what mood He's in. But let's look on the bright side and cheer ourselves up with bunches of pink-rooted spinach, whose spear-shaped leaves make the finest salad going. I add bacon to mine in a moment of unsurpassable originality, but I insist it must be cooked almost (but not quite) to a crisp to be really good and there must be a decent blob of mustard in the dressing. On a warm note, I often add lemon to the steamed leaves when I eat them hot. There is something quietly perfect about limp, emerald-green spinach, butter and lemon.

The fishmonger will probably have some small crabs, a treat on a sunny day with the spring light filtering through and a bunch of loud, cheeky daffs on the table. He will have wild salmon, too, perhaps to steam for a change, and halibut steaks to go with the smallest of meticulously scrubbed new potatoes.

Goat's cheeses fill the gap left by the departing Vacherin. There is a sharp, grainy freshness to the snow-white ones, barely firmer than strained yogurt. Names to hunt for are Banon, complete with its tiny sprig of Provençal savory, Saint Marcellin (which is often made with cow's milk), tiny Bouton d'Oc, barely ten days old and sold on a little wooden stick, and then there are gentle English ones such as the Innes buttons. It is worth remembering that many cheese shops do mail order. Look out, too, for tiny discs of melting Cabécou with their parchment-like crust. It seems a shame to cook with the first of the season's young *chèvres*, their lightness and charm will be lost. I give them pride of place on the table, devoting a whole meal to them and their fragile, fluffy rind. There will be bread, too, of course, a ficelle and maybe some toasted sourdough cut thin and chewily crisp. Chilled radishes will be in a small bowl if I am lucky, as will some tiny mauve and black olives.

The time seems right for a chicken or even a young turkey to roast. Rub butter, mashed with chopped tarragon and mint (yes, mint) over, up and under, and then, as the bird comes sizzling from the oven, dissolve the pan scrapings, carefully decanted of fat, with a glass or two of white wine. More fresh herbs and you have a golden, herbal juice with which to wet the pale, golden-skinned meat.

The worst month for local fruit so no one can blame us for turning to chocolate – it's an obvious step. Dig out a recipe for a classic chocolate mousse or melt some chocolate with a small amount of butter and cream to make a sauce for pouring over a somewhat vulgar sundae of the season's best bananas with a ssshlurp of softly whipped cream.

May

The first teasing signs of summer abound. The palest apricots and peaches, the early runner beans, so sweet, so slim, and baskets of claret-coloured imported cherries catch our eye. So welcome are such things after the roots and old apples that we pounce on the first we see, but it is a false start and we are invariably disappointed. We should know they won't be ready yet. But asparagus is, boxes of the stuff, English, Spanish, French, and all of it worth a look. Keep an eye out for crisp, tight tips and moist, freshly cut stalks – though in reality the ends will be hidden in paper. We must trust our greengrocer.

I am an asparagus pig, never tiring of platefuls of the boiled stalks with a puddle of melted butter. I know asparagus makes your wee smell funny, but who cares when it is so good? It used to be hideously expensive, yet like pineapples and grapes, asparagus is now within reach of most of us who choose to spend rather than save money on our dinner. But there is much else, too. Tiny broad beans, the size of a child's thumbnail, hide in fluffy green pods; the first peas; watercress in lush bunches to dress with olive oil, wine vinegar and Dijon mustard. I sometimes add black grapes or blood oranges, too.

I hope you are not sick of cabbages because there may be some beautiful primo around, sage green and flushed with mauve. Cut them into wedges and steam them, then toss the tender leaves briefly in soured cream and eat them with the first of the pale, firm-fleshed wild salmon (wrap the fish in foil with a slice of butter and a glug or two of white wine, then seal tightly and let it bake in its own steam). But this is really the month of the new potato. The price of tiny Jersey Royals will be high but hopefully not exorbitant. In my house the first of these kidney-shaped, flaky-skinned potatoes tend to get steamed over boiling water and eaten with salt, no butter. Then, as the season progresses, out come the pots of crème fraîche and the melted cheese. I do crave them, and have been known to make a meal of them with just a bundle of thin asparagus, almost a packet of butter and a slice or two of Parma ham. As an early summer lunch, it is blissful and only works out at a couple of quid a head.

145

June

Bundles of asparagus are still hard to resist. If you have had enough of sweating over the hollandaise on page 179, then simply let half a packet of butter soften – rather than completely melt – on a plate over the boiling asparagus and lift it with a squeeze of lemon juice. Broad beans are fattening up now and will need skinning. Try them briefly boiled, skinned and stirred into a pan of cubed pancetta or streaky bacon, heated till its fat starts to melt, then toss with lots of vivid green chopped parsley. This is good with salmon or mackerel.

June is also the time for Little Gems and old-fashioned floppy-leafed butterhead lettuces. Serve their tender leaves with the season's poached salmon and mayonnaise for a peaceful garden lunch. This could well be the month to buy a freshly cooked crab and tear it limb from limb with hammer and pliers. You will get a pile of sweet rust and cream flesh to scoop up and claws to wiggle

your tongue in. Even a crab bought ready-dressed is fine if you know and trust your fishmonger, though you won't have as much fun with it as you will with a whole one. And don't forget sardines – they just need a hot grill, some sea salt and lemon juice.

Puddings slide towards the lazy, no-cook variety. English strawberries are at their sweetest; offer them in overflowing platters with jugs of double cream and bowls of caster sugar. Italian cherries are worth buying by the bagful to scoff as you work, and the appearance of gooseberries marks the start of dog-day afternoons. Stew them with a little sugar, then mash to a thick slush, stirring them through with softly whipped cream to make the ultimate June dessert to follow your salmon or crab – a classic gooseberry fool.

June marks the start of the summer slowdown. I don't cook as much, or as often, during June, July and August. Not that I live on salads, I don't, but I am much less likely to do battle with a fish pie or a steamed pudding when the sun is high in the sky. If cooking is to remain a pleasure rather than a chore, I suggest you do the same. The grill gets used almost daily for lamb and pork steaks, for squid and for aubergines, all of which tend to get eaten with a salad rather than hot vegetables. If a pan is puttering away on the stove, then the chances are it contains new potatoes and mint rather than plum pudding.

A typical June meal for friends might be the classic asparagus, salmon and strawberries hat trick. Hardly original, but who cares when such glories come together for such a short while? The salient point is that the meal should be one of understated perfection – don't even think of apologising for your lack of originality – so you can make your own mayonnaise and serve nothing fancier than a simple, ice-cold salad of lettuce, cucumber and watercress. The berries must be sweet, ripe and unblemished, the cream yellow and old fashioned and offered in a generous quantity in a pretty jug. If you are going to serve a meal of such classic nakedness, then make no attempt to get fancy. A last-minute panic ('am I doing enough?') into doing two puddings or a fancy salad will miss the point. This sort of simplicity only works if you keep to the rules, and one of those is not trying to gild the lily.

147

July

Things taste better in the open air. I do as much cooking outdoors as I can. At the very least, now is the time to sit on a windowsill with a bag of peas and a colander. If there is room to eat out of doors, then better still. The markets and greengrocer's shops are piled high with classic English salad stuff – especially thick, juicy cucumbers, new-season beetroot, lettuces, radishes, spring onions and sweet-tart tomatoes. An unfussy, fridge-crisp salad of some or all of the above, some thinned-down mayonnaise and a plate of cold roast chicken must be the meal of the month. Especially if you can contrive to eat it in the garden.

This is also the time that the tomato and basil salad is at its best: both the tomatoes and the herbs have had a chance of getting some of the intense sunshine they need to concentrate their flavour. I like to wrap a small ball of mozzarella in thin streaky bacon and grill it until the cheese starts to ooze. Look out for piquant, fudgy goat's cheeses to eat with English cherries; paper-thin

slices of San Daniele ham to lay gracefully over drippingly ripe Charentais or honeydew melons; and French and Italian peaches to poach with sugar and vanilla or to slice over vanilla ice-cream or lemon sorbet. Raspberries abound. Offer them in a huge bowl with a jug of double cream just like last month's strawberries, then, as the month wears on, put a pile of berries, a few crumbly meringues and a mound of whipped cream on the table and get everyone to make their own voluptuously fruity, creamy mess.

A July meal for friends could well be out of doors. I suggest a summer roast – a chicken or piece of lamb massaged with lemon, oil and robust herbs – served warm with a green salad; or grilled squid with chopped raw chillies and coriander. No one will thank you for any potatoes other than new ones, scrubbed and served with thick cold soured cream. Dessert, however unoriginal it may seem, could not be better than summer pudding. A glorious purple hat of a dessert, rich and sloppy with tart, magenta juice.

August

Summer blazes on. There is still plenty of fat white garlic about for roasting or crushing into mayonnaise. It squashes juicily under the knife. Deepest scarlet peppers, new season's garnet beetroot and wax-fleshed salad potatoes such as Pink Fir Apple add substance to salads. A luscious and silky-slithery salad can be made by grilling peppers till their skins blacken, peeling them and dressing their scarlet and orange flesh with olive oil and some shredded basil. Long, curly runner beans with their mauve beads inside and juicy, green-shouldered tomatoes are the vegetables in glut. Courgettes are ripening as fast as you can pick them. Try them sliced and slowly fried in butter and olive oil with basil leaves. Basil, cheap and plentiful, is the herb of the month.

Sardines are in fine fettle. Eat them grilled with hunks of bread and halves of lemon. Prawns, too; buy them raw and grey if you see them, then put them over the grill till their shells turn pink. Prise it away with your fingers and scoff the juicy flesh inside with salt and melted butter.

August is the month of sweet juice. The sticky dribbles down your chin from perfectly ripe nectarines, the splodges of crimson raspberries on a child's summer dress, the sweet, cool syrup that runs from a melon as you cut yourself a wedge. And as nectarines and blackberries ripen, juice is everywhere. The joy is trying to catch it. Make a last summer pudding whilst there are still red and black currants about.

If you find yourself with people to feed this month you could do worse than to offer them grilled prawns (bring them to the table on a huge platter and let everyone peel their own) followed by grilled chicken or rabbit. Yes, I am thinking barbecue here. Marinate the chicken pieces – I suggest boned legs or breasts – in lemon, olive oil, garlic and mint for a good few hours before grilling. For dessert, offer a huge bowl of drippingly ripe peaches. No cream, no sauce. Just perfect peaches, preferably white.

I do everything to hold on to the summer, eating in the garden as often as I can, taking it easy with lazy summer salads and grills, but at some time during the month I know that there will be a whiff of autumn in the air and the first flash of a saffron-coloured pumpkin at the greengrocer's.

149

September

The golden month. The farmers' market is a mass of wooden boxes and wicker trugs in the mellow, faded shades of early autumn: the rose-fleshed Discovery apples, bloomy damsons and dusty yellow pears tempt. There are punnets of dark-claret raspberries, some tiny strawberries still, and gold and ruby Victoria plums and purple Warwickshire Droopers. Best of all there are red and gold tomatoes with their green shoulders, tiny fresh-green jalapeño chillies and early squashes.

There are apples, too, though next month will see many of them at their best. There will be mixed-size Worcesters, with their welcome crunch, and of course, there are the juices from single varieties of apples – an innovation that makes the anonymous blended juices seem so flat. Lovely runner beans still, and the first small, round pumpkins. There is often a glut of basil, both green broad-leafed and ruffled purple. There will be red chard and fat, juicy cucumbers. The first purple cabbages appear now, a startling sight next to ochre pumpkins. Autumn is pulling at our apron strings for pies and crumbles. But I don't want to let go of summer. Don't miss treats such as ears of sweetcorn still in their husks, or any of the orange-fleshed melons still around.

The first signs of autumn – tiny pumpkins and the first good pears – serve to remind us to hold on to the summer as long as the evenings are warm enough to eat outside. But the game season starts now and plump wood pigeons tempt, as do the scallops and bags of blue mussels on the fishmonger's slab. A loin of pork would make a fine late-summer roast, perhaps with a few fennel stalks under it in the roasting tin, with a jumble of harlequin-coloured plums to follow.

150 Lunch of the month – if possible eaten outside in a sunny corner – has to be bread and cheese with some of the new-season's pears and walnuts. Try something melting, like an artisan-made Taleggio or a Camembert. The oozing cheese marries well with crisp fruits and walnuts. Brie de Melun and many of the blues are perfect at this time of year, too.

October

Apples, apples, apples. The plums have gone, apart from a few punnets of dusty, slightly overripe damsons. A few raspberries, oozing with scarlet juice and almost alcoholic to the nose, are still around and there are bunches of dark and winey grapes. But this is the month for apples and pumpkins. Farm shops, proper greengrocer's and farmers' markets will be stacked with apple crates – English Gala, Worcesters, Russets, Spartan, early Cox's ... apples, apples, apples.

On the vegetable front you will find things crisping up. Heads of celeriac, leafy cabbage and early kale. There should be some decent-sized carrots and parsnips for an early stew. Earthy, red-stemmed chard, glowing on a cold October morning, is irresistible. Cook the stems first, then add the leaves at the last minute, draining both, then tossing them in melted butter as you would spinach.

With Hallowe'en at the end of the month you can expect pumpkins to be piled high and as cheap as chips. Make soup, or roast them with butter and a little chopped chilli. Look for decent-sized potatoes for baking and chestnuts for sticking in the embers of a real fire (make a cut along

the plump side before you bake them; the skin will split cleanly, taking the annoying fine hairy underskin with it). This is sausage weather, too, to be cooked slowly till their skins are sticky and covered in mahogany-coloured goo.

Make the most of the figs coming in from the Eastern Mediterranean. Split them and bake them with honey and cream, or cut them into wedges and serve with parchment-thin slices of coppa. There will be apricot-coloured chanterelles to fry with butter, parsley and garlic, and – for the rich – porcini to bake with pancetta and thyme.

Dish of the month is thick, golden pumpkin soup, with crumbled bacon, rough-chopped parsley and perhaps a chilli or two as the weather cools towards the end of the month.

November

We are entering the comfort-food season. Even with today's global menu, the baked potato still rules here, either as ballast for a plate of grilled meat or, better still, as a meal in itself, the fluffy flesh squashed with butter and cheese through the tines of a fork. The orange-fleshed sweet potato, less substantial and with a softer skin, should be in good supply now, as will most roots. Parsnip mash is worth trying with roast lamb or beef.

Cabbages such as the frilly green Savoy, the deep-purple red and the crisp, hard white are rarely better than in the long run-up to Christmas. You can get fancy with them by adding apples and juniper but I still like the green varieties boiled and bathed in butter, though some of this may be pure nostalgia.

Mussels, oysters and scallops are in good nick at this time of year and need only the most modest of treatments. Scallops can be flashed briefly in a pan of frothing butter and garlic, while those mussels will provide the most sensual of feasts, to be torn apart and sucked by those not too proud to use their fingers.

Game could be in our shopping bags at a reasonable price this month. Pheasant – just roast it in a deep pot with celery, onions and Vin Santo – and chubby little partridge wrapped in bacon are the easiest to find. Look out for birds without any blue bruising and whose skin is without tears. The skin is important; game birds have little enough fat to keep them moist as it is.

Keep a look-out for the majestic, pear-shaped yellow quince. Baked with honey or stewed with apples and sugar, it is a deeply fragrant fruit and deserves our patronage. Those who rate the pear as highly as I do can exercise their gums on the glassy white flesh of the long Conference or wallow in the softness of the drippingly ripe and buttery Comice. Figs, too, both fresh purple-black ones in their paper cases and the soft, squidgy dried variety from Turkey, make a sumptuous end to a meal.

December

We are led slowly to the feast. First by the sight of tangerines, with their glossy green leaves, then by piles of pomegranates, with their spiky crown and jewel-like seeds. I sometimes just rub the halved fruit on the citrus press and mix the seeds with my breakfast orange juice. Passion fruit are around in quantity – split them in half and up-end them over deep, snowy meringues. Look out, too, for deep amber pineapples to slice and sprinkle with orange or passion fruit juice.

The vegetable racks are dominated by Brussels sprouts. Their green pungency has grown on me but they are hardly my favourite vegetable. They work at Christmas on the same plate as roast turkey (I have finally given in and succumbed to the inevitable), though they still need lashings of melted butter. But there are other vegetables, too: golden pumpkins for roasting; crisp white chicory in its blue waxed paper for that great winter salad with crumblings of Roquefort and a mustardy dressing; red cabbage, too. Preserve its gorgeous colour by adding a splash of cider vinegar as you stir-fry it with oil, butter and juniper berries.

Smoked salmon is a certainty on Christmas plates in our house, but smoked trout and eel can be good, too. A plate of smoked fish is light enough to precede the Christmas roast. I think you need only one type rather than a mishmash of different fish on the same plate. Simplicity combined with generosity is impossible to beat. Oysters should be at their best right now; I buy a couple every time I go to the fishmonger's, as a treat for putting away the shopping.

You should order your turkey in advance. Even then you can expect to queue when you go to pick it up. The best, by which I mean the feted Kelly Bronze, are in huge demand now that every cookery writer and their dog has sung the bird's praises (which is, of course, what we are here for).

I see no real reason to sidestep the obvious Stilton, it should be in good supply. But there are other fine cheese, too, namely Vacherin Mont d'Or – a cheese so blissfully runny you will need a spoon to lift it from under its soft, apricot-coloured crust. A whole one comes in a wooden box for you to pass around the table, along with the spoon and some scrubbed celery. The other unmissable treat is The Pudding ...

some really
useful stuff

a really good, and very easy white loaf

Nothing gives me a bigger buzz than baking a loaf of bread. Well, almost nothing. I played around with home baking for years, rarely producing anything to be proud of, then one day I made a really fab loaf that looked like one of those crackle-crusted artisan loaves you find in posh bakeries and I was hooked. Now I make bread all the time. Nothing fancy – I hate those loaves with olives, herbs and sun-dried this and that in them. I just want a plain white loaf with a crisp crust to have with a bit of cheese or some pâté. That's all.

Makes 1 large loaf (or 2 smaller ones)

white bread flour – 1kg, and a little more for kneading
instant dried yeast – 2 x 7g sachets
salt – 20g
water – about 700ml

Take your largest, widest mixing bowl and tip in the flour, yeast and salt. Pour in almost all of the water and mix it to a sticky dough. Keep mixing for a minute or so – the dough will become less sticky – then add a little more flour until you have a dough that is soft and springy and still slightly sticky to the touch.

Generously flour a large, flat work surface and scoop the dough out on to it. Work the dough with your hands, pushing it flat with your palms, then folding the far edge towards you and pushing it back into the dough with the heel of your hand. Continue pushing and folding the dough. Work firmly but gently, with none of that brutal banging people tell you about, folding and pushing the ball between your hands. It should feel soft, springy and alive (which, of course, being full of yeast, it is). The technique is less important than you may have been led to believe. What is important is that you carry on gently but firmly pummelling the dough. As you do so, you will feel it get lighter and more springy. Keep this up for almost ten minutes. If you find it exhausting, then you are pushing the dough too hard.

158

Place the ball of dough back in the bowl, cover it with a clean tea towel and put it somewhere warm, but not hot, for an hour or so. It should be well out of a draught. An airing cupboard is ideal. I don't have one, so I end up balancing the bowl on a thick towel over the radiator. The dough should almost double in size. The time this takes will depend on how hot or moist your room is, the exact type of flour you have used and the age of your yeast, but it will probably be about forty-five minutes to an hour.

Once the dough has doubled in size, you need to tip it out on to the floured surface again, scraping out the dough that has stuck to the bowl, and give it another short session of pushing and squeezing; a couple of minutes will do fine. Bring the dough into a ball again and place it on a floured baking sheet. Dust it heavily with flour, then cover with a tea towel and return it to its warm place to rise again. Set the oven at 250°C/Gas 9. After an hour or so the dough will have spread, and somewhat alarmingly. You want it to be twice its original size – or as near as damn it. Gently, and I do mean gently, tuck it back into a neat, high ball, then place it softly in the hot oven. Don't slam the door.

Leave the loaf to bake for ten minutes, then turn the heat down to 220°C/Gas 7. After twenty-five or thirty minutes you can check the loaf for doneness. It should sound hollow when you tap its bottom. Like a drum. Let the loaf cool on a wire rack. Try not to cut straight into it; give it time to settle before slicing.

161

and more

- **who can bake their own?** Take no notice of anyone who tells you that bread-making requires a certain gift or magic. If I can make a loaf to be proud of, anyone can.

- **dough too wet?** If your dough is sticky and won't come off your fingers, then just add a bit more flour.

- **dough feels tight?** If it feels tight and dead when you are kneading it rather than soft, springy and alive, then it needs a bit more water.

- **how to knead.** Don't worry about the intricacies of kneading – just push and fold the dough with both hands. You only need to do this enough to develop the protein in the flour (the gluten), which will eventually trap the gas in the loaf as it rises. There is no real art to it. The point is to be firm rather than bullying. In other words, push and fold rather than knock the hell out of it.

- **getting a crisper crust.** Some people swear by spraying the oven with water from a plant spray as you put the loaf in, to give it a nice crisp crust. It's worth giving it a try.

- **pizza too.** It is worth remembering that bread dough also makes a fine, crisp pizza crust. The trick is to press the dough into thin plate-size rounds and shake some really good olive oil over them before you add the topping. Don't go mad, add only what feels right, by which I mean truly Italian things like mozzarella, garlic and sautéed mushrooms.

a really great tomato sauce … and a few good things to do with it

A tomato sauce will brighten up a cold, grey day especially when you have roasted the tomatoes first to bring out all their sweet richness. Is there anything more useful in the kitchen, except perhaps a bowl of chicken stock? I spoon thick, scarlet tom sauce over roasted aubergines and baked mushrooms, toss it with spaghetti and penne and even stir it in at the end of a risotto. For a tomato sauce that will coat enough pasta for four, I use about twelve medium-sized or thirty cherry-sized tomatoes. That is to sauce it in the authentic Italian way, which is less copiously than we do.

garlic
olive oil
tomatoes
basil

The amount of garlic you put in your tomato sauce is up to you, but I tend to allow one juicy clove per four or five tomatoes. This doesn't sound a lot, I know, but the garlic is only meant as a back note here, rather than an upfront flavour. Whatever, it will need to be peeled and sliced very thinly and left to cook over a gentle heat in a little olive oil. Just enough to make a very thin layer on the bottom of the pan.

When the garlic has softened, but long before it has coloured, add the tomatoes, chopped up a bit, but neither seeded nor skinned. Let the tomatoes cook down to a slush over a low to moderate heat. This will take half an hour or so. Towards the end of cooking, tear up a handful of basil leaves and add to the sauce, seasoning with salt and black pepper. If your tomatoes were a bit on the sharp side you might need a tiny bit of sugar, too. Just keep tasting till you have something you like. You now have a thick, slushy sauce for pasta or as an accompaniment. You can rub it through a food mill to make a smoother sauce or you can whiz it in a blender.

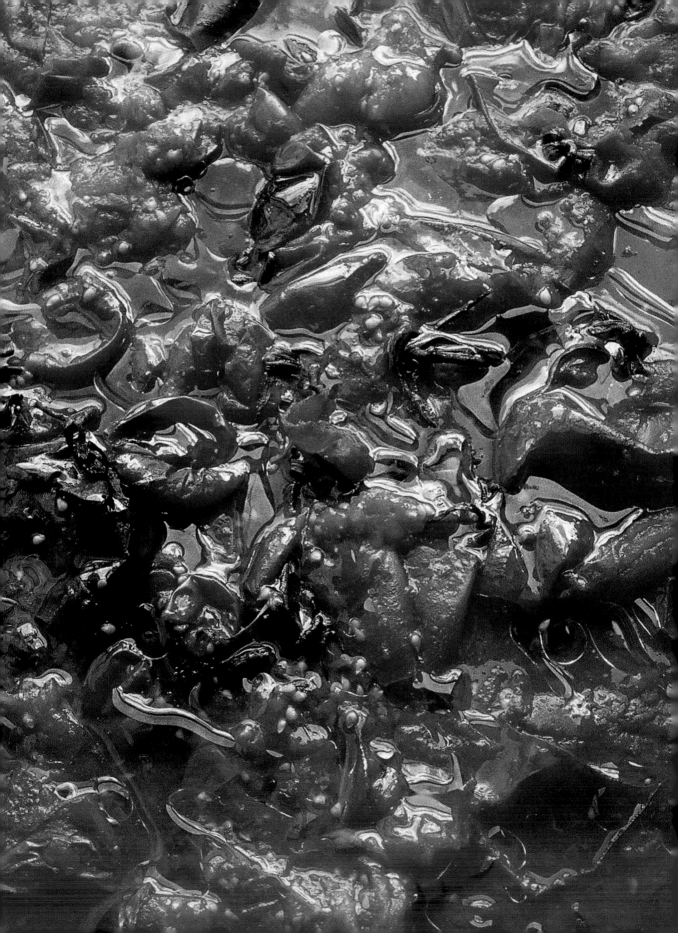

and more

♦ **a roast tomato sauce and some pasta suppers.** The more interesting the tomato, the more interesting the sauce.

tomatoes
olive oil
bay leaves
red wine vinegar

Put your whole tomatoes into a roasting tin or baking dish – be they beefsteak or cherry, they should fit snugly in a single layer. Pour over enough olive oil to wet the fruit – no need to use your extra virgin – and to form a thin layer at the bottom of the dish. Season generously with salt and black pepper, tuck in a couple of bay leaves and sprinkle a little red wine vinegar over, probably a couple of teaspoons' worth. Now leave in a hot oven (200°C/Gas 6) for about thirty minutes, until the skins have started to blacken here and there and there is much juice in the dish.

Crush the tomatoes with a fork, pulling off their black skins, then return them to the oven for fifteen minutes. You now have a choice: you can either push the tomatoes and their juice through a food mill, whiz them to a thick slush in a blender (the sauce will turn vivid orange) or leave as is. Whichever way you choose, check the seasoning, then use as you want.

♦ **pasta with chilli tomato sauce.** Any pasta you happen to have in the cupboard; either of the sauces above. If you are making the stove-top sauce, then add either a chopped fresh chilli or a large pinch of crushed dried chillies for every five or six medium-sized tomatoes, letting them cook a little with the garlic before adding the tomatoes. If you are making the roast tomato sauce, add the fresh chillies, whole and unseeded, to the tomatoes as they roast. You can remove them just before you crush the sauce.

♦ **baked pasta with tomato sauce and mozzarella.** On cold nights I sometimes cook macaroni or penne, drain it, then pile it into a dish with thin slices of mozzarella and either of the tomato sauces, crumble grated Parmesan over the top and bake until the sauce is bubbling and the mozzarella has melted into strings. A sauce of twelve medium tomatoes (two cloves of garlic and a handful of basil) will cover 300g of pasta and two balls of mozzarella, and will feed four.

167

a simple, useful sauce for every day

Integral sauces, made from the pan juices of meat, fish or vegetables, are to my mind the best of all because they contain some of the heart and soul of the main ingredient. The juices, the marrow, the sugars, the intense flavours give the sauce a sense of point. But it cannot always be so, and sometimes we need a sauce – hollandaise or tomato, perhaps – that comes from outside. It still flatters whatever you put it with but it is a separate item, put there to add something in the way of texture or flavour or simply to lubricate something that may not have its own juices. I usually fall back on sauce hollandaise, mayonnaise, tomato sauce or salsa verde, the unctuous green sauce overleaf. They seem to work well with so many dishes. I include the sauce below, which is something I make when I want a sauce that will work with grilled chops, fish, anything in fact where a creamy sauce with a little sharpness would be appropriate. Its pepperiness is complementary to a chargrilled chop or even a steak. Its tang of acidity makes it less cloying than other dairy-based sauces. It doesn't split like hollandaise either. And it is so useful.

Enough for 2

168

tarragon or white wine vinegar – 100ml
a shallot
mint – a small handful of leaves
black peppercorns
crème fraîche – 200ml
smooth Dijon mustard

Pour the vinegar into a small saucepan and add a similar amount of water, then bring it slowly to the boil while you peel and very finely chop the shallot. Tear the mint leaves and add them to the vinegar with the shallot and four or five lightly crushed black peppercorns. Within a few minutes the liquid will have reduced to a couple of tablespoons. Turn off the heat.

Scoop the leaves and bits of shallot out of the reduction, squeezing them against the pan as you do so, then discard them. Turn the heat on again and stir the crème fraîche into the seasoned vinegar. Stir in a couple of teaspoons of mustard, although you could add more if you want to. Let the sauce come to the boil, then turn the heat down to a simmer, till it has thickened to the consistency of double cream. A matter of two minutes or so. Taste it and add a grinding of salt.

and more

♦ **a green peppercorn sauce for steak or lamb.** Those darkly sinister jars of frog-coloured green peppercorns in brine are a much underrated seasoning, offering a unique aromatic warmth. Their brine is a boon for lifting the deadening effect of cream sauces. It is rather like a spicy, salty vinegar and I treasure it. Add a small palmful of the peppercorns to the sauce above after the vinegar has reduced (their flavour will be too strong if you add them at the beginning), taste the sauce when you have added the crème fraîche and, if you feel it could take a little more sharpness, add a nudge or two of brine from the peppercorn jar. Not surprisingly, this is especially good with steak.

♦ **a dill version for fish.** The soft, aniseed notes of feathery dill seem to do the most for oily fish such as salmon, mackerel and trout. Normally I would be against spooning a cream sauce over pink fish, and certainly over mackerel, but the inherent sharpness of this sauce makes it an exception. A small bunch of dill fronds in place of the mint will be enough.

a gutsy, piquant sauce to serve alongside grilled lamb, chicken or fish

Or pork for that matter. Or, come to think of it, baked ham or grilled vegetables.

flat-leafed parsley – just the leaves from a large bunch
mint – the leaves from a small bunch
anchovy fillets – 3–6
capers – 2–3 tablespoons
Dijon mustard – a tablespoonful
olive oil – start with 6 tablespoons or so
lemon – the juice of half

Stuff the parsley and mint into a food processor or blender with the anchovies, capers and mustard, switch it on, then pour in enough olive oil to reduce the ingredients to a lumpy slush. I don't think you should go too far; the sauce seems more interesting with some texture to it. Taste the sauce and add lemon juice as you go. What I suggest you are looking for is a sauce that is bright, herby, salty and piquant, with a consistency that allows it to ooze lazily across the plate rather than stand up in a mound or run amok.

and more

♦ **seasoning.** Capers and anchovies added in quantity usually mean a dish has plenty of salt, but should you decide to leave either out then you might need to think about adding some. Taste, taste, taste.

♦ **when it is at its best.** There is nothing quite like this wonderfully herby, mildly astringent mixture with cold roast beef and boiled, unbuttered potatoes.

♦ **a basil or coriander version.** You can add other tender herbs instead of or as well as the mint but the parsley needs to stay to give it some body. Try a couple of handfuls of basil or coriander leaves.

♦ **a feast.** I am so seduced by the luscious piquancy of this sauce that I have been known to dip my chips in it.

a lovely, wobbly mayonnaise

There are plenty of times when a jar of bought mayonnaise fits the bill perfectly. But I do think that there are some occasions when only a bowl of wobbling, greeny-yellow home-made will do. If you think of making mayonnaise as a pleasure, something to do late on a searingly hot summer's morning before everyone turns up for lunch, then it loses all, or much, of its capricious reputation. There are few better ways to say welcome than to put a big bowl of hand-made garlic mayonnaise and a crusty baguette on the table when everyone sits down, no matter how much whisking it takes. Once people start dipping in and passing it round, the effort becomes worth every stroke.

egg yolks – 2 large, free range
groundnut oil – 100ml
fruity extra virgin olive oil – 200ml
lemon

Put the egg yolks into a large, round-bottomed bowl. Sprinkle a pinch of salt over them and stir briefly with a whisk. The salt has the effect of thickening the yolks very slightly, which will only make the whole process easier.

Add a drop of groundnut oil – no more than half a teaspoon at first – and whisk it in. Now add another and whisk that in, then a few more drops, still whisking constantly. You can now start to let it run in a trickle, but you cannot stop whisking. Go slowly, firmly and with confidence (mayonnaise can misbehave terribly if it thinks it can get away with it). Once you have finished the groundnut oil, then start adding the extra virgin. At this point you should be able to feel the whisk becoming heavier, a sign that the mayonnaise is thickening. By the time you have almost finished, the mixture should be thick enough to wobble. Once all the oil is finished, give it one more really good beating.

I should add at this point that sometimes the eggs will take more, or less, oil than at others. Much depends on the weight of your oil. Don't add the whole amount of oil if you feel the mayonnaise is thick enough, just stop when it is as thick as you want it to be. You can always thin it down later with a little hot water.

Season with lemon juice – just a teaspoon or so may be enough – some more salt and a little pepper. You might find that you don't need any pepper – some oils are peppery enough in their own right, so it depends on the oil you are using.

and more

◆ **what if it all goes wrong?** Occasionally mayonnaise can split on you. In my not inconsiderable experience this usually happens early on. It is not difficult to sort out. Just start again in a clean bowl with a new egg yolk, then slowly, slowly, bit by bit, add your previous attempt to it, whisking all the time.

◆ **a garlic mayo for dipping things into.** You could, and I sometimes do, lazily add a few crushed garlic cloves to the recipe above. You will get garlic mayonnaise, fair enough, but I am not sure it is as good as it could be. Better, I think, is to crush the garlic first – it should be young and mouthwateringly juicy – with a good pinch of salt (a couple of cloves of garlic is enough for a discreet whiff – you will need more if I am coming to lunch). Then start adding the oil as usual, except that in this case I would be tempted to add much more extra virgin than groundnut. Its peppery, dark greenness is right for lunch in the garden in high summer, when it is too hot even for the bees and butterflies to come out. The sort of mayonnaise you make in a big, quivering bowlful and dip celery, lightly cooked green beans and chunks of bread into. You will need some chilled rosé on the table, too. Even better is to eat it with cold baked cod in great chalky flakes, as they do in the Provençal *grand aïoli*, and new potatoes, still warm from the pot. And then there's the grilled vegetables, cold roast meat (especially underdone beef) and grilled fish that I think it goes with so perfectly.

◆ **a herb mayonnaise.** You can let mayonnaise down so that it is rather more of a sauce than something that sits and quivers. I use hot, not-quite-boiling water for this. Just a spoonful or two will soften your mayo into something that will form a puddle on your plate. It is in this sloppy state that I use it with fish, peppered heavily with chopped herbs. The aniseed herbs – dill, chervil, tarragon – all work superbly here, offering a gentle whiff of anise that is so pleasing in the summer. I add fresh parsley too, and occasionally capers and a few chopped gherkins, by which time we are virtually into tartare sauce.

◆ **I am very fond of eating garlic mayonnaise with grilled meats.** I know it sounds strange, but think about it: we are not that far away from sauce béarnaise, are we? It's just oil instead of butter. I have also been known to creep down in the middle of the night and attack the garlic mayo, slathering it on to any bread I can find.

a simple gravy

You have a delectable piece of meat that has been roasted to perfection, its fat crisp and jelly tender, its meat hot, toothsome, juicy. This could be good enough. But there is much, so much, pleasure left in that roasting tin. The same goes for a sauté. Left behind in the pan is the real treasure, the intensely flavoured bits and pieces stuck to the bottom, the caramelised meat juices that have turned to an interesting goo. These are the best bits of all, and it would be a shame and a waste to throw them down the sink.

There is so much flavour in these concentrated juices just waiting to become an impromptu sauce – and to my mind so much more interesting than any of those fancy sauces you can make from veal stock and butter. They might impress the little man from the Michelin guide but they do little for me. An integral sauce, made from the pan scrapings and some wine, stock or even water, is far better because it has a history and a connection with the meat. A sauce made separately might be good but it can never really be part of the dish. It can never *belong*.

the roasting tin and its fat, aromatics and debris
wine, stock, Madeira, Marsala or even water

Remove the roast chicken/lamb/pork/beef from the tin and set it aside to rest. Tip the excess fat from the tin, leaving just a thin layer of the dark juices under the fat, then fish out the bay leaves, lemon, onion, garlic, thyme, whatever, and throw them away. Now put the tin with its brown juices and sticky bits over a low to moderate heat and pour in enough liquid to make a thin layer in the bottom. As the liquid comes to the boil, stir it with a whisk or wooden spoon, scraping away at the stuck bits and dissolving them into the juices. Let the mixture bubble and reduce for a minute or two, then taste and add a little salt and some black pepper. It will not thicken, so take it off the heat once it has concentrated to a rich, aromatic liquor. Spoon it over the roast meat.

and more

♦ **a thick gravy.** There are times when only a thick gravy will do. In my book this means sausages, beef and sometimes chicken. Luscious and savoury and thick enough to soak your Yorkshire pudding. You could, I suppose, thicken the juices above by beating in butter or stirring in cornflour but I see no reason other than misplaced snobbery not to use a bit of flour. The trick is not to use too much. Tip the fat out of the roasting tin and leave just the juices and any stuck-on goodies. Sprinkle in a tablespoon of flour – it won't seem like enough but you only need the smallest amount to get a good thick gravy. The important bit is to cook it out for a minute or so to get rid of the uncooked flour taste and give your gravy a warm, nutty flavour. Once the flour, fat and juices it soaks up start to cook (you need to move it round the pan to stop it burning), then you can pour on whatever liquid you fancy.

♦ **which liquid you add will depend on the meat the gravy is to accompany.** You can make perfectly good gravy with boiling water if there are enough caramelised juices in your pan. For a chicken I tend to add a little stock first, made by sticking the giblets in a pan with water to cover and seasoned with some thyme, carrot and onion and left to simmer for an hour until it is a thin, brown liquor. This adds much depth to the gravy. You can then add anything you like in the way of flavourings. I particularly like white wine or dry vermouth in my chicken gravy. For pheasant, partridge, guinea fowl, lamb or pork, I would always prefer something sweeter, such as Madeira or dry Marsala.

♦ **some good things to do with leftover gravy.** A jug of gravy, providing it is not more than a day or two old, can provide untold pleasure. The trick is to get it piping hot.

♦ **greens in gravy.** Trim and rinse soft, tender greens such as spring greens, spinach leaves, Chinese greens or watercress. Drop them into a pan, still wet from rinsing, and place over a moderate heat. You will need to cover the pan tightly with a lid so that the greens soften in their own steam. When they are soft, dark green and collapsed, drain them and stir them into your steaming hot gravy.

♦ **fried mashed potato.** Shape leftover mashed potato into round patties, fry them in a little butter till they are golden on both sides, then serve with very hot gravy. The best bit is mashing the potatoes with their crisp shell and velvety insides into the luscious, reddish-brown sauce.

a luxurious sauce for anything

Hollandaise is the scariest of sauces to make but, God, is it good. Gentle, soothing, a bowl of creamy-yellow bliss in which to dunk your asparagus, your potatoes, your sole. I make it day after day in May and June when the English asparagus is up.

It must be heated gently while being constantly whisked but without getting too hot. This is the crux of it. Without-Getting-Too-Hot. You will need a round-bottomed, heatproof bowl and a saucepan for it to sit on snugly. Oh, and a plump balloon whisk.

eggs – 3 large free range
butter – almost a full 250g packet
lemon – you'll need half, perhaps less if it is particularly juicy

Break the eggs, dropping the yolks into a heatproof bowl and putting the egg whites in the fridge for later. Half fill the pan with water and put it over a moderate heat. Sit the egg bowl snugly on top – it shouldn't touch the water – then add a small splash of water to the eggs and stir gently for a few seconds. Cut the butter into twelve cubes and add four of them to the egg. Whisk firmly but slowly until the egg yolks have taken up the butter, then slowly whisk in the rest. You will need slightly less than a whole packet. A nuisance, I know, but it will do for toast.

Squeeze in the lemon juice, still whisking. The colour should be almost that of custard. Grind in a little salt and white pepper. Use black if you don't have white. Turn off the heat. The sauce will keep warm over the water for half an hour or so but whisk it now and again. This is the point at which it may curdle. No one is immune – a bowl of it did the dirty on me last week and I have made it a million times. But I really do think it is worth the sweat. We are talking heaven here.

and more

♦ **if it really has split into thousands of tiny grains,** then try adding a splash of either boiling water or very, very cold water (strangely, both seem to work) or even an ice cube and beating like hell. I find this works almost every time. I once threw in the ice from a friend's gin and tonic. It did the trick.

♦ **take the sauce on a bit, if you want,** by adding chopped soft herbs to it such as basil, dill or tarragon. The latter is quite sublime with grilled chicken or chips.

a clear, savoury broth

People can be very snotty about stock cubes. No single item on your kitchen shelf is guaranteed to get you more withering looks and raised eyebrows than a little foil-wrapped cake of salt, flavourings and boiled-down bones. Such looks suggest that no one who takes their cooking seriously could ever be caught crumbling a cube into their soup. Well, I use stock cubes – or, to be more accurate, stock powder – and, what is more, so do many of the chefs and writers who self-styled 'serious' cooks hold in such great esteem. The simple truth is that commercially made stock is fine for some things. The sad cooks are not the ones who on occasion resort to using stock powder but those who spend their day boiling down bones and vegetables as a sort of culinary one-upmanship.

I don't use beef, chicken or lamb stock cubes because I find them too salty and with a chemical aftertaste. But I do recommend the instant vegetable stock powder, which is lighter and less salty. The best I have found is made by Marigold. It is a pleasantly savoury, light and clear broth that is fine for most everyday uses. It is, I suggest, the only good thing ever to have come out of Switzerland. It makes those recipes with the dreaded word 'stock' in them a real possibility.

But there are times when stock, or broth as I prefer to call it, becomes the star of the meal – the very point of your supper, if you like. In that case I suggest you might prefer to make the real thing with a few chicken bones, some sweet vegetables and a handful of herbs. The resulting golden liquid is the most soothing, comforting, sustaining, satisfying, warming, healing bowl of stuff on earth. It needs little or no fuss: just an onion, a carrot, some celery, a tomato and some leek and parsley, simmered with either Sunday's roast chicken carcass or a whole fresh chicken. Either one will give you something so blissful to sup that you will wonder why you haven't bothered to do it before.

If you choose a fresh chicken, I suggest you lift it from the stock after an hour or so and serve it in thick, juicy slices with garlic mayonnaise and plain, crisp lettuce. And whichever method you use, I recommend you tuck a few chicken wings in, too. They will enrich the broth like nothing else.

181

You will need:

**either the remains of a roast chicken (don't forget the bits of jelly in the dish) or,
much better, a fresh free-range chicken**

a handful of chicken wings

an onion and a leek or two

a couple of celery sticks

a tomato or two

a few peppercorns – I use about 8

a small bunch of parsley stalks and 3 or 4 bay leaves

Get out your largest pan. The deeper the better. Stuff the chicken or its bones, the wings, the vegetables – rinsed but not peeled or cut up – and the peppercorns and herbs into it, then pour in enough water to virtually cover the bird. You may find you have to turn it over or top up the water during the cooking. Bring the water to the boil, then turn down the heat so that – and this is important – the liquid bubbles only very gently. What you should hear is blob, blip, blop rather than hubble bubble. From time to time, shove anything sticking up down under the water.

After a couple of hours the liquid will be pale gold in colour, depending on how many tomatoes and onions you have used, and should smell deeply appetising. Lift the fresh chicken out and set aside, then strain the liquor through a sieve into a bowl. Leave to cool, then refrigerate.

and more

♦ **running with it.** You can drink the hot broth, seasoned with salt, as it is, or use it in any recipe that calls for stock. You can also use it as a base for your supper.

♦ **layer thinly sliced potatoes and onions in a shallow buttered dish.** Season with salt and pepper as you go, then pour over hot broth to cover lightly. Bake in a low oven till the onions have softened and the potatoes have soaked up most of the stock. You will need a salad and some cold meat or a wedge of cheese here.

♦ **make a bowl of noodle soup.** You can, of course, put every herb and flavouring in the cupboard into a noodle soup but I think this destroys the purity, and therefore the point, of the clear, herbal soup. I prefer to keep such suppers as simple as possible. Chillies are obvious and appropriate bringers of heat; lemon juice, lemon grass or lime leaves will add tartness and piquancy; and fresh herbs or greens will bring the necessary freshness.

a smooth and creamy pâté

There is a constantly recurring lunch in my house that consists of little more than deli shopping laid out on the kitchen table, eaten from its wrappers and cartons. It is a Saturday morning thing, really. Hunks of bread, either freshly baked sourdough or a crisp ficelle, some tiny, purple-black olives, miniature gherkins, a knobbly salami and a couple of fat wedges of cheese are pretty much what we seem to have. Yet it is a favourite meal, one I enjoy as much as any other. I like a pear with mine, too, or a huge bunch of sweet, muscaty grapes. The star of such a meal is often a white china dish of home-made pâté to go with the little gherkins, or cornichons as they seem to be called nowadays. It is so difficult – almost impossible – to find a commercial pâté that is both velvety and pink enough that I think it worth making your own. The method that follows may sound pedantic but it is small points such as the sieving after the initial blending that make the difference between a good pâté and one that is truly sublime. Some swamp-green canned peppercorns, hot, soft and addictive, to scatter on as you eat will bring untold rewards.

Enough for 6

chicken livers – about 400g
milk – enough to soak the livers in
butter – 110g, plus 50g at the very end
whipping cream – 90ml
brandy

184

Trim any dark or green bits from the livers, cover them in milk and leave them for thirty minutes. This will rid them of any bitterness. Soften two thirds of the 110g butter, not so far as to melt it but just so it takes a finger easily. Melt the remaining third in a shallow pan. When it starts to foam, drop in the livers, drained of their milk. Take care – they will spit at you. Let them develop a pale, golden crust on one side, then turn them over and do the same to the other. It is essential that the butter is hot enough for this to take only a few minutes, otherwise the centre will not stay pink and the pâté will lose its magic.

Now tip the livers, their butter, the softened butter and a generous seasoning of salt and black pepper into a blender or food processor with the cream and blitz to a smooth purée. Pour a couple of good glugs of brandy into the empty pan, put it over the heat and bring to the boil so the alcohol burns off (some people ignite it at this point but I have never found it makes that much difference). Pour the brandy into the creamed chicken livers and continue to blitz. No matter how much you whiz the pâté there will still be some graininess, but it should remain pink.

Now, using a rubber spatula, push the mixture through a stainless steel sieve into a bowl. I know this is deeply boring, and the sieve is yet another thing to wash up, but it really does make a crucial difference to the pâté, turning the grainy and the mundane into the blissfully velvety. The point is to have as smooth a texture as possible, and you can only get that by sieving. Scrape the whole lot into a terrine or bowl, smooth the top and put it in the fridge to set.

Half an hour later, and no longer because the mixture will discolour, melt the 50g of butter and scrape off the froth that rises to the surface. Pour the butter over the pâté and return it to the fridge to set. I tend to leave mine for most of the day or overnight, but it should be ready in three or four hours. It will keep for a day or two.

and more

♦ **a more pungent pâté.** I add cream to my chicken liver pâté because I like the mild, silky feel it gives to the basic liver and butter mixture, but you could leave it out. The result will be a more strident flavour and a deeper pink colour.

♦ **a green peppercorn pâté.** Fold a palmful of bottled green peppercorns into the pâté just before you put it into the dish.

♦ **a duck liver pâté.** If ever you come across quantities of duck livers, do have a go at substituting them in the blueprint pâté above. The effect will be (slightly) richer.

♦ **some good things to serve with your pâté.** Green peppercorns to scatter over each scoop of pâté as it goes on the bread; some mild pickled chillies; plenty (and I really do mean plenty) of hot toast or crusty bread.

a simple, extremely useful pastry

You can make a pastry crust with nothing more than flour, fat and a little water. The amount of fat you add, be it butter, lard or olive oil, depends on how crumbly or 'short' you like your pastry. You can go on to enrich the basic dough with egg yolk, sweeten it with sugar or flavour it with spices or ground nuts if you fancy, but a plain, unsweetened shortcrust pastry, made with lots of butter to flour, is a perfectly appropriate, though strangely unfashionable, crust.

Pastry making is one type of cooking you need to get the measuring scales out for. I like to use the American cup measuring system – so straightforward – but some people get in a terrible tizwaz about it (and what, may I ask, is so difficult about dipping a cup measure into a bag of flour?), so I have added metric measures too. I recommend any doubters pick up a set of cup measures. Once they get into the habit of using them they will not be surprised that half the world does so.

plain flour – 1½ cupfuls or 180g
butter – a loosely packed cupful or 100g, cold from the fridge
ice-cold water

Don't bother to sift the flour, it won't make the slightest bit of difference. Cut the butter into small chunks and rub them into the flour, pressing the ingredients over your fingertips with your thumbs. Keep rubbing the butter in until you have a mixture that looks like coarse fresh breadcrumbs. I know you can do this in the mixer but what is the point? It takes only a minute or two by hand, is as relaxing as stroking the cat and makes less washing up.

All you need to do now is bring the crumbs of butter and flour together to form a soft, but rollable dough. Use a little water for this. I have found that adding ice cubes to chill the water really does make the pastry lighter and easier to roll. Don't ask me why. Add a tablespoon or two of water, gingerly, because too much is difficult to correct, until the dough looks as if it will come together to form a smooth ball. You are looking for a dough that is firm enough to roll but soft enough to demand careful lifting.

Flatten the dough slightly, fishcake style, then wrap it in clingfilm, greaseproof or a clean tea towel and put it in the fridge for half an hour. Don't miss this chilling time, no matter how tempting it may be. It is essential for the pastry to relax a while, otherwise it will shrink in the oven. I promise.

custard, how to stop it curdling and some good things to do with it

There are three types of custard: the stuff you make from powder in the blue and yellow tin; the sort you buy ready-made from the supermarket chiller; and the one you make yourself from eggs, sugar and creamy milk. There is room for all of them, and I find I finish a carton of ready-made all by myself without even bothering to heat it up. But there is nothing quite like a bowl of pale and creamy home-made custard. I include it in this book because it is something I feel we have got out of the habit of cooking – if we ever did – and it is one of the most soothing, comforting and calming things you can make. If you have never made it, a word of warning. Custard curdles. It is one of those wretched things that can burn, split or scramble in a blink of an eye. That does not mean to say it is difficult. It just needs a bit of tender, loving care.

milk – full cream, 500ml
a vanilla pod
egg yolks – 5
caster sugar – 5 tablespoons

Pour the milk into a saucepan. Split the vanilla pod open lengthways with a sharp knife, then drop it into the milk and bring to the boil. When the milk looks as if it is on the point of boiling – it will be shuddering, bubbles will be visible and maybe a little steam – remove it from the heat and leave for about twenty minutes – this allows the vanilla pod to do its stuff. Lift out the vanilla pod and scrape the little black seeds into the milk with the point of a knife.

Whisk the egg yolks and sugar together until they are thick and pale in colour, then add the milk and stir. Rinse the milk pan, pour the custard into it and put it over a low heat, then stir almost constantly until it thickens somewhat. The consistency should be that of double cream. On no account let the mixture get too hot – if it boils it will curdle and there will be tears. Pour the warm custard into a jug and use immediately or cool, cover loosely with clingfilm and refrigerate until needed. It will keep for a day or two.

and more

♦ **how to stop your custard curdling.** I suggest you make it in a non-stick saucepan and stir it with a wooden spoon. Rinse the pan out and shake it dry after boiling the milk, otherwise the bits of skin will catch on the bottom. Don't let the custard get too hot, or boil. Keep stirring once it goes back on the heat.

♦ **rescuing your custard if, even despite your best efforts, it curdles.** Put the plug in the sink, turn the cold tap on hard and pour the custard into a clean bowl. Dunk the bowl in the water so that it comes half way up the sides, then whisk energetically with a balloon whisk. If you are lucky it will come back to normal. If not, you could always try giving it to the cat.

♦ **banana custard.** I could eat gallons of this stuff. It is good made with custard powder but better still when you can be bothered to make the real thing. The reason being that the bananas somehow flavour the thinner home-made custard more than they do the thick packet variety. I don't know why, I only know that they do so, therefore becoming banana custard rather than bananas-in-custard. Reckon on the above ingredients being enough for four, and allow two bananas per person, fewer if there are children to feed.

♦ **sponge and custard.** Custard has an affinity with those almondy sponge cakes such as the one on page 431. I prefer to chill the sauce for this, letting it get thoroughly refrigerated before pouring it around my slice of sponge. For sheer bliss, try poached pears or damsons, warm sponge cake and cold custard.

♦ **an indulgent way with custard and meringue.** Try home-made or even shop-bought meringue, crumbled into large chunks and stirred through with raspberries (as if you were making Eton Mess), then folded into enough cold custard to make a trifle-like dessert.

191

an appetite for
soup

a fast, warming bowl of soup for tonight, tomorrow, for now

Few suppers are so satisfying. The chillies will perk you up no end.

Per person:
chicken stock
small, hot red chillies – 2 or 3, depending on your heat threshold today
lemon grass – a couple of thick, young blades or several thinner supermarket stems
noodles – a small handful
greens – such as spinach, mustard greens or dark, tender cabbage

Using a soup bowl as a measure, pour as much chicken stock as you want to eat into a deep saucepan. I suggest you allow two deep bowlfuls per person, giving you some to evaporate during cooking plus a little for seconds. Bring the stock to the boil, meanwhile slicing the chillies very finely and removing the seeds if you wish (they carry some heat). The amount you need will depend on how hot your chillies are. I reckon on two very small, very hot chillies per person. Smash the lemon grass blades with the handle of a cook's knife so that they splinter but stay together, then add them to the hot stock with the chillies. Turn the heat down so that the stock bubbles gently and leave it until the lemon grass has given up some of its flavour. Taste the stock regularly, but you can reckon on about fifteen minutes.

Meanwhile, cook the noodles for only a minute or two in boiling water. They need a bit of bite to them to be good. Drain them and drop them into cold water so they don't stick together. Sort through the greens, throwing out anything that isn't perky, then tear them into pieces that won't fall off your spoon.

Fish the lemon grass from the stock and discard it, then add the greens to the bubbling stock. Taste it for salt, adding some if you think it needs it. Once the greens have softened to a velvety texture – about a minute in the case of spinach, a bit longer for cabbage and for mustard greens – divide the noodles between warm soup bowls and ladle over the hot stock, greens and chillies.

and more

- **the crux of it.** The quality of the chicken stock is crucial here.

- **how to eat it at its best.** The soup needs to be really hot to do the trick.

- **adding a few scraps.** You can add shredded chicken or cooked prawns if you want.

- **adjusting the seasoning.** Try chilli oil, lemon juice, *nam pla* (Thai fish sauce), fresh coriander leaves, Thai basil.

- **a very fragrant version.** To the original recipe add a last minute seasoning of torn basil and mint leaves and lime juice.

- **a deeper spicing.** Add star anise, sugar and *nam pla* to the broth.

- **a mushroom soup.** Slice or quarter a few mushrooms per person, then fry them in a wok with a little garlic until nutty. Add them to the stock with the noodles.

- **an Italian version.** Don't. I know there is this idea that pasta and noodles are interchangeable but I really cannot agree. Whilst tortellini is an Italian version of the wonton and spaghetti hardly a world away from the noodle, they are, I think, as different as chalk and cheese. There is something that feels wrong in the mouth about Italian pasta in a broth or sauce flavoured with soy and fish sauce. It is a touchy-feely thing rather than anything else. Having said all that, I have used orzo, the rice-shaped pasta, in Asian soups and got away with it.

196

- **prawn noodle soup.** What is it about prawns and noodles that seems so right in the mouth? Use them here, dropping a handful of peeled defrosted jobbies into the pan, or mixing them up with the noodles. Either way, the less you cook them the better. Mint, lime and basil will work well in a seafood variation, as – strangely – will the chicken stock.

a clear, reviving soup

Groovy noodles. This and similarly straightforward bowls of soup are a permanent fixture in my kitchen. They seem to fit in so comfortably day or night. They have a clean, smart edge to them (that's lemon grass for you) and a deep, soul-enhancing savour from the fish sauce, not to mention the soothing quality of pasta.

Per person:
garlic – a medium-sized clove
shallots – 1
!emon grass – 1 stalk
mushrooms – a large handful of button or chestnut mushrooms
groundnut oil
chicken stock (or, at a push, vegetable bouillon) – enough to fill a large soup bowl
to season – star anise, sugar, *nam pla* (Thai fish sauce)
noodles – a handful (depending, of course, on your appetite) of whatever type you fancy
to serve – basil, mint leaves, limes

Peel and crush the garlic, peel and finely chop the shallot, discard the outer leaves of the lemon grass and finely slice the inner heart. Slice or quarter the mushrooms. Get a wok or frying pan hot, add a tablespoon or so of oil and let it shimmer for a second or two before adding the garlic, shallot and lemon grass. Let them sizzle briefly – you don't want them to colour too much – then add the mushrooms and stir-fry for a few minutes till tender, juicy and appetisingly golden in patches.

Pour over the stock and bring it to the boil. Let it simmer for a couple of minutes, then season gingerly - a star anise, a big pinch of sugar, a few shakes of fish sauce, a pinch of salt, some black pepper. Go easy on the fish sauce but keep tasting till you have got something you really like.

Meanwhile, drop the noodles into boiling water (I often just pour a kettle of water over them), then whip them out as soon as they are tender and put them into a large, deep, soup-type bowl. Stuff a few herbs into the bowl – torn-up basil leaves, some finely shredded mint – and a good, big squeeze of lime juice. Then ladle over the sauce with its mushrooms.

a main-course soup for a winter's day

The most satisfying version of this soup is invariably the one where I manage to include the end of a Parma ham bone. Italian delis are usually more than happy to hand them over to regular customers for little or nothing. Failing that, a bit of ham hock from the butcher will suffice – the bone and some fat being essential if the soup is to warm you right through to the marrow.

Enough for 6

dried beans – borlotti, cannellini or chick peas, 200g
carrots – a large winter one or 2 smaller ones
celery – a stalk or two
leeks – a thick one or 2 smaller ones, thoroughly cleaned
garlic – 2 or 3 large cloves, or more if you want
parsley – a small bunch
a little oil, butter or fat in which to sweat the vegetables
bacon or ham – either a small unsmoked ham hock or the end of a Parma ham

The beans need to be soaked overnight in cold water. The next day, drain them, then tip them into a large, deep pan and cover with water – and, if you like, a few drops of olive oil and some bay leaves to flavour. Boil them hard for ten minutes, then turn the heat down and simmer briskly until the beans are tender but far from squashy. The time this takes will vary according to the age of the beans. You should allow twenty-five to forty minutes, or an hour if you are cooking chick peas.

Meanwhile, dice the carrot, cut the celery quite finely and shred the white and pale green of the leek into thick coins. Discard the tough, dark green parts. Peel and chop the garlic and roughly chop the parsley.

Drain the beans and put them in a little oil or fat in a deep pan with the vegetables and most of the parsley. Set it over a low heat until the vegetables shine and start to soften. Add the ham in one piece and pour over enough water to cover it, then bring to the boil. Turn down the heat so that the soup is bubbling gently around the ham and leave it for at least an hour and a half. You will get the best results, by which I mean the most flavoursome, by letting the soup cook slowly, blipping and glupping rather than bubbling, for two hours or more. Check for seasoning; it will need salt, black pepper and the rest of the parsley. The beans should be soft, almost squashy, and have thickened the liquor to a velvety broth.

and more

♦ **adding other roots.** Chop and change the vegetables according to what you have an appetite for or what is in the fridge. I often throw a diced parsnip in with the carrot, or sometimes a bit of swede. I also find this a good use for those winter tomatoes that aren't anything like tasty enough for salad. They seem to come to life with long, slow cooking.

♦ **a herbal soup.** Add tough herbs such as thyme or bay at the beginning of the cooking. If you want to add tender-leafed herbs such as tarragon or coriander, then do so at the end. Add the tough herbs in sprigs so that you can pull them out when you feel they have added enough of their flavour to the soup. Add the fresh herbs chopped and by the tablespoon at first, adding more as you wish.

♦ **adding vigour and freshness.** You will probably be tempted to hack off bits of ham to drop into your soup, but you can also add vegetables such as cabbage or spinach leaves at the last minute. Shred them finely and add them to the hot soup ten minutes before you intend to eat. Tough-stemmed vegetables such as white cabbage need to be dunked briefly into boiling water first. I reckon on a small handful of greens per person.

♦ **a meatless version.** I cannot say that this is strictly vegetarian, but you will find that a few thick Parmesan rinds can be used instead of the ham bone to add depth and general savour. I know people who remember to store theirs in the deep-freeze, but they are more organised than I am. I tend to cadge them off my grocer.

an earthy, meal-in-a-bowl-type soup

Deep, dark, bass notes here. One of those swamp-like soups that gives much in the way of sustenance and warmth. I have offered this at big lunches for friends, a vast bubbling cauldron of it, setting it down amongst the bread and cheese.

Enough for 4 as a main course

onions – 2 small ones or 1 large one
olive oil
garlic – 3 or 4 cloves
unsmoked bacon or pancetta – a good handful, diced
flat-leafed parsley – a small bunch
green or brown lentils – maybe Puy or Castelluccio – a good 2 handfuls (250g)
stock or water – enough to cover the lentils completely, about a litre
spinach – 2 or 3 big handfuls
a lemon
mint – a small bunch, the leaves only

Peel the onions and chop them quite finely, then let them cook over a moderate to low heat with a little olive oil, the peeled and sliced garlic and the diced bacon. You want all to be golden and fragrant. Chop the parsley and stir it in.

Wash the lentils thoroughly and pick them over for little stones, then stir them into the onions and bacon. Pour over the stock or water and bring to the boil, skimming off any froth that appears on the surface. You can add a bay leaf or two if you like. Turn the heat down so that the lentils simmer merrily, then almost cover the pot with a lid and leave until they are tender but far from collapse. About thirty minutes, depending on the age of your lentils.

Wash the spinach very thoroughly and tear it up a bit. While it is still wet and dripping, put it into a shallow pan over a high heat and shut the lid tightly – you want it to cook in its own steam. After a minute or so, it will be limp and bright emerald green. Lift it out, squeeze it dry (I do this by pressing it against the side of the pan with a draining spoon), then divide it between four warm bowls.

Season the soup with salt, black pepper, lemon juice and the torn mint leaves, tasting it as you go. Ladle the hot soup on top of the spinach and serve with more lemon and mint for those who want it.

and more

♦ **haricot and tarragon soup.** Soak 250g dried haricots overnight, then simmer them in unsalted water for 30 minutes. Drain and add to the onions and bacon. Continue as in the lentil soup above, but obviously without the lentils. Instead of mint, try tarragon leaves, but add them earlier, say fifteen minutes or so before the soup is due to be ready. There is no need to offer more herbs at the table but the lemon juice will still be welcome, as will some lovely crusty bread.

♦ **cannellini and chilli soup.** Soak and cook the beans as in the haricot and tarragon soup above but this time add a couple of seeded and chopped fresh red chillies to the onions and bacon. Serve with a slick of olive oil floating on top, plus the lemon and the mint.

♦ **lentil soup with celery and mushrooms.** Add a stalk or two of celery, finely diced, to the onions and garlic in the basic recipe above. Some button mushrooms, cut into quarters, can be added just before the lentils, so that they colour and sweeten. They will add even more earthy notes to the soup. You may need a little more lemon.

♦ **lentil and bok choi soup.** Spinach leaves are not the only greens. Use any of the Chinese leaves, such as bok choi, mustard greens or Chinese broccoli. Don't be tempted to try this with the tarragon mentioned in the haricot soup above. It won't sit comfortably.

♦ **other good things to add to the basic soup.** Worcestershire sauce; mushroom ketchup (or mushroom seasoning as it is called nowadays); dark soy – stir it in at the end of cooking; a wine glass of Madeira (fabulous) about fifteen minutes before the soup is due to be ready; crushed dried chillies added with the onions and garlic; a few florets of broccoli instead of the spinach – too healthy-sounding, I know, but it is just brilliant if you have used the purple sprouting sort.

206

萬里香牌

新竹

米粉王

HSIN CHU PY MEI FUN
(RICE STICK

an appetite for
pasta and noodles

a quick, soothing weekday cheese and pasta supper

No matter which recipes I hold dear, the most downright useful are those weekday pasta recipes whose sauces cook in less time than the pasta takes to boil. Is this book invaluable or what?

Per person:
pasta – an overflowing handful, or more if you think you can eat it
broccoli – a thick stalk of 5 or 6 large florets, or 3 or 4 stalks of purple sprouting
Gorgonzola – seriously ripe and creamy, about 150g

Get a large, deep pan of water boiling furiously – the pasta needs room to move around – salt it generously and throw in the pasta. Let it boil with gusto, loosening any stuck pasta from the bottom of the pan with a long spoon. Dried pasta takes about nine minutes to come to tenderness but the exact timing will depend very much on the shape you choose and how soft you like your pasta. Tubes such as rigatoni, for instance, take longer than ribbons like fettuccine.

Bring a second, smaller pan of water to the boil and salt it lightly. Trim the broccoli, cutting it into small florets and thin pieces of tender stalk (don't use the tough stuff at the bottom), then let it simmer to tenderness. Taste a piece for doneness after two or three minutes, then drain it.

Put the cheese into a warm serving bowl – it will start to ooze – then add the hot, drained broccoli followed by the lightly drained pasta. A little of the cooking water adhering to the pasta will prevent it sticking together and help the sauce coat it easily. Toss the cheese, broccoli and pasta – the cheese, incidentally, will now be melting under the heat of the pasta – and spoon into shallow bowls.

and more

♦ **other cheeses, other pastas.** Work this idea through with any shape of pasta and any very ripe and runny cheese. Successes in my house have included rigatoni, penne and macaroni with Gorgonzola, an oozing Taleggio, and, more than once, a running Camembert. The softer blues, such as Irish Cashel, work satisfyingly with flat ribbon pastas like fettuccine and the wider pappardelle. The trick is to choose a cheese that is meltingly ripe and to work quickly so as to keep the pasta hot.

♦ **other greens.** If you don't fancy broccoli or purple sprouting, try spinach (just wash it and dump it, still wet, into a shallow pan with a lid, then let it cook in its own steam for a minute or two over a high heat). Avoid peppery, bitter oriental leaves. They don't feel quite right with this.

♦ **and another ...**

butter – a thick slice
bacon – smoked streaky is good here, 3 rashers per person
leeks – 2 medium ones per person
pasta – an overflowing handful for each person, or more if you think
    you can eat it
cream – 100ml should be enough for each person

Melt enough butter in a saucepan or high-sided frying pan to cover the bottom – this will be about 50g for a medium pan – then cut the bacon into short, thick strips (or pieces the size of a postage stamp, if you prefer) and let them cook in the butter for a few minutes. They should colour a little. Cut the leeks in half lengthways and then into pieces no thicker than your little finger. Add them to the bacon and leave to cook until they are soft and squashy, stirring them from time to time.

Put a large pot of water on to boil, salt it and add the pasta. Let the pasta boil until it is tender, yet with a bit of bite to it (nine minutes or so for rigatoni or penne, less for ribbons such as fettuccine). When the pasta is almost ready, pour the cream into the leeks and bacon and let it bubble gently. Drain the pasta lightly (a little of the cooking water will help the sauce to coat the pasta), then tip it into the leeks and cream.

a cheap spaghetti supper

It's not just that this is a cheap supper but that it is put together from things we tend to have knocking around anyway. Its practical, almost puritan background is a bonus. The point is that crisp bacon and breadcrumbs work brilliantly with the long strings of pasta. It makes a change to have pasta without a sauce. A few glugs of oil at the end are lubricant enough. You can safely use any of the thin pasta family here instead of spaghetti: tagliatelle, tagliarini, fettuccine or linguine. I have used the wide, floppy ribbons of pappardelle before now. They all work. Try to get a mixture of breadcrumb sizes, they are more interesting to eat.

Per person:
white bread – 2 thickish slices, crusts removed
spaghetti – a thick handful, about 125g or so
butter – a thick slice
olive oil
bacon – 2 good-sized rashers of streaky
parsley – a small bunch, the leaves only, roughly chopped

Whiz the bread to rough crumbs in a food processor, or grate it by hand. It won't hurt at all (in fact it will be a bonus) if some of the crumbs are on the large side. Put a big pan of water on to boil, salt it generously and shove in the pasta. Let it cook for about eight or nine minutes, till it is tender but chewy.

Meanwhile, melt the butter in a frying pan with a little olive oil to stop it burning. Cut the bacon into short pieces and fry it in the butter till its fat is golden and the kitchen smells wonderful. Scoop the bacon out with a slotted spoon into a large, warm serving bowl. Add a bit more butter and oil to the butter and bacon fat in the pan and tip in the breadcrumbs. Stir them from time to time in the sizzling butter till they have turned a rich gold. You need to keep an eye on them because they appear as if they are never going to brown, then suddenly they are almost black.

Drain the pasta and toss it with the hot crumbs and any of their butter, the bacon and the parsley, and just a little olive oil to moisten and flavour.

and more

◆ **spaghetti with bacon, breadcrumbs and garlic.** Crush a clove of garlic per person into the butter before you fry the crumbs.

◆ **and with chillies.** Crushed dried chillies seem to work better here than fresh. The quantity depends on your heat threshold but start with a fat pinch or two per person, stirring them in with the crumbs.

◆ **and with lemon and thyme.** Remove fine, young thyme leaves from their stalks and add them to the pan with the bacon. Squeeze the juice of half a lemon into the bowl as you toss everything together.

◆ **thin pasta with anchovies and parsley.** Chop two or three anchovy fillets per person and cook them in a little olive oil over a low heat with a small handful of chopped parsley and a couple of cloves of finely chopped garlic. When the garlic is soft and pale gold – the anchovies will have almost melted – tip into a warm serving bowl, then continue with the crumbs as in the blueprint above. A pinch or two of dried crushed chillies, added with the anchovies, goes well here, too.

◆ **with roast tomatoes and basil.** Toss any of the thin pasta here with the roast tomatoes on page 250. I think it worth squashing them a little, and including their seedy juices. Basil leaves, torn to shreds, and some black pepper will produce a heady, sweet-sharp supper. There is nothing to stop you shaking some toasted crumbs over at the end if you fancy.

◆ **and with butter and Parmesan.** For each person grate 60g Parmesan or pecorino. I know this will look like a lot but generosity is the only route to take here. Toss the hot pasta with a thick slice of your freshest butter (you really should open a new packet for this, as the sweetness of the butter is the whole point) and the grated cheese. The two will melt into a thin sauce that will lightly coat the spaghetti. Spoon over more cheese at the table – or on the floor or the sofa or in bed or wherever else you may be eating this.

a creamy, calming pasta dish

We eat not just to please our mouths and fill our bellies but to satisfy our bodies' needs. Clear, hot noodle soups fill us with energy, while anything with pasta and cream can virtually send us to sleep. What follows is a soporific supper for those times when you want to curl up and do absolutely nothing for the rest of the night.

Per person:
garlic – fresh and young, a whole head
olive oil – a few glugs to drizzle over the garlic
thyme – a few sprigs
pasta – shell or tube shaped, 125g
double cream – a small carton (150ml or so)

Set the oven at 200°C/Gas 6. Trim any long stems from the garlic, then put the bulbs, whole and unpeeled, in a baking dish, drizzle with olive oil and scatter with some of the thyme. Roast until the cloves are soft, sweet and virtually caramelised. They should be tender enough to squash between your fingers. This will take thirty to forty minutes, depending on the age of your garlic.

When the garlic is ready, tear the heads apart and squeeze the golden cloves from their papery skins, then mash them to a pulp. They should be as soft as butter.

Put a large, deep pan of water on to boil and cook the pasta till it is as you like it. I suggest about nine minutes. Warm the creamed garlic in a pan over a moderate heat, then pour in the cream and let it bubble briefly before crumbling in a little salt, some ground black pepper and the rest of the thyme leaves stripped from their branches.

Drain the pasta, but not so thoroughly that it becomes completely dry. Tip the pasta into the sauce and toss gently until all is warm, bubbling and sweetly fragrant.

and more

♦ **pasta with roast garlic, cream and pancetta.** Add crispness to the overall softness by cooking thin slices of pancetta or streaky bacon under the grill, then crumbling them over the pasta as you serve. I reckon on two rashers per person.

♦ **pasta with sausage and thyme.** Skin a butcher's sausage, crumble the meat into a frying pan with a slick of oil and fry it till golden. Toss with the cream and pasta. A fat, herby butcher's sausage for each person.

♦ **and with mustard and Parmesan.** Stir in a spoonful or two of grain mustard with the garlic, tasting as you go, then shake over some grated Parmesan.

♦ **pasta with cream and mushrooms.** Wacky fungi, now available from most supermarkets and the more adventurous greengrocers, will add a warm, woodsy flavour. Toss a handful of mushrooms, cut up if larger than a mouthful, in some sizzling butter, then add the roasted garlic and cream as above.

♦ **or with asparagus, lemon and black pepper.** Boil a few asparagus spears until soft and truly tender, then chop them into short lengths and fold them in with the cream. Stir grated lemon zest and a grind or two more than usual of black pepper in at the end. When I make this I use slightly less of the roasted garlic purée.

♦ **or with ricotta and herbs.** You will need a small handful of ricotta and a good, big handful of soft and fleshy herbs, such as parsley, basil or tarragon, per person, folded into the drained pasta and cream.

♦ **with Gorgonzola and toasted breadcrumbs.** Melt some ripe Gorgonzola with the cream – about 100g per person – and scatter over breadcrumbs that you have fried first in butter till crisp and golden at the end.

♦ **or how about a few chopped anchovies**, some shredded sun-dried tomatoes in oil, chopped steamed spinach, or maybe some broad beans briefly boiled and popped from their skins?

♦ **a suitable salad.** Add crunch to your supper in the form of a salad and use it to mop the garlicky cream off your plate. Frisée or chicory, both crisp and bitter, will be a great contrast to the general sweet creaminess.

deeply savoury noodles as hot as you like

There is a tendency to assume that warm, nourishing food needs to be stodgy. Hardly surprising when you think of our heritage of pies, puddings and dumplings to keep out the cold. But we only have to look in the direction of the noodle dishes of Southeast Asia to find food that will nourish us without making us grind to a halt. For midweek suppers I often want food that is warming yet light to eat. The basic noodle and greens dish below, plus the variations that follow, are suppers that I turn to over and over again. I use any greens, any noodles. I suggest something juicy, like bok choi or mustard greens, and, for the sake of speed and to save a pan, I also suggest you use thin noodles that can be cooked with water from the kettle.

chicken stock – 500ml will be enough for 2
greens – such as bok choi, spinach, mustard greens, a small handful per person
noodles – 50g fresh per person, or slightly less of dried noodles
to season – dark soy sauce, *nam pla* (Thai fish sauce), chilli sauce, lemon juice

222

Bring the chicken stock slowly to the boil. In a separate pan (boring, I know, but it really must be) bring a little water to the boil also. Rinse the greens under running water, then lay them in a steamer of some sort. If you don't have a steamer you can improvise with a colander or sieve, covering it with a plate for want of a lid. Steam the greens over the boiling water until they are tender but still have some life in them. The time will depend on what sort of greens you are using but you can reckon on about three or four minutes for bok choi or mustard greens.

There are several ways of cooking the noodles. If they are very fine dried noodles (about the thickness of the lead in a propelling pencil), simply put them in a heatproof bowl and pour boiling water over them, then leave to soak for a minute or two. Anything wider or thicker and you will need to add them to boiling, salted water for a minute or two. I have tried using the water under the steamer but in truth find it easier to boil them separately. They need to be tender to the touch. Drain them.

Now season the stock. I suggest starting with just half a tablespoon of soy, a whole tablespoon of fish sauce, a scant tablespoon of chilli sauce and the juice of half a lemon added to the simmering stock. Taste as you go, remembering that it is easy to add too much soy. Go carefully with the chilli sauce, too. For the record, I leave the seasoning at that, then put the chilli sauce, soy, lemon and *nam pla* on the table for everyone to help themselves.

Drain the greens, cut them up a little, then put them into a couple of warm bowls with the noodles and the hot, seasoned stock. Eat straight away, so hot that you have to blow on each spoonful and while the soup still has its warming, healing qualities, seasoning gingerly as you go.

and more

♦ **noodles with salty-sweet grilled chicken.** Make up a little pot of sauce with a couple of tablespoons each of dark soy sauce and rice wine, then stir in a teaspoon or so of sugar. Rub this over a boned chicken breast and put it under a hot grill. Brush the chicken from time to time with more of the sauce until it is glossy and firm to the touch. Slice it thickly and dunk the pieces into your bowl of noodles, greens and stock. One chicken breast is enough to feed two.

♦ **noodles with Chinese-style pork.** Pick up a bottle of Chinese *char siu* sauce from a Chinese grocer's – it is sometimes labelled barbecue sauce – and use it to marinate a small pork fillet or a short piece of pork belly. It will need a good hour or two in there. Roast the meat on a wire rack over a roasting tin half filled with water (this is simply to stop the fat burning) until it is a sizzling, burnished brown, then slice it thinly and add to the noodles and soup above. You can prepare the pork several hours in advance if you wish; it will warm up in the hot broth.

♦ **a Japanese fish noodle supper.** Brush small fillets of skinned salmon with the rice wine, soy and sugar mixture used for chicken above (or a good commercial brand of teriyaki sauce) and grill for a few minutes, till glazed and deep golden brown. Swap the chicken stock for fish, then slide in large pieces of the salmon. Another light and warming noodle supper, though it must be said that this is not quite as sustaining as one made with chicken.

a luxurious and deeply aromatic noodle dish

I know this looks like a load of trouble but in practice it is more about a trip to a really good supermarket or Asian grocer's. Once you start cooking, the hot, creamy and piquant result will be yours within half an hour or less. There are few things I find more exciting to eat. Don't even think of making it without a food processor.

Enough for 4

For the spice paste:
chillies – 4 or 5 small, hot red ones
garlic – 2 or 3 small cloves
ginger – a small lump, about the size of a walnut in its shell
lemon grass – 2 or 3 plump stalks
coriander seeds – a few
coriander leaves – a small handful, plus 2 or 3 of their roots if possible
ground turmeric – a teaspoon
vegetable oil – a little

For the soup:
stock – preferably chicken, 500ml
coconut milk – 400ml
a lime – just the juice
nam pla (Thai fish sauce)
mint – a small handful of leaves

To finish:
noodles – a handful (about 50g) per person
crab-meat – brown and white, a small handful per person
shelled prawns – about 16 large ones

Halve and seed the chillies. Peel the garlic. Peel and shred the ginger. Finely slice the tender, innermost leaves of the lemon grass. Grind the coriander seeds or crush them in a mortar. Blitz it all to a thick paste in a food processor with the coriander leaves and any well-scrubbed roots, plus the turmeric. You may need a few tablespoons of vegetable oil to help it go round but add as little as you can.

Place a fairly deep pan over a moderate heat, add half the spice paste (keep the other half in the fridge for tomorrow) and fry it, moving it round the pan, for a minute or so, then pour in the stock and coconut milk and let it come to the boil. Turn the heat down and let the soup simmer for ten minutes. Meanwhile, cook the noodles briefly in boiling water and drain them.

Lower the crab-meat and prawns into the soup. The prawns only need a minute or two to cook, then season with a little lime juice, salt, a teaspoon or so of fish sauce and the mint leaves, torn up if they are large.

Divide the noodles between four large, deep bowls and ladle over the hot soup.

and more

- **making the dish your own.** Chop and change the ingredients to suit your taste and appetite. I find myself introducing a few shredded lime leaves to the spice paste and sometimes cutting back on the garlic, other times I use more coriander and maybe fewer chillies. If I want a thicker sauce I let it simmer for longer, if I need something that is more soupy then I add more stock. I find that sometimes I yearn for a sauce that is milder, in which case I use less of the spice paste and more coconut milk (gently uplifting and soothing, that one), whilst other days have me chucking all the spice paste in and sweating it out.

  What else I stick in it depends on what I feel like. This is a dish that is perfect for tinkering with, adding and subtracting to suit your mood.

- **hot and creamy chicken noodles.** Forget the prawns but still use the fish sauce (it is not really fishy, just very savoury) and add either a handful of cooked chicken per person or some pieces of raw chicken fillet as the soup comes up to the boil. Coriander and Thai basil leaves are good stirred in at the end.

- **a small knob of grated galangal,** a pinch of cumin seeds or a couple of teaspoons of shrimp paste can be added to the spice paste if you fancy to make the whole thing closer to its Malaysian roots.

- **and some other good things to throw in your noodles.** Pieces of boned and shredded roast duck leg; strips of salmon (they will cook in seconds); cubes of tofu; shelled raw oysters; Thai basil leaves, or even Italian basil for that matter; finely shredded spring onions.

an appetite for
rice

a rice supper to soothe and comfort

There is something consoling about a plate of risotto. Anyone who doubts the ability of what we eat to alter our mood might like to try making this for supper next time they are feeling tetchy. The limpid, velvety texture of the warm, soft rice is at once soothing and soporific. If your risotto is truly to hit the spot, though, the texture must be right, by which I mean pleasingly moist, the chubby grains soft but with a little bite to them and suspended in a creamy stock.

As the rice cooks it absorbs the stock, swelling slowly to tenderness. You have to keep an eye on the liquid, adding more as it is taken up by the grains. There is no real short cut, such as adding the stock in one fell swoop – it doesn't work like that, but in this instance I am not sure it matters. We are only talking about thirty minutes and anyway, making risotto is pure, mood-enhancing therapy.

Enough for 2

a small, sweet onion
butter – a thick slice (about 30g)
rice – arborio, carnaroli or vialone nano, 3 or 4 handfuls
hot chicken stock – up to 1 litre
to finish – saffron, a bunch of parsley, chopped, more butter and a big lump of
  Parmesan cheese

Peel the onion and dice it finely. Melt the butter in a heavy-bottomed pan (it can have deep or shallow sides, but not as shallow as a frying pan), stir in the onion and let it bubble gently for five minutes or so, until it is soft and translucent. Tip in the rice and stir it gently through the butter. Pour in a ladleful of stock and let it come up to the boil. Adjust the heat so that the liquid bubbles around the rice and stir almost constantly with a wooden spoon.

Pour in more stock, just enough to cover the rice, and continue stirring gently. The stock will be absorbed and the rice will swell. As the liquid disappears and the rice becomes heavier on the spoon, add more stock. There is deep pleasure to be had here, watching the grains gradually plump up and the liquid that surrounds them become almost limpid. At some point you could sprinkle in the saffron. You will need two or three pinches of the deep scarlet stamens but no more. As you stir now, the rice will turn a deep amber.

Stop adding stock when the rice is tender but still keeps a little (just a little) of its chalkiness. The only way to find out is to taste it (timing is, as always, impossible to check by the clock alone, but twenty minutes or so should find the rice approaching tenderness). The risotto should be moist but not soupy and should slide lazily off the spoon. Stir in some chopped parsley – as much as you fancy – a generous slice of butter and a big handful of grated Parmesan. The butter and cheese will melt into the goo suspending the rice, and the risotto will at once become unctuous, voluptuous even.

Spoon the buttery, creamy rice on to warm plates or into bowls, ignoring the purists who say it should be eaten tepid, and tuck into one of the world's most soothing, blissful suppers.

and more

♦ **mushroom risotto.** It is usual to make a mushroom risotto with dried porcini and, while I would never disagree with this, I am not convinced fancy fungi are any improvement here. I much prefer to find thick nuggets of fresh mushrooms in my rice. Ordinary chestnut or even diminutive button varieties are fine for this; Cut them into halves or quarters, then add them to the onion before you add the rice. Only you know how many mushrooms you can eat but I suggest a small handful – say four or five chestnut mushrooms – per person will do fine.

♦ **artichoke risotto.** A rather luxurious plateful, this, but so sublime as to be worth every penny. You will need two or three bottled artichokes per person, cut into segments and added with the first ladle of stock so that they do not overcook.

♦ **pea and Parmesan risotto.** Kids seem to love this one. At least this kid does. Add a handful of frozen peas per person towards the end of cooking, or use fresh ones, briefly boiled in salted water. A generous hand with the Parmesan adds even more pleasure. I have always liked peas and cheese.

♦ **other good things to put in your risotto.** Celery – sliced quite thin and added when the onion is soft; pancetta – in little cubes, to add deep savour; chopped Taleggio – totally unauthentic but you probably won't care when it melts into creamy strands; skinned broad beans and bacon; some wodges of chalky goat's cheese; asparagus – cook it first, then add the chopped tender stems after the rice, the fragile tips and some butter and Parmesan just before serving.

235

a fragrant, healing bowl of rice

I find rice both calming and restorative, and will happily eat a bowlful, unadorned by any sauce or curry, for a mid-week lunch or supper. Interestingly seasoned with whole spices and flecked with chopped herbs, a bowl of rice is the perfect antidote to almost any kind of overindulgence you can think of. Food to soothe and revive.

Enough for 2

oil – either groundnut or vegetable
a small onion
basmati rice – a large cupful, or 2 or 3 handfuls

The aromatics:
garlic – I suggest 1 large clove per person but you may want more
green cardamom pods – 4 or 5
a cinnamon stick
cloves – 2 or 3
a small, hot chilli
coriander leaves – a handful, chopped

Warm a little oil in a small saucepan. You need just enough to cover the bottom. Peel and finely chop the onion and fry it gently, over a low, simpering heat, until it is soft but not coloured. Squash the garlic flat and add it to the onion with the cardamom pods, cinnamon stick and cloves, then let the spices cook briefly in the oil. You need to warm their essential oils but not let them colour.

Tip in the rice, then tuck in the chilli. Pour three times as much water as rice into the saucepan and bring to the boil. Add salt generously and turn down the heat so that the water is simmering gently, then cover the pan tightly with a lid. After ten minutes you should switch off the heat. Avoid the temptation to lift the lid. Leave the rice for ten minutes, maybe a little less, then lift the lid and sift through the rice with a fork. You can pick out any whole spices at this point if you wish, or leave it to everyone to police their own. Grind over some black pepper and stir in the chopped coriander leaves.

and more

- **fragrant lemon rice.** Tuck two stems of lemon grass, smashed so they splinter but still hold together, into the rice. Leave out the garlic but do leave in the cloves, they have a wonderful affinity with lemon. The effect will, of course, be more Thai or Vietnamese than Indian, but gently fresh and fragrant. A lovely, peaceful rice to eat with fish. If we are being purist about things then we should really swap the basmati rice for a Thai fragrant rice. I am not convinced this is absolutely necessary, though you may feel more comfortable with it.

- **lime leaf rice.** Not only soothing but fresh and cool, lime leaf rice is what I eat with hot Thai curries or plain grilled fish or pork. You need little more than four or five leaves to scent a small pan of rice. Leave out the cinnamon, cloves and garlic and tuck the whole leaves in before you pour the water on, pulling them out before you eat.

- **a sticky rice.** Fans of glutinous, sticky textures could swap the long-grain rice for a short-grain Thai sticky rice. This is particularly appropriate for a dish flavoured with lemon grass or lime leaves. There is something deeply nannying about such a supper.

- **saffron rice.** One of the most gently pleasing of all rice suppers is a pilau scented with saffron and flecked with sultanas and pine kernels. Halve and thinly slice the onion rather than chopping it, so you get golden strands flecked throughout the rice. Stir in the saffron stamens before you add the water and the sultanas just after. The pine kernels will keep their crunch if you toast them first, then fold them through when you fork up the cooked pilau.

- **pea and mushroom pilau.** Fry a handful of quartered mushrooms with the onion so that they become sweet and juicy, then add the rice. Just before eating, fold in as many cooked fresh or frozen peas as you like. They lift the dish and give it a bit of life, yet it still remains comforting and somehow peaceful.

- **other good things to add to your bowl of rice.** Bottled artichokes, drained and sliced; slices of garlic sausage cut into matchsticks; cubes of soft cheese such as Port Salut, Camembert and fontina (wonderful with peas but you should miss out the spices); and chopped skinned tomatoes.

an appetite for
vegetables

some extraordinarily good but simple salads

I guess there is a salad leaf to answer our every whim, from the peppery bitterness of watercress to the soft, buttery crunch of an old-fashioned garden lettuce. I cannot go along with those who extol the pleasure of mixed salads containing a dozen different varieties of leaf. For me, a salad is (yet) another case of less is more.

Much depends on how you are going to eat your salad. Is it, for instance, something with which to start a larger meal, a side dish to accompany something substantial like a chop or a piece of fish, or is it going to be the principal dish? Surely I cannot be the only one who often chomps his way through a big white bowl of salad and croûtons with a mustardy dressing as his main meal? It goes without saying that freshness is all, so be ruthless and use only the juiciest, squeaky-fresh leaves, and dress them appropriately.

soft, hot, peppery leaves – rocket, watercress, the red chicories, mizuna

Such assertive leaves respond well to a simple dressing of mild, creamy-tasting olive oil and lemon juice, or you could use the velvety Parmesan one below. You want something that will cool their ardour a little without smothering their character. Any of these bold leaves are particularly suited to sweet, rich meats such as roast pork, duck or grilled lamb. Just shake the leaves through with oil and lemon and pile them next to the meat.

To serve them as a main dish in their own right, match them to something cool, sweet and soft textured, such as folds of Parma or San Daniele ham, thick slices of milky buffalo mozzarella, ripe peaches or luscious pears.

crisp bitter leaves – chicory, frisée

The tart crunch of these leaves makes them a sound bet for a first course. Dress them with the creamy vinaigrette overleaf or a plainer oil and vinegar dressing with a good dab of mustard in it. I find walnut oil good here, too. You could eat them as a side salad but to me these stunning leaves shout out for a starring role as a light lunch. Scatter them with cubes of sizzling pancetta, warm toasted walnuts or soft blue cheese, such as ripe Gorgonzola, and revel in it.

243

crisp sweet leaves – Cos lettuce, Little Gem, iceberg lettuce

If you really must make a complex salad, these are the leaves to do it with. They are flattered by the addition of anchovies, lightly cooked French beans, tuna, white haricot or flageolet beans, and work well with a mustardy or creamy dressing. These are also the leaves to use with croûtons. Try frying cubes of white bread in butter and garlic, then tossing them over the unadorned, roughly torn leaves dressed with the creamy cheese dressing on the opposite page.

soft, sweet leaves – butterhead lettuce, mâche, young spinach

My advice is not to overdress; light olive oil and lemon juice are more than enough. These are the sweet, soporific leaves that I like with cold salmon, thinly sliced cucumber and salad cream for summer lunch. Those who find their bland gentility boring have obviously never used them for what God intended: to mop up the warm, thin gravy of a roast from your plate. They virtually melt in the hot, savoury juice.

dressing your salad

You will probably find that the more bitter the leaves, the less pungent you will want the dressing to be, so up the oil a little and use slightly less vinegar. Softertasting, though crisp leaves such as Little Gem or Cos do seem to like creamy dressings.

a good, mustardy dressing for a simple leaf salad

red wine vinegar – 2 tablespoons
smooth Dijon mustard – 2 teaspoons
olive oil – 5 tablespoons

In a screw-top jar, a blender or a bowl with a fork, mix the ingredients together, adding a couple of good, big pinches of salt and several grinds of black pepper. You can, and I often do, make a large batch of this and keep it in a jam jar in the fridge (you know that feeling when you really want a salad but can't be bothered to make the dressing?).

a creamy dressing to make a salad seem more substantial

red wine vinegar – 2 tablespoons
smooth Dijon mustard – 2 teaspoons
egg yolks – 2
light olive oil – 200ml, or 100ml each of olive and groundnut
grated Parmesan – 3 generous tablespoons

Pour the vinegar into a small bowl and add the Dijon mustard and egg yolks. Beat them briefly with a fork, then slowly pour in the oil, continually beating with a fork, as if you were making mayonnaise. Stir in the grated Parmesan cheese and season with salt and black pepper. Set aside for ten minutes or so for the flavours to marry (I am not being precious here, it really does make a difference). I often add chopped tarragon leaves to this dressing and use tarragon vinegar instead of red wine vinegar.

a walnut dressing for lettuce, frisée and chicory salads

Don't just swap the olive oil for walnut in the mustardy dressing or you will overpower the salad leaves. Instead use fifty-fifty of each or, even better, slightly less of the nut oil. Goes wonderfully with sharper, more bitter leaves such as rocket and chicory.

some clean-tasting greens

I often think that the Chinese and Vietnamese meals I enjoy the most are those where I remember to order greens. The pure, clean, fresh taste of bok choi, choi sum or mustard greens, cooked in steam and dressed with a slather of oyster sauce, seem to make the whole meal gel. A contrast, perhaps, to the addictive salty-spiciness of the rest of the dishes. What really appeals is the sudden smack of juice from the thick, watery leaves of, say, bok choi. They refresh.

I cannot see why we need to leave such things to the professionals – it takes no great skill to put some greens over a pot of boiling water, then toss them in oyster sauce.

greens – a small handful per person, either short, fat bok choi, mustardy, loose-leafed gaai choi or thin-stemmed Chinese broccoli
groundnut oil
oyster sauce
chilli sauce

You will need some sort of steamer here. As I mention in How to Do It (page 61), you can either use a made-for-the-job steamer or you can improvise with a colander and saucepan lid. Either way will work. Put a pan of water on to boil – the pan should be big enough for your steamer to sit comfortably on top without touching the water.

Wash the greens thoroughly, checking for any grit or insects hiding in amongst the leaves. I say this as someone who has occasionally cooked a caterpillar along with the broccoli. Put the greens into a steamer basket, colander, what you will, and sit them on top of the pan of boiling water. Cover with a lid.

Warm a tablespoon of oil in a small pan, add four or five good big glugs of oyster sauce, then stir in some chilli sauce. The amount will depend on how hot you want your sauce to be and what sort of chilli sauce you are using. For the record, I start with half a teaspoon (for which you can read one small squirt) of thick Vietnamese chilli sauce and taste as I go. Remove the sauce when it is warm, lift the steamed greens on to a plate and drizzle over the sauce.

and more

♦ **steamed broccoli or bok choi with three seeds.** I know this sounds like something from one of those depressing eat-yourself-younger cookbooks but I stand by it all the same. Put a handful each of pumpkin and sunflower seeds in a small, non-stick frying pan over a low to moderate heat. Watch them, shaking them around now and again, till they turn a pale, nutty brown – a matter of seconds – then add a handful of sesame seeds. Once they start to colour, remove them from the heat and tip them out of the pan (watch out – they burn if you so much as blink). Add them to the vegetables with or without any of the sauce above.

♦ **steamed bok choi with oyster sauce and garlic.** If there is one thing better than greens in oyster sauce it is greens in oyster sauce with lots of garlic – sticky, salty-sweet and deeply garlicky. Pour a tablespoon of oil into a frying pan and when it is hot add four crushed cloves of garlic plus a thumbsized knob of ginger, peeled and shredded. Then, working quickly, add three or four tablespoons of oyster sauce. The smell will be wonderful. Roll the steamed, drained greens in the sticky sauce and eat straight away.

♦ **spinach with spiced browned onions.** For those who find all this a bit too green and pleasant, here's a warmer-tasting way with spinach. Slowly fry a couple of onions, peeled and finely sliced, in lots of butter so that they colour deeply. Season with a big pinch of crushed dried chillies, a very little salt and a tablespoon or slightly less of mild garam masala. Let it continue cooking for a minute or two (garam masala does not need cooking like other spices, since it has already been roasted and ground), then scatter it over the drained spinach.

249

grilled vegetables for a salad, light lunch or antipasto

red peppers – 1 per person
olive oil
aubergines – a large one will be enough for 2 people
herbs – a few soft-leafed ones, such as basil and oregano
garlic – a clove per person will be enough
lemon – half a small one per person

Set the oven at 200°C/Gas 6. If the peppers are particularly plump, slice them in half; smaller ones you can cook whole. Put them in a roasting tin or baking dish, drizzle with a very little oil and bake till their skins are blackened and their flesh soft – about thirty to fifty minutes. Leave them until they are cool enough to handle, then seed and skin. Save any juices that come out.

While the peppers are cooking, put a ridged grill pan over a low to moderate heat and wipe and slice the aubergine. Slices that are too thin will burn on the grill; too thick and they won't cook in the middle, so aim for slices no thicker than your little finger. Brush the aubergine with a little oil, grind over a little salt and place them on the grill. After three or four minutes they will be starting to brown. Turn them over and let the other side cook till it is golden, with deep black lines on it from the grill bars. These are what will give the aubergine a smoky flavour. Each slice should be crisp on the outside and juicy in the middle – it is essential that they are cooked through right to the centre. Take them off the heat too soon and they will be truly indigestible, but leave them till they are crisp and soft inside and they will melt in your mouth.

Remove the aubergine from the grill and place them in a serving bowl with the peppers. Tear up a small handful of herbs. I suggest three times as much basil as oregano, though a little flat-leaf parsley would be good in there too. Scatter them, along with peeled and thinly sliced garlic, over the grilled aubergine and baked, skinned peppers.

Generously crumble some sea salt and grind some black pepper over the vegetables, then drizzle with olive oil, any of the sweet, reddish-brown cooking juices from the peppers and some lemon juice, gently tossing them around with the herbs as you go. Set aside until the vegetables are at room temperature.

and more

- ◆ **as an antipasti.** Keep the peppers and aubergines apart but use the same dressing, remembering to include the cooking juices from the pepper. Offer in small dishes, together with some little round toasts spread with olive paste or tapenade and some slices of prosciutto. I suggest you don't do much more than this though; preparing lots of dishes at once, even simple ones, is actually quite a lot of work.

- ◆ **a summer lunch.** Make a large bowl of grilled aubergines and peppers and toss it with handfuls of rocket leaves, rounds of toasted bread brushed with garlic and drizzled with olive oil, and some shiny purple-black olives.

a side dish of stove-top vegetables

When non-leafy vegetables are cooked slowly in butter they take on a deep, earthy sweetness that makes them a brilliant accompaniment to grilled meat or fish. During half an hour or so over a low heat, thin, intense juices develop in the pan and the vegetables become sweet and tender. Any robust root or stem-type vegetable is suitable, such as celery, fennel, Jerusalem artichokes, small potatoes or parsnips. They brighten up a plate of cold roast meat like nothing else.

Although I call this a side dish, I have eaten celery cooked to this recipe as a main course with nothing but brown rice and a glass or two of white wine.

the vegetables: either fennel – 1 bulb per person; celery – a small head will do
   for 2; Jerusalem artichokes or young turnips – 3 or 4 per person; small potatoes
   – 4 or 5 per person
butter
Parmesan – or pecorino if that is what you have – grated
juice of half a lemon

Cut the vegetables into very large pieces. They should have flat sides so they will lie flat and go sweet and golden against the pan, so the cut fennel into thick wedges and the heads of celery, the artichokes, potatoes and parsnips in half lengthways.

Melt enough butter in a large, shallow pan to cover the entire bottom with a deep pool – about 75g. When the butter is just starting to bubble, add the vegetables, cut-side down, in a single layer, then pour in enough water to come a quarter of the way up the vegetables, and let that come to the boil. Add a little salt and set the heat so that the buttery liquid bubbles around the vegetables, then cover the pan and leave until the vegetables are completely tender to the point of a knife. The timing will, of course, depend on the vegetables – their age and variety – but you should expect them to take a good thirty minutes over a low to moderate heat.

Turn the vegetables over, sprinkle over a handful of grated Parmesan, squeeze in the lemon juice and cover with a lid. Once the cheese has melted, a matter of just a minute or two, remove the lid, turn the heat up slightly and boil until the liquid has reduced to just a few spoonfuls. You want to end up with buttery, soft vegetables and a drizzle of slightly piquant juice.

a potato supper

I suppose we all know the health advantages of a diet based around carbohydrate rather than protein – the Asian and Mediterranean diets that include potatoes, vegetables and rice rather than hunks of red meat as the hub of the meal. But I think they are also worth considering purely from the pleasure angle. There is much comfort, warmth, solace and satiety in a bowl of starch, especially in cold weather. As much as I love meals based around rice or pasta, and eat them on an almost daily basis, there is something about a potato supper – be it a baked potato dripping with butter and grated cheese, a plate of chips or a potato curry – that appeals to my northern European soul. The basic idea below, and the ideas that follow it, turn up as supper in my house time and time again.

**waxy potatoes such as Charlotte or Belle de Fontenay – about 5 small ones
      per person**
oil – a little groundnut or light olive
butter – just a little for buttering the dish and a few knobs on top
bacon or pancetta – about 2 thin rashers per person
stock – preferably a good chicken one, though Marigold or similar bouillon will do
sage leaves – 1 per person

Set the oven at 180°C/Gas 4. If the fine, pale skin doesn't bother you, there is no need to peel the potatoes but you should give them a good wipe. I must say I invariably peel mine, or at least scrape them well, but others think I am being pernickety. Whatever, you need to slice them no thicker than a pound coin. Warm enough oil to cover the bottom of a frying pan, then fry the sliced potatoes in it just long enough to colour them lightly on both sides. Lift them out on to kitchen paper.

Generously butter a shallow baking dish or roasting tin. Cut the bacon into pieces about the size of a postage stamp. Layer the potatoes in the buttered dish, scattering the bacon, sage and a grinding of salt and black pepper over them as you go. Dot the surface with a few little knobs of butter, then pour over enough stock to cover. Bake in the preheated oven for about an hour, until the potatoes are soft enough to crush between your fingers.

and more

♦ **a quicker version.** I fry the potatoes because I think it gives them more flavour but you can cut out this step if you wish. They will need baking a little longer.

♦ **an onion and potato bake.** Peel and thinly slice one small onion per person and tuck it in with the potatoes. I suggest you fry it with the potatoes, too.

♦ **a sausage and potato supper.** Those who remain unconvinced that this is suitable as a principal dish might like to tuck thick slices of herby butcher's sausages amongst the potatoes. Something with a little garlic in, such as one of the Toulouse variety, can be good here. Or try fresh chorizo, the Spanish chilli sausage.

♦ **a mushroom and potato supper.** Use large, velvety field mushrooms instead of the meat. You will need to slice them thickly and fry them briefly in butter before adding them to the potatoes. Allow one really large flat mushroom per person.

a creamy, unctuous potato dish

A shallow earthenware dish of *gratin dauphinoise* is a perfect thing, the slices of potato scented with garlic and wallowing in cream, its top lightly browned. It seems sacrilegious to add or subtract from the classic recipe. Yet I think we can, and should, in order to turn a side dish into a voluptuous occasional main course. Should you take the main-course option, you will need some crisp and astringent salad on the side – say chicory and watercress.

Despite the almost obscene quantity of cream, there is still a frugal simplicity to this dish.

Enough for 6 as a side dish

potatoes – waxy-fleshed if possible, about 1 kg
garlic – 2 large, juicy cloves
butter – just enough to butter the baking dish thickly
double cream – enough to cover the potatoes (about 600ml)

You will need a moderate to slow oven, so set the heat at 160°C/Gas 3. Peel the potatoes and slice them thinly. This, by the way, is one of those dishes where you really must peel: strings of brown, 'healthy' skin are totally at odds with the gratin's hedonistic overtones. The slices should be no thicker than a pound coin. If the garlic is really juicy, cut the cloves in half and rub them round and round an earthenware or enamelled cast iron dish, pressing down hard to release the juices. Otherwise it might be better to slice it thinly and tuck the slices between the potatoes.

Smear the dish generously with butter. Please don't be tight – you are only cheating yourself. Lay the potato slices in the dish, orderly or positively hugger-mugger, it matters not, seasoning with salt and black pepper as you go along. Pour the cream over the potatoes – it should just come to the top of the slices. Bake for an hour to an hour and a half, until the potatoes are virtually melting into the cream.

and more

◆ **a bacon *dauphinoise*.** An addition of pancetta or smoked streaky bacon may sound like gilding the lily but I recommend it nevertheless. The smoke mildly permeates the cream, the meat adds something in the way of texture. Have a crisp, bitter frisée salad waiting.

◆ **a creamy smoked fish and potato supper**. In *Real Food*, I made a gratin of potato and smoked mackerel; those who haven't tried it might like to add some smoked mackerel to the recipe above. You need do nothing more than peel the fish from its skin and slide large, juicy pieces in between the slices of potato. You will only need a fillet or two for the quantity above. I usually drop the garlic for this one. Wonderful preceded by a watercress salad.

◆ **with salt cod.** Salt cod is a splendid thing to add here. You need about half the weight of salt cod to potatoes. Soak it overnight, poach it in water for ten minutes and pull it from the bone, then sneak it in between the potatoes. This is not my idea but a classic. I once had a version of this at Simon Hopkinson's house and, as you might expect, it was truly, utterly sublime.

◆ **a mushroom gratin.** I often add mushrooms to my potato gratin. You could add posh ones, such as chanterelles and slices of porcini, but I have had equal success with good old field mushrooms, sliced, fried gently in butter, then patted dry on kitchen paper and snuggled in with the potatoes.

◆ **the Swedish way.** The Swedes often poke a few anchovies into the general creaminess. You will need only six or so for a kilo of spuds. The salty fishiness is extremely good with the potatoes and cream.

◆ **as a side order.** Served as a side dish, this is a heavenly, unsurpassable match for roast lamb, cold roast beef or, I think, a green salad. The latter will sound strange but a soft, tender lettuce leaf is perfect for mopping up the warm, garlicky cream from your plate.

a spicy vegetable stir-fry

I am not sure one can ever replicate at home the sizzle, splutter and sheer excitement of a stir-fry in a good Chinese restaurant. Some things are probably best left to the professionals. But I still make stir-fries at home. OK, it's not quite the same because my kitchen does not have the high-power gas jets of a restaurant kitchen, but I don't think we are after perfection here, just the fun of throwing squeaky greens at hot oil and smelling the garlic rise up and fill the kitchen. At home a stir-fry only really works for one, two at a push. The point here is heat and speed, and large quantities of ingredients will slow down the process to more of a stir-steam. Get all your ingredients ready first, the gas up high, then get your wok really smoking hot. If the ordeal isn't a bit scary you probably aren't doing it right. There should be much crackling of hot oil and shaking of pans but it will all be over in minutes. A great supper for those who can stand the heat.

Enough for 1
mushrooms – 2 good handfuls of shiitake or buttons
cornflour
baby bok choi – about 3 or 4
spring onions – 1 or 2
ginger – a thumb-sized knob, peeled
garlic – a couple of large juicy cloves or more
to season – Chinese rice wine, dark soy sauce, chilli sauce
oil – groundnut or vegetable

If the mushrooms are large you might like to cut them into quarters so that they cook through more quickly. Toss them in enough cornflour to coat them all over. The bok choi will need tearing up into pieces and the stalks kept separate from the more tender leaves. Shred the spring onions and ginger into fine matchsticks; peel and finely chop the garlic; get all the other ingredients by the side of the cooker. You don't want to be hunting for the chilli sauce at the last minute.

Put your wok over a high heat so that it is smoking hot (there is no point in half measures here), then pour in enough oil to make a shallow pool – about three or four tablespoons, depending on the depth of your wok. It will shimmer within seconds. Add the spring onions, garlic and ginger; they will immediately sizzle and pop (or at least they should). Quickly, so that they stand no chance of burning,

move the food around the wok with a chopstick or one of those Chinese scoops if you have such a thing (I haven't), then add the mushrooms and the bok choi stalks. Again they will bubble furiously and you need to move them round the pan so that the onions and garlic brown without singeing. When they are tender, which will take barely a minute or two, pour in a good slosh of rice wine and several shakes of soy sauce. The sauce will immediately darken and thicken a little. Then add the green leaves, pushing them down into the hot sauce.

Things should still be bubbling at this point, though they will have quietened down somewhat. As soon as the leaves darken, season with chilli sauce – a teaspoon's worth for a start, then taste the sauce and add more if you wish – checking the salt level as you go (remember that the soy you have added already might make it salty enough). Eat immediately, while all is hot and steaming.

and more

♦ **stir-fried broccoli with ginger.** Cook large florets of broccoli in boiling water for a few minutes before adding to the blueprint above in lieu of the bok choi. I think ginger is great with broccoli, so shred some up as fine, or even finer, than matchsticks, and add it with the spring onion and garlic.

♦ **stir-fried broccoli with oyster sauce.** Boil the broccoli briefly and drain it, then toss it in a little cornflour. Soften and colour the spring onions and garlic with a little oil in the wok, then add the broccoli, stir-frying for just over a minute. Pour in a little oyster sauce, rice wine and stock or water and let the mixture darken and thicken slightly before adding a little salt and black pepper. Eat as a side dish.

♦ **garlic bok choi.** Luscious. Get your wok smoking hot over a high heat, then pour in a little pool of groundnut oil – this won't be much more than a tablespoon – and let it shimmer. Add three or four chopped cloves of garlic and let it sizzle and colour. Quickly, before it turns dark brown, add six small heads of bok choi, quartered lengthways. Toss them around with the garlic, then pour in a couple of splashes of water or, better still, vegetable stock. Eat immediately, as a side dish, though I will admit to liking this so much I sometimes eat it on its own, for a weekday lunch.

269

a hot, fragrant, lively curry (and several other options)

The recipes in this book are simple, clean and uncluttered. There are no unnecessary ingredients; nothing is there unless it has a point. I love — adore — Thai green curries and have tried over the years to prune their long and intimidating ingredient lists, but to no avail. Everything is there because it needs to be. You may have to make a trip to a big-name supermarket or, of course, Chinatown. But this is as good as eating gets. Both fiery and soothing — the chillies being cooled by the coconut milk — and at once invigorating and luxurious. I know it's a lot of shopping but there is not much cooking involved. Just do it.

Enough to feed 4 (with rice)

For the green curry paste:
lemon grass — about 4 stalks, the tender, inside leaves only, chopped
green chillies — 6 medium-hot small chillies, seeded and chopped
garlic — 3 cloves, peeled
galangal or ginger — a thumb-sized piece, peeled and chopped
shallots — 2, peeled and roughly chopped
coriander leaves — a good fistful
lime zest — a teaspoon, or 5 – 6 lime leaves, chopped
lime juice — use 1 lime to start with; you can always add more later
nam pla (Thai fish sauce)
black peppercorns — ground, a good half a teaspoon

The rest of it:
a small pumpkin or squash
aubergines — 4 small ones, or 8 egg-shaped ones, or 2 whoppers
oil — groundnut or vegetable, 2 or 3 tablespoons, maybe more
   (depending on how much the aubergines soak up)
shiitake mushrooms — 2 or 3 per person
coconut milk — a 400ml tin
stock — Marigold bouillon or similar vegetable powder, 400ml
green peppercorns — fresh if you can find them, a small palmful
coriander leaves — a handful
Thai basil leaves — a handful, roughly torn

Whiz the curry paste ingredients in a food processor till you have a vivid, spicily fragrant slush.

Peel and roughly chop the pumpkin or squash. Cut the aubergines lengthwise into quarters and then into fat chunks (small round ones can simply be quartered). Fry them in the oil – a deep frying pan will suffice – until both pumpkin and aubergine are softening, then add the mushrooms. The heat should be quite high, as the vegetables need to brown here and there. Spoon' in about four tablespoons of the paste (more can be added later but it is too early to taste yet) and let it fry and sizzle. Stir so it doesn't stick.

Pour in the coconut milk and stock, scatter in the green peppercorns and leave to simmer until the vegetables are fully tender. Taste the curry, adding a little more paste if you think it needs it, in which case you will have to cook it for a few minutes longer. Either way it should be ready within ten minutes. Scatter the herbs over. You will need some rice here, either fragrant Thai rice or unauthentic but nevertheless delicious basmati.

and more

♦ **a green chicken curry.** Swap the vegetables for 750g boned chicken pieces and fry them off instead of the vegetables. This is unauthentic (Thai cooks just slide the raw chicken into the curry sauce) but I find frying it gives a better flavour.

♦ **a green prawn curry.** Use 500g large prawns instead of the aubergines and squash. No need to fry them off, just throw them in the curry sauce after you have added the coconut milk.

♦ **a fish curry.** Check out the Indian one on page 305, but you might like to make a Thai version from the blueprint above. Try adding approximately 750g mixed prepared fish (can I suggest monkfish, briefly cooked-open mussels, and prawns?) just after you have added the coconut milk. The fish will need just ten minutes to cook.

♦ **a mushroom and spinach curry.** Drop the aubergine and squash from the ingredients above and increase the quantity of mushrooms to 650g. Chestnut, button and oyster mushrooms are good – add the more fragile ones last, in this case the oyster mushrooms. Cut up any that seem very big before you fry them. When the coconut milk comes to the boil, slide in some spinach leaves – a fat handful per person – that you have quickly cooked and squeezed dry.

a no-fuss puff-pastry vegetable pie

I have never understood why some people come over all sniffy about ready-made puff pastry. It is a perfectly good commercial product, light, crisp and a joy for people like me who imagine they have better things to do than making their own. (Shortcrust is different altogether because they never put enough butter in the commercial stuff and anyway, it's as easy as toast to make.) You can buy prepared puff pastry chilled or frozen and now made with butter instead of vegetable fat. But the best invention must be puff pastry that is ready rolled and cut to size. The sort that comes in a long, thin rectangle is the most useful of all – it can become a pie or a millefeuille in the time it takes you to find the rolling pin, though you might like to roll it just a tiny bit thinner, so that it becomes even lighter and crisper.

Enough for 4

onions – 5 medium-sized
butter or oil – enough to cover the bottom of a medium-sized shallow pan
mushrooms – 350g of any firm variety, or a mixture
chopped herbs – thyme, lemon thyme or oregano, just enough to sit in the palm of
  your hand
crème fraîche – about 200g
puff pastry – 425g
a little beaten egg or milk to glaze the pastry

Peel and roughly chop the onions and let them cook slowly with the butter or oil over a low heat for twenty minutes or so, until they are golden, soft and almost transparent. Tear or slice the mushrooms into large, bite-sized pieces and add them to the onions, adding a little more butter or oil if they soak it all up. Leave them to turn golden and tender but stir them from time to time so they do not stick and burn. Season them with the chopped herbs and stir in the crème fraîche, grinding in a little salt and pepper as you go. You want a mixture that is creamy rather than runny, so let it bubble for a minute or two to thicken.

Heat the oven to 200°C/Gas 6. The pastry needs to be rolled into two rectangles about 35cm by 20cm (this is conveniently the same measurements as the ready-rolled frozen stuff). Lay one piece on a lightly floured baking sheet and spread the mushrooms and onions over, leaving a good finger thickness of bare rim around the edge. Brush a little beaten egg, milk or even wateraround the rim, lay

the second rectangle of pastry over the top and squeeze the rims together to seal. It is worth being quite zealous about pinching the pastry, there shouldn't be any possibility of the filling escaping. Brush with more of the beaten egg or milk so that the pastry will take on a rich golden shine in the oven, then cut a couple of little holes in the top to let the steam out.

Bake the pie until it has puffed up like a cushion and is the colour of honey. You can expect this to take about twenty-five minutes. It is worth sneaking a look at the bottom to check if the pastry is crisp underneath (it should be fine because this is not an especially wet filling).

and more

- **some other good things.** There is magic, at least there is for me, in the bringing together of mushrooms, cream and puff pastry, but there are other fillings you can try here too.

- **a Gorgonzola and broccoli pie.** If broccoli ever seems just that bit too 'good-for-you', you can always take the smugness off its face by mixing it with cream and cheese. It works well in a pie like this in place of mushrooms. Cook the florets briefly, drain them, then fold them in with the onions and crème fraîche above. As we're lacking the savoury note of the mushrooms, I would suggest some cheese – a blue perhaps, such as a creamy Gorgonzola, a little Roquefort or the delightful Cashel Blue from Ireland.

- **garlic, cream and potato pie.** In the unlikely event of you having any *pommes dauphinoise* (see page 262) left over, I suggest you add a few softened onions and stuff it all between two sheets of pastry as in the pie above. I know potatoes in pastry sounds like a carbohydrate overdose but the effect is softened by the garlic-scented cream and buttery onions. Pushing your fork through golden, flaking pastry and slices of melting, cream-sodden potato is utter bliss.

- **pumpkin pie (but not *that* pumpkin pie).** When I say pumpkin pie I mean a savoury one with onions and cream, not the bland, overrated tart that I have never managed to get the hots for. Peel a small pumpkin, cut it into chunks and roast with a generous amount of butter. When the golden flesh is soft and sweetly caramelised, add it to the softened onions above with the crème fraîche and a very little ground cinnamon. Pile it on to the pastry and top as usual. Great as a side dish for sausages.

a tart for lunch, supper or a party

A large, thin tart is perfect crowd food. You can serve it in long fingers or neat little squares, or as a cut-and-come-again thing. If you are making more than one, get the filling done before and the pastry ready to roll and you're laughing. Especially if you use ready-rolled puff pastry. But I do think this sort of food works well for weekend lunch, too. Of course it is the marriage of cheese and crisp pastry that really rings my bell. Add some sweetly incandescent golden onions and I am ready to pop my cork. Any onion – sweet white, red, even leeks, and any melting cheese – Taleggio, Camembert, fontina, will do the trick here; you want something oozing and molten with the crisp pastry and buttery onions.

This is something to serve on those occasions when you are not sure whether your friends are expecting something substantial or just a snack.

Enough for 4 as a light lunch, or 12 as nibbles

onions – 6 small to medium
butter – a thick slice, about 50g
puff pastry – 200g or thereabouts
Taleggio, or similar semi-soft cheese – 120g
thyme – enough leaves to make a little pile in your palm

Peel the onions, cut them in half from stem to root, then into thick segments. Put them into a shallow pan with the butter and leave over a moderate to low heat until they are soft. Let them take their time. They need to be translucent, golden and sticky. This only comes with slow cooking and it is pointless to try and hurry it. The actual timing will depend on the type of onion (some contain more water than others) but you can expect them to take a good thirty minutes.

Set the oven at 220°C/Gas 7. If you are using a sheet of ready-rolled pastry, simply unroll it on to a lightly floured baking sheet. If you are using a block of pastry, roll it out into a rectangle (or square or round) no thicker than a ten-pence piece. Score a border 2cm in from each edge and prick all over with a fork.

Tip the onions on to the pastry, pushing them almost, but not quite, to the border. Brush the rim with some of the onion butter. Slice the cheese thinly, then break it up into small pieces, tucking it in amongst the onions. Scatter over the thyme. Bake until the pastry is golden and puffed and the onions browning – fifteen to twenty minutes.

and more

- **a leek and Taleggio tart.** As above, but with leeks. The essential point is not to let the leeks colour too much – they turn bitter when even slightly charred you may find you need a little more butter. I find it helps to put a piece of greaseproof paper and a lid over the leeks while they are cooking, to stop them browning.

- **an onion and Camembert tart.** I have used Brie, too. Both work and give a deeply savoury, melting result.

- **a tomato and basil tart.** Something for summer and autumn. Spread a thick layer of pesto on the puff pastry, then cover it with thin, though not too thin, slices of tomato. Lots of black pepper and sea salt, then bake till crisp and golden.

- **a mushroom and Taleggio tart.** Toss mushrooms – one variety, such as chanterelle, chestnut or field, or a mixture – in olive oil. Add a crushed clove or two of garlic, some herbs, such as thyme or oregano, and some salt and black pepper. Fry them with a generous amount of butter – by which I mean enough to cover the bottom of the pan – till tender and golden, then scatter them over the pastry. Tuck in the cheese – you will need about half as much again as in the blueprint above – and drizzle with some of the butter you cooked the mushrooms in.

- **a pancetta and onion tart.** I think there are two ways you could go about this. I have added chopped pancetta – about the size of Dolly Mixtures – to the cooked onions as the tart goes in the oven but I have also had success (if that's what you call it when every last crumb gets eaten) with scattering thin slices of pancetta, cut into pieces the size of a postage stamp, over the onions before I tuck in some Camembert or Brie.

- **a red onion and Parmesan tart.** You get that wonderful sweetness with red onions so redolent of contemporary Italian cooking, and they work well, as you might imagine, with the depth of savour you get from Parmesan cheese. Cook the onions as above, spread them over the pastry, cover them with a thick layer of grated Parmesan (some thyme would be good here too) and bake as above. Be generous with the cheese.

an appetite for
fish

a solitary and utterly luxurious fish supper

A deeply delicious and satisfying fish supper. Nevertheless, you will need some bread to mop up the garlicky juice and, as this is not a filling meal, a pudding of some sort to follow.

Enough for 1, with crusty white bread and something to follow

butter – sweet, pale and unsalted, as always
scallops – as many as you fancy, but I suggest about 4 large ones
garlic – sweet, juicy and young; a large clove, peeled and chopped
parsley – a small palmful or so, chopped, but not too finely

Take a small shallow pan, one that is light enough to pick up and shake, then melt enough butter in it to cover the bottom thinly. Let it sizzle and froth over a high heat. When the foam subsides and the butter falls silent, lower in the wobbly, glistening scallops and let them cook (they will spit at you) for two or three minutes, until a sticky, golden crust has formed on the underside. Turn them, let them colour underneath, then whip them out on to a warm plate, throw out the browned butter and put in some more, sweet and fresh. Then, as it froths, add the crushed garlic, swirl the pan quickly around, toss in the parsley and tip it all, sweetly frothing, over the scallops. Now eat up.

and more

♦ **a prawn supper.** Raw tiger prawns work here too, though they will probably end up even more expensive than scallops. You could peel them if you wish, in fact some shops even sell them so, but I prefer to cook them shell on, in which case I get to suck at the crunchy shells before tearing them away from the flesh with my fingers. They are cooked when their shells have gone from grey to pink.

a thirty-minute fish supper

Sometimes you just want huge, chalky white flakes of fish and a mound of fluffy potato. It is difficult to think of cod and mash as being an expensive supper but that is what it has become. I must say I like haddock almost as much as cod. In fact, any thick fillet of white fish appeals to me when it has been cooked in butter in a hot oven till its flesh is as white as snow and full of juice. How much you enjoy the result will, I think, depend almost entirely on the quality of the fish – by which I mean its freshness and flavour – and whether you get the timing right. The trick is to ignore the clock and to cook the fish only until a flake of its flesh will come easily away from the skin and bone when you pull it. Simple as that.

potatoes – a large, floury one per person
olive oil
butter – a thick slice for cooking the fish and another for the mashed potato
cod or haddock – a thick piece, about 200g, per person
lemon – a quarter per person

Peel the potatoes and cut them into halves or quarters, depending on their size. Drop them into boiling salted water and let them cook till tender to the point of a knife. You can expect this to take about fifteen to twenty minutes, depending on the variety of potato.

Meanwhile, get the oven good and hot. It should be at least 200°C/Gas 6. Put a thin pool of olive oil – just enough to cover the bottom – into a metal-handled frying pan or a roasting tin. Warm the oil over a moderate heat, then slide in a thick slice of butter. The butter will bubble, then foam, and this is when you should lower in your piece of fish. Do this skin side down.

Tweak the temperature so that the bubbles surrounding the fish are lively but not so excited that the butter burns. Leave the fish, without nudging or turning, for a minute or so. Lift it gently to check how it is coming on. You want the skin to be touched with pale gold. Now turn the fish over with a fish slice or palette knife, crumble over some sea salt and black pepper and put it in the hot oven. Bake until the fish is opaque, juicy and will come away easily from the skin and bone. Test it for readiness by gently tweaking a flake. You will find the thickest piece of fish, about 200g in weight, will take about eight minutes.

Drain the potatoes, mash them with a potato masher and beat in the butter. How far you go with this depends on how much washing up you feel like doing but I believe the fluffiest mash is that which spends a minute in an electric mixer armed with a beater attachment. Serve the mash with the roast fish and some lemon for squeezing over.

and more

♦ **with a soothing butter sauce.** Sometimes I like to swap the clean, biting addition of lemon with my fish for something richer. A butter sauce, thickened with egg yolks and rescued from cloying with lemon juice, is my first choice. There is something quietly perfect about a forkful of white fish, a bit of steamed or mashed potato and a trickle of hollandaise sauce. I know there are those purists who screech that you should always use a reduction of white wine vinegar rather than lemon juice in a classically made hollandaise. Well, I prefer lemon in mine, so they can just shut up. If you fancy something more than lemon with your fish, turn to the recipe on page 168.

♦ **with an uplifting green and piquant sauce.** A blender salsa verde is another idea. The piquancy of the capers and the saltiness of the anchovy are singularly appropriate with white fish. My basic recipe is to whiz all or most of the following in the blender: the leaves from a large bunch of flat-leaf parsley and a few sprigs of mint, 6 anchovy fillets, a couple of cloves of garlic, a spoonful of Dijon mustard, a couple of tablespoons of capers and 2 tablespoons of lemon juice. Now pour in enough olive oil to reduce it all to a lumpy slurry the colour of that green stuff that floats on the pond in summer. Taste and check; you might find you want it with more mustard or lemon.

♦ **let's leave it at that.** There are some things it is best not to meddle with too much, and I think this is one of them.

293

a whole baked fish for midweek

Few suppers give me more pleasure than a whole fish, baked on the bone. No fancy sauces with it, thank you, just some olive oil and a sprig or two of herbs. I find a whole fish is often more succulent than one that has been filleted and, once the fishmonger has done the horrid bits for you, it must be one of the easiest suppers around.

You can cook most fish whole, the fierce, dry heat from the oven or grill adding a smoky flavour that flatters firmer fish such as sea bream, snapper, red mullet and mackerel. Such fish also benefit from robust aromatics, like garlic and thyme (the gentler herbs such as chervil and dill will do nothing for them).

The basic roasting method here, with garlic and woody-stemmed herbs, can be applied to any firm-fleshed fish, oily or not, the only difference being the time they will take to cook. Size wise, it depends on your appetite, but I usually reckon on one mackerel or sea bream per person, or two red mullet or four to five large sardines.

whole fish – such as large sardines, red mullet, sea bream or small mackerel, gutted
olive oil – enough to drizzle over the fish
garlic – 1 or 2 large, plump cloves per large fish, peeled and thinly sliced
thyme – the leaves torn from a few sprigs for each large fish
lemon – a quarter of a large, juicy one per large fish

Set the oven to 220°C/Gas 7. Rinse the fish, pat them dry with kitchen paper and lay them in a roasting tin or baking dish. Drizzle over a little olive oil to moisten the fish and to stop it sticking, then add your seasoning of garlic, thyme leaves and lemon juice. Crumble over several flakes of sea salt and a few grinds of black pepper and put the fish into the oven to bake. It is done when the skin peels away readily and the flesh will slide easily from the bones, which you can test by inserting a knife into the spine of the fish and gently teasing the flesh from its backbone. If it comes away without much pressure from you and looks juicy and opaque, then it is ready. Any transparency and reluctance to come from the bone and it needs a bit longer in the oven.

Place the fish on a warm plate, first removing the head for the squeamish, and spoon over the meagre, though delectable, pan juices.

and more

- ♦ **a piquant fish.** Something sharp will naturally bring out the flavour of the fish. Lemon, obviously, but also try adding tomatoes, halved if they are small, or chopped and tossed with a little oil and thyme if they are larger. Scatter them round the fish so their juices mingle.

- ♦ **and one baked in butter.** You could anglicise the recipe above by swapping the olive oil for butter – you will need one or two walnut-sized lumps per medium-sized fish.

- ♦ **or with baked vegetables.** Rather than serve green vegetables or a salad alongside or after the fish, you could cook the vegetables with it. This is not purely to save on washing up but rather to let the flavours marry. Thinly slice fennel, young, slim leeks or chestnut mushrooms and cook them briefly in the olive oil over a moderate heat. Place the fish on top and bake until the fish comes cleanly away from the bone.

- ♦ **with extra roasting juices.** If you would like more juice with your fish – to mash into your potatoes, say – then once the fish is done, lift it out, together with any vegetables, put the dish over a high heat and add enough vegetable or fish stock (I think you can get away with powdered bouillon here) to make a few tablespoons of juice. Stir to mix the fish juices and stock, letting it bubble away until it tastes as you would like it to. Expect this to take all of a minute or two.

- ♦ **a few other ideas.** Other good things to add to the roasting tin include a glass of white wine; a couple of spoonfuls of sherry vinegar; a few bottled green peppercorns (about 8 per fish); even fewer capers (about 6 per fish); a small handful of pancetta, cut into thin strips.

a mild, juicy and aromatic fish

I am not good at formal eating, the special-occasion dinner party or lunch. I feel uncomfortable with it because showing off or standing on ceremony is not what my food has ever been about. For a start, I never know what to cook for such occasions. Yet as much as any formality goes against the grain, there are times when it isn't appropriate to stick a big pie on the table and say tuck in. Times when a certain restraint is called for. It is on these occasions that I go for gentle, understated food that is easy to eat and also, from a practical point of view, that can be prepared a little while before I need to cook it.

a small, whole fish per person – sea bass, trout or sea bream, cleaned
chillies – 2 or 3 small ones per fish
lemon grass – 2 stalks per person, or 6 to 8 lime leaves
rice wine – a small glass
coriander – a few sprigs

Set the oven at 200°C/Gas 6. Lay each fish on a piece of greaseproof paper or foil. Finely slice the chillies and bash the lemon grass stalks so that they splinter but still stay together. Tuck the smashed lemon grass or the lime leaves, scrunching them up to release their zest, inside the body as well as over the fish, then scatter the chillies on top. Pour over the rice wine and tuck in a few sprigs of coriander and some salt. Fold the paper over and seal with a fold and a paper clip or two. You can leave it like this for an hour or two. Bake until the fish is juicy and fragrant (you have to peep inside to see). A 500g sea bass will take about twenty minutes.

and more

♦ **getting the timing right.** Every fish takes a different time to cook. There is no hard and fast rule on this, no matter what others may have you believe. Fish of any sort is cooked when it is opaque right the way through and will come away from the bone without resistance.

♦ **a dipping sauce.** Boil an equal amount (say, 6 tablespoons) of rice vinegar and sugar. When it starts to become syrupy, remove it from the heat, add a tablespoon of dark soy sauce and a couple of finely chopped small, hot red chillies. Stir in the juice of a lime and use this as a dip for each mouthful of fish.

298

a fishcake to console and another to excite

There is something peaceful and faintly reassuring about a fishcake. Old-fashioned food that reminds us of less frantic times. It is not for the sake of convenience that fishcakes are made with equal amounts of potato to fish. It is simply that the ratio seems right: not enough potato and the cakes lack substance, too much and they lack flavour. As always, it is up to us to nudge the two to make the recipe our own.

Enough for 4–6

potatoes – 500g
fish – salmon, haddock, cod, hake or any large-flaked white fish, 500g
milk – for baking the fish in
flour – a little for coating
butter and oil – for frying
white wine – a large glassful, not too dry
tarragon – a small bunch
cream – a medium carton (about 300ml)

301

Set the oven at 200°C/Gas 6. Peel the potatoes and cut them into large chunks, then boil them to tenderness in salted water. Meanwhile, put the fish into a baking dish, almost cover with milk – you can add a bay leaf or two if you like – then bake until the fish is opaque and will come easily from the bone or skin when you pull it. You can expect this to take about ten to fifteen minutes, bearing in mind that different types of fish take slightly different times to cook.

Drain the potatoes, putting them back into the empty pan over a moderate heat for a few minutes if they seem wet, then mash them with a potato masher. Lift the fish from its milk, reserving the liquid, then pull the flakes away from the bones and skin. Tip the fish into the mashed potato, add salt and grind over some black pepper (if you wish to add any of the additional seasonings below, do so now), and mix briefly and gently, so as not to crush the flakes of fish too much.

Shape the mixture into patties, as large or small as you like – I favour ones the size of a digestive biscuit and the thickness of an English muffin – coating each one lightly in flour as you go. I think you should avoid the temptation to err towards perfection. Wobbly cooking has a certain charm about it.

Melt a little butter and oil in a frying pan – you need enough to coat the bottom of the pan – and fry your cakes till they are softly golden. This should take no more than a couple of minutes on each side. Keep them hot in a low oven.

Wipe the pan out with kitchen paper, add the glass of wine and let it bubble down over a high heat until there are just a few tablespoons left; strip the tarragon leaves from their stems and drop them into the wine as it bubbles. Pour in the cream and a wine glassful of the fish milk and bring to the boil, turning it down to a fierce simmer so that it thickens somewhat. Season with salt and pepper, then pour it over the fishcakes.

and more

- **some good things to add to your fishcakes.** Chopped, vivid green parsley leaves; 5 or 6 mashed anchovies; a few shakes of anchovy sauce; chopped tarragon leaves; chopped dill; chopped leeks cooked in butter till soft.

- **a chilli-hot, citrus-scented fishcake.** Forget the potatoes. Skin the fish (500g will be enough for 4 people). Blitz 2 spring onions, 2 cloves of garlic, a couple of small, seeded red chillies and 6 lime leaves together with a handful of coriander leaves in a food processor to make a thick sludge. Mix in a tablespoon of *nam pla* (Thai fish sauce) and tip it into a bowl. Whiz the fish to a coarse paste, then mix it with the seasonings and shape into small cakes. Some flour on your hands will be useful here. Fry till golden brown.

- **a smoked fishcake.** The smoky flavour of cured haddock, Arbroath smokies or even smoked salmon makes a beautiful, rather homely-tasting fishcake, reminiscent of Victorian high tea. It is flattered enormously by a cream and parsley sauce (simply substitute parsley for the tarragon above, then whiz the sauce in a blender). Cured haddock and smokies will need cooking in milk, as above. Smoked trout or salmon can be added directly to the potato.

- **tinned-fish fishcakes.** Lovely. Canned salmon and sardines make deeply flavoured fishcakes. You will need the same quantity as fresh fish, and you will have to drain them of their oil or water. Squeeze wedges of lemon over.

- **little prawn cakes.** Make these in the same way as the chilli-hot cakes above but using defrosted cooked prawns. I sometimes add a dollop of mayonnaise and a little flour to these, the mayonnaise adding lusciousness, the flour holding the fragile little cakes in one piece.

302

a fresh-tasting and really quite spicy fish curry

There was a time when you tended to play safe when making food for friends, and I doubt whether fish or curry would have been on the list. Our tastes have changed and almost everyone seems to be prepared to try spicy food.

When you multiply a recipe such as this you need to take care with the spices – you do not need to double or triple them like everything else. Taste as you go, using just a shake more, until you come up with a flavour and heat that you like. It is not really something that you would make earlier and reheat – though you could – but more the sort of meal you could cheerfully carry on with whilst talking. It is not something you must concentrate on, though I would get all the fish prepared first before anyone arrives. I would offer a bowl of rice, too (the rice pilau on page 236 would be fitting), and follow with some ice-cream and a whole load of wrinkly purple passion fruit, cut in half and piled hugger-mugger in a bowl.

Enough for 2–3

onions – 2 medium
vegetable oil
550g assorted fish and shellfish – monkfish, salmon, bream, haddock, squid,
**   mussels, prawns – whatever looks good**
mustard seeds – the black variety
red chillies – hot and medium sized, 2 or 3
garam masala, ground turmeric, mild chilli powder – a teaspoon of each or slightly
**   less of the chilli**
tomatoes – 4
stock – chilled ready-made fish stock or Marigold vegetable bouillon, about 500ml
coconut milk – 100ml

305

Peel the onions and chop them roughly, then let them cook slowly with a small amount of oil in a heavy casserole over a low heat, until they are soft and pale gold. Scrupulously remove any skin and bones from the fish, cutting it up into large chunks, and scrub the mussels. If you are worried that they may be gritty inside, cook them for a minute in a small pan with a lid over a high heat; they will open in seconds, and you can then sieve the juice and add it to the sauce.

Sprinkle a teaspoon or so of mustard seeds into the onions, then seed and chop the chillies and add them too. Continue cooking, stirring in the ground spices, till you have a fragrant, warm-smelling base to which to add the rest of the ingredients. Chop up the tomatoes (you can skin and seed them if you wish but it seems to make little difference in this instance) and stir them in, letting them cook down for five minutes or so, then pour in the stock. Bring to the boil, then slide in the prepared fish – white fish first, then the squid, then the mussels and prawns. Simmer until the fish is tender, a matter of six or seven minutes. Stir in the coconut milk, season with salt and simmer for a minute or two longer before eating.

and more

♦ **a shellfish curry.** I have used white fish in the recipe above because I think it stands up well to the hot spiciness of the seasoning but there is no reason why you could not make this purely with shellfish. I would certainly keep the mussels because they add much in the way of flavour, but you could add clam-type shellfish if you fancy. If you like your curries exceptionally rich, I suggest you stir in a few handfuls of crab meat at the end.

♦ **fish and mushroom curry.** Button mushrooms, pure and ivory coloured, are worth adding here. They give it some bite and flavour. Cut them in half and fry them off with the mustard seeds and chillies, letting them colour only slightly. I have also added spinach to this curry before now, cooking a handful of well-washed leaves per person in a lidded pan with a small amount of water, then squeezing it dry and folding it into the curry just before we eat.

♦ **other good things to add to your curry.** A large clove of garlic with the onions; some potatoes, peeled and diced quite small, with the onions; a couple of small aubergines, cut into wedges and added with the onions; a little ground coriander instead of the garam masala; a handful of fresh peas added a few minutes before the end of cooking; a small handful of fresh curry leaves with the spices; a handful of chopped coriander leaves at the very end.

♦ **and to follow.** The ice-cream and passion fruit mentioned above; halved very ripe papaya sprinkled with lime; slices of mango marinated in orange and passion fruit juice.

307

an extremely versatile fish soup

The big rustic fish soup to put on the table when friends come round always sounds like a lot of work, indeed many recipes for it are, but I am not sure it has to be. I generally make a tomato base – using very juicy fresh tomatoes when I can get them, but more often than not tinned – with a couple of small onions and some garlic. I add chilli and usually saffron to introduce a mildly spicy earthiness to it – the rustic bit, I suppose – then add whatever fish looks good when I go shopping. Mullet, both grey and the smaller red, and monkfish are good firm fish that give body and flavour to the soup. I then pick whatever looks good from mussels, scallops, prawns and clams and add them a few minutes after the fish. They are done when the mussels or clams open.

Enough for 4

olive oil – just enough to cover the bottom of your pan
onions – 1 or 2, small and sweet
garlic
dried chilli – crushed
to season – 1 or 2 of the following: dried oregano, orange peel, white wine, bay
**   leaves, flat-leaf parsley**
saffron – a big pinch of threads
tomatoes – 750g, tinned or skinned and seeded fresh ones
fish – 1kg, an assortment of skinned and filleted white fish and some mussels,
**   prawns and clams; ask your fishmonger**

Warm the oil in a large, heavy pan, chop the onions and let them cook gently in the oil until they are soft and pale. It is best not to let them colour. Peel and chop as much garlic as you want to add. I suggest a clove per person but much depends on how young and sweet your garlic is and how much you like it. Stir it in with the onions and continue cooking for a minute or so before adding about a teaspoon of crushed, dried chilli flakes, any other seasonings you fancy and a pinch or two of saffron stamens. You can use a whole chilli instead of crushed chilli, if you prefer, fishing it out when you think the soup has enough heat, but you will miss the brick-red colour the crushed chilli lends. Introduce the tomatoes and let them cook slowly, bubbling gently, squashing them with a spoon. Once they have collapsed into a rough sauce, pour in enough water to make a loose, soupy stock – about 500ml for a kilo of fish – and bring to the boil.

Check the fish over, removing any scales, skin or bones left by the fishmonger, cut it into large, meaty chunks, then add it to the stock. You should add the firmest fish first (mullet, monkfish or bass) and cook until it is firm but opaque – a matter of ten minutes or less – then add the shellfish and carry on cooking only until the mussels and clams open and the prawns change colour from grey to pink. Serve steaming hot, with the garlic toasts below.

and more

♦ **on the side.** Bread of any sort adds the obligatory satisfying note for those who don't feel they have eaten unless they have had some starch. I simply cut a ficelle or baguette into thick slices and toast them on both sides, then rub them with a cut clove of garlic and give them a heavy-handed slosh from the olive oil bottle.

♦ **a shellfish soup.** Ever trying to simplify a recipe, I often find myself leaving out all the fish and making up the bulk with mussels, prawns and clams. Mussels, I think, are essential for their salty, fishy liquor, and I often drop in half a dozen shelled oysters. Prawns just don't have enough liquid to offer and need to play a supporting role rather than a main one. The cooking time from when you add the mussels should be a matter of four or five minutes, or until the majority of them have opened. Rather than letting everyone do battle with them, I quickly pull most of the mussels from their shells, stopping when I can't stand their heat any more and leaving the rest for everyone to do for themselves.

♦ **saffron and orange fish soup.** If I have included red mullet, I often add a couple of strips of orange peel, though no more than that and a couple more pinches of saffron and some chilli flakes. Strong, memory-inducing flashes of the Med in high summer here.

♦ **a fish soup with summer herbs.** Basil, with its deep, peppery, Italianate notes, is not a herb I use much with fish but it works here. Stir lots of those blousy leaves, torn up at the last minute, into the hot soup. You could even do it at the table. I do the same with coriander, too, but checking that everyone likes it first. People are either passionate for it or cannot be within a mile of it.

♦ **pesto fish soup.** Stir spoonfuls of home-made, or perhaps very good-quality ready-made, pesto into the soup just before you ladle it into bowls.

311

a big fish pie for friends

Whilst I swear by all the pared-down, if-in-doubt-leave-it-out cooking to be found in these pages, there is one supper I am happy to sweat over and that is fish pie. This is 'brace yourself' cooking, by which I mean you will need several pans, the sieve and the potato masher, perhaps even the electric mixer. You will have to peel potatoes and chop parsley, skin fish and make a white sauce. You will have to scrub mussels and pull them from their shells. Then you will have to clean up the kitchen. I include it because it is a meal of pure piscine pleasure. Soothing, soul-warming and peaceful. You can make it in advance, then proudly put it on the table for your guests to help themselves. It needs no accompaniment other than a bowl of peas and a few cold beers or bottles of white wine.

Enough for 6

mussels – 2kg
white wine – a wine glass full
smoked haddock – 1kg
bay leaves – 2 or 3
milk – 500ml
butter – a thick slice, about 50g
plain flour – 4 tablespoons
parsley – the leaves from a small bunch, chopped

For the mash:
floury potatoes – 1.5kg
butter

Discard any dodgy-looking mussels such as those with broken shells, then tip them into a large pan with a lid, pour over the wine and bring to the boil. Let them cook in their own steam until they have opened (a minute or two), then tip them into a sieve with a basin underneath to collect the juices. Tweak each juicy little mussel from its shell, then sieve the juices thoroughly to rid them of any grit.

Put the smoked haddock into a saucepan with the bay leaves and add the milk and as much water as you need just to cover the fish. Let it simmer for a few minutes, until you can pull the fish from its skin with ease, then turn off the heat.

Peel the potatoes and cut them into large chunks, then put them in a pan of water and bring to the boil. Salt them and simmer until tender enough to mash. Drain, add one or two thick slices of butter and two or three spoonfuls of the haddock cooking liquor, then mash to a fluff.

Rinse the mussel pan and melt the 50g butter in it. Stir in the flour, letting it cook over a low to moderate heat until it is biscuit coloured and nutty. Pour in the mussel liquor and 500ml of the haddock cooking liquor, then leave to simmer, with a regular stir to stop it catching, for ten minutes.

Skin the haddock and check for bones, keeping it in large, juicy flakes. Nothing is worse than a fish pie with its heart and soul mashed to a pulp. Stir it into the sauce with the mussels and parsley. Grind in some black pepper but go easy with the salt. You may not need any at all. Scoop the lot into a large pie dish (I often use a roasting tin) and leave to cool.

Set the oven at 200°C/Gas 6, then pile the mash on top of the fish. It may sink a little into the creamy filling. Bake until the top is crusty and the filling is bubbling up. About fifty to sixty minutes. This is not a pie you can slice – there is little less appetising than a dry pie – but one with an unctuous, oozing filling.

and more

♦ **a creamy fish pie.** Smoked fish has a deep affinity with cream and there is every reason to add some cream to a fish pie. The filling, already gorgeous, becomes silkier and more luxurious.

♦ **a pastry-topped pie.** If you fancy a pastry crust, you will need about 250g to cover the pie above and you should wait until the filling is fully cold before putting the topping on. In the absence of a traditional pie funnel, an inverted egg cup will help support the pastry in the middle.

♦ **a haddock, prawn and parsley pie.** I cannot pretend the above recipe isn't quite hard work but you can cut down some of the preparation time by using peeled prawns instead of the mussels. You will need four or five handfuls – a large bag, if you like. Make up for the missing cooking liquor with a glass of white wine.

♦ **other good things to add to your fish pie.** Skinned chopped tomatoes; cooked peas; quartered mushrooms fried in butter; a little saffron; chopped dill; and a few chopped anchovies all add interesting notes to the creamy filling, though, as always, I suggest you add only one new flavour at a time.

an appetite for
meat

a big chop for one (and two, and three, and a party)

If you have chosen a chop for your supper, then I guess you are after a take-no-prisoners lump of meat that is succulent and deeply aromatic. It is worth taking five minutes to season it with thick-stemmed, woody herbs that will stand up to the sweet gaminess of the meat and a fierce grill.

rosemary or thyme – a couple of bushy sprigs
garlic – start with one big clove
olive oil
a pork chop – about 250g, and no thicker than your finger
a lemon – half per chop

Run your fingers down the herb stems, loosening the needles or leaves, then chop them roughly. Put them in a mortar and pound them with the garlic – one clove should be enough, use a second if you want – a big pinch of salt flakes and a few grinds of pepper, then pour in enough olive oil to make a thick, fragrant slush. You need to be able to rub it over the chop without it running off.

Smear the flavoured oil and herbs over both sides of the chop. Turn on the heat under a ridged grill pan. Hold your hand over it from time to time. It is hot enough when you can barely hold your hand a few centimetres above it (this is not a contest). You want it to be hot enough for the chop to sizzle immediately you lay it down. There should be smoke, too.

Put the chop on the grill and press it down firmly with a palette knife. Turn the heat down just enough so that the chop is sizzling appetisingly and smoking quite seriously. After four or five minutes, lift one edge with your kitchen tongs. How does the underside look? Golden and brown in patches, the fat translucent? Are there black lines across it? Then turn it over, press down and leave it till the other side is similar – another five minutes or so. Feel the chop with a finger. Is it firm and springy? If so, cut into it at its thickest part with a small knife. If you see any blood or hint of pink, it is not ready.

Lift the chop on to a plate, then squeeze over the lemon. Don't forget to pick up the bone and gnaw it – there is much flavour and succulence there.

and more

♦ **grilled chops for friends.** I see no reason why you cannot cook something like this for six or more. It is a question of organisation and, I suppose, having either two ridged grill pans or one of those grills that fits over two gas jets. Get the chops ready an hour or so before you want to eat and let them sit in the oil and herbs; they will be better for it. I hope you have a powerful extractor fan.

♦ **baked chops for a houseful.** If you have lots to feed at once, you could always bake your chops instead. Make a good amount of garlic paste but use a little more olive oil, so that there is enough to spread over the chops and a bit for the pan. Rub the chops with the garlic seasoning and set aside for an hour or so. Get the oven really hot (about 230°C/Gas 8), lay the chops in a baking tray, so they are snug but not actually touching one another, drizzle over any extra seasoning – or some more oil if you have used it all – then roast them for about forty-five minutes or so, till they are tender and golden. Squeeze over plenty of lemon juice as the hot chops come from the oven. Some baked potatoes and butter would be fun here.

320

♦ **on the side.** Potatoes cooked in stock, page 259 (start them forty minutes before the chop) or the riced potatoes on page 282. Green beans, boiled in salted water till they go dark green and slightly limp (put them in the boiling water as you turn the chop).

♦ **to follow.** Some ripe pears and a knob of young Parmesan or a piece of Beaufort, Wensleydale or Caerphilly.

lamb on the grill

The branding-iron scars that you get from cooking meat on the bars or ridges of a grill are guaranteed to add to its savour. The ideal is surely a discreet charring on the surface with a thick layer of juicy, very pink meat within. There is no point in pussyfooting around with this. If that is what you have an appetite for, plus the bonus of a bone to chew, then I suggest you go for lamb chops cooked with scorching heat and robust seasonings. Think garlic, lemon, thyme, rosemary, mint, anchovy (strange but true) and oregano. I would also vote for mustard but I know many who would disagree. The French mixture of dried herbs known as herbes de Provence, made from rubbed thyme, savory, fennel seed and often lavender, is good here, too. Whatever, you want a cooking method that produces smoke rather than steam, and woody herbs that can stand the heat of the grill. In other words, only cook and season lamb with something that will make your kitchen smell like a Mediterranean village on a summer's evening.

garlic – a small clove per chop
olive oil – fruity and green
oregano, rosemary or thyme
lamb chops – one heavy chump chop per person
lemon – half per chop, big and juicy

Mash the peeled garlic cloves to a paste with a little sea salt. You can do this with a pestle and mortar if you have several to feed, but squashing the garlic and salt on to a chopping board with the flat of a kitchen knife will work for one or two. Add enough oil to make the garlic paste loose enough to massage into the chops. Mix in a few good pinches of chopped oregano, finely chopped young rosemary leaves (they should be dark green and tender) or chopped young thyme leaves per chop. Grind in some black pepper. Now massage the paste into the meat with your hands.

Warm a ridged grill pan over a moderate heat. It is hot enough when you can feel the heat rising if you hold your hand a few inches above it. Put the chops on the grill pan, pressing them down on to the bars with a palette knife. You want the meat to have formed a thin, deeply savoury crust on the outside with charred black lines where it has been on the ridges of the grill pan. This will take about three minutes. Now turn the chop over, crumble over some sea salt and cook the other side. It is ready when the centre of the chop is as you like it. For me, that is deep rose pink and juicy.

and more

♦ **the juicier cut.** I much prefer the plump chump chops from the rear end of the animal to the more demure cutlets from the neck. I like their marbling of fat and the ease with which the meat comes away from the bone. Lamb steaks cut from the leg are an alternative, cooking in much the same way.

♦ **when to season.** This is something that cooks love to argue about. I have found that if you salt meat before you grill it the juices seem to pour out and you get a dry chop. If you season after cooking then somehow the salt seems to stay on the outside. If you salt a chop during cooking, in other words when you turn it over on the grill, then you end up with a tasty chop. Of course, others would disagree. I tend to add pepper both before and after cooking. The early grind seems to bring out the flavour of the lamb, while the last-minute grinding adds a heady whiff.

♦ **when is it done?** Despite what other people would have you believe, watching the clock is a hopelessly inaccurate way to get your chop cooked to perfection. At first, it is probably best to slice neatly into it to see if it is done to your liking inside. The more you cook, the more you will probably find that simply touching the surface of the meat is a better guide, and saves those precious juices being lost. Poke a rare chop and your finger will leave an indentation. Poke a medium rare one and it will give a little but start to bounce back into shape. You don't need to know about well-done lamb chops.

♦ **a deeply savoury version.** I often grill a chop that I have seasoned with nothing more than oil, sea salt and black pepper, then, as it comes sizzling from the grill, I shake over a few drops of mellow, black-brown balsamic vinegar.

♦ **chops with robust herbs and garlic.** Marinating always sounds like a load of trouble. In fact it is as simple as putting your chops in a dish, pouring over some olive oil, tucking in a few herbs such as thyme and bay (tear the bay first to release its oil), or a scattering of herbes de Provence, and some sliced garlic (slicing gives a more subtle effect than crushing) and then going off to work. When you come back you will have heavenly, scented chops all ready for the grill.

♦ **a piquant accompaniment.** Whiz up a batch of the blender green sauce on page 170. It sounds unlikely, I know, but anchovies, mint, parsley, lemon and olive oil are all traditionally used to flatter lamb, so why not?

grilled chicken for a summer barbecue

I will not pretend to be a fan of the barbecue but, perversely, I do love eating out of doors. Of course, food eaten in the open air cannot make even so much as a nod towards sophistication. It must be punchy, loud and spicy. What I call Food With Balls. In reality you may find that all you need is a slightly heavier hand than usual with the salt, which seems to have a magical effect on anything cooked over the embers of a fire. Chilli, garlic, ginger and mint are my favourite barbecue flavourings. I may be alone in this, but to me they just seem to feel right with anything that has a slightly charred skin, such as chicken or lamb that has caught on the bars of the grill.

Makes enough for 4 skewers

yogurt – a large teacup
mint leaves – a loose handful
red and green chillies – 1 or 2 of each, depending on their heat
ground turmeric – a teaspoon
garam masala – a mild one, about a teaspoonful
ginger – a thumb-sized piece
a lime
chicken – 500g boned white and brown meat

Scoop the yogurt into a mixing bowl. Chop the mint leaves and chillies and add them to the yogurt with the turmeric and garam masala. Peel the ginger and grate it coarsely, then fold it into the yogurt with the grated zest of the lime and a few grinds of pepper. Keep the lime for squeezing over the finished chicken.

Cut the chicken into large chunks. They should be small enough to thread comfortably on to a skewer but large enough to remain juicy. In other words, about the size of a chicken liver. Dunk the chicken pieces into the spiced yogurt and set aside for at least an hour. If you can leave them for twice as long, then so much the better. No longer though; leave them overnight and they will get wet and woolly. Thread the chicken on to metal or wooden skewers. If you are using wooden ones it is best to soak them first so they do not burn. Get your griddle pan or barbecue warm (I will not go into the intricacies of barbecuing here, you probably know more about it than I do, anyway).

When the grill is really hot, place the skewers of chicken on the bars and let them sizzle unheeded for a full two or three minutes, until they have come cleanly away from the grill, leaving thick black lines. Turn and cook the other side. You can test to see if they are ready by breaking off a lump of chicken from a kebab. It should be cooked through, with no sign of pink in the middle, yet still juicy.

and more

♦ **barbecued chicken with woody herbs and lemon.** There are countless changes you could make to the spice, mint and yogurt marinade above, by chucking in ground cardamom, paprika or cumin, or you could opt for something even simpler and with European rather than Indian back notes. Leave the chicken in a marinade of olive oil, thyme leaves, crushed garlic and thick parings of lemon zest, twisted to release a spray of their oil. The chicken will need a good couple of hours in this before grilling, and rolling in some flakes of sea salt, crumbled black pepper and lemon juice after. Chicken wings, soaked in this, then grilled till their pointy bits are as brown as wenge and chewy as a pork scratching are perhaps the best of all.

♦ **grilled rabbit with a herb marinade.** It would not be inaccurate to say that the aromatics and flavourings that work so well with chicken sit just as comfortably with rabbit – well, they would, wouldn't they, their flesh is not dissimilar – but some seem more appropriate than others. Garlic, lemon, thyme, juniper and aniseed herbs such as tarragon and fennel all flatter rabbit as well, if not even more so. But it is the smoky notes of pancetta, bacon and dried mushrooms that are probably the most successful of all with the meat's slightly gamier flavour, and the pork's fat will minimise the rabbit's tendency to dryness.

Soak pre-barbecue rabbit joints in a shallow bath of olive oil, thyme, crushed garlic and squashed juniper berries for several hours, then grill over hot coals, dusting with coarse black pepper and sea salt as they come from the grill. Pass around lemon halves to squeeze over them. Alternatively, wrap your bits of marinated bunny in bacon and roast them on a high setting till sweet and completely tender.

a steak supper

There are meals that you fancy, or feel like. There are those you desire or even crave. Then there are those, like a bloody chargrilled steak, that you simply lust after. And I do think lust is the appropriate word here. It would be my last meal, steak, béarnaise sauce and *frites* (there simply have to be *frites*). Few meals arouse quite such passion or contention. A steak, more than any other meal, is something that you must get absolutely right. Shape, size, colour and, above all, timing. Otherwise it misses the mark. None of us wants to eat that much meat any more so when we do it must be perfect. The point of the whole thing is when bloody meat meets velvety, piquant sauce meets long, crisp, salty chip meets savoury juice on the same fork. This is not an especially easy meal – so many things can go wrong – but get it spot on and it is a truly sensational plate of food.

steak – a slice of rump as thick as your thumb and as big as you fancy
   (200g per person is about right)
olive oil

Rub your steak all over with olive oil, not too much, just enough to give it a good gloss, then grind a little black pepper over both sides. I put salt on later. Get the grill pan hot (there are some notes on this in How To Do It on page 62), then slap on the steak and press it down on to the bars with a palette knife. Let it cook for two full minutes. Do not move it. Now turn it over (long metal tongs are useful here), press it down again (this is when I usually add the salt) and let it cook for a further two minutes. The best way to tell if your steak is done is to press it with your finger. Timing is a hopelessly inaccurate measure because so much depends on how your meat has been hung and butchered. The best – by which I mean the juiciest – results will come from a steak where your finger has left a slight indentation. Until you get to know the 'feel' of your steaks you may have to make a small cut into them, but you will lose juice this way. If you want a well-done steak, with no blood in it, then I can't help you. Well, I could but I won't.

Incidentally, I sometimes pour a little wine on to the grill pan after removing the steak and let it bubble, then pour the meagre, intensely beefy juices over my steak. Eat with the béarnaise sauce overleaf and a dish of *frites*.

330

For the sauce (enough for 2, at least):
shallots – a small one
white wine or tarragon vinegar – about 3 tablespoons
peppercorns – black, whole, about 6
tarragon – 3 or 4 healthy stalks and their leaves
egg yolks – 2
Dijon mustard (not traditional this, but I like it)
butter – 150g, soft, almost melted

Peel and finely chop the shallot and put it in a small saucepan with the vinegar, peppercorns and the tarragon leaves and stalks. Bring to the boil and watch it while it reduces to a tablespoon or so. Put the egg yolks and a little mustard into a glass bowl (not a steel one, they get too hot) and place it over a pan of very gently simmering water. The bowl should sit snugly in the top of the pan. Whisk the reduced vinegar into the egg yolks, holding the debris back in the pan, then slowly add the butter, a soft cube at a time, whisking almost constantly until it is thick and velvety. You can turn the heat off halfway through; the sauce must not get too hot. It may need a little salt. It will keep warm, with the occasional whisk, while you grill your steak and fry your *frites* – which, by the way, I tend to buy very thin and frozen and cook in deep groundnut oil.

and more

♦ **if your béarnaise sauce should separate.** It does happen, even to people who make it all the time. I find adding a spoonful of the boiling water from the pan underneath often brings it back. Sometimes, when things have gone completely pear-shaped, I take the bowl off the pan and put it into a sink of cold water, add a spoonful of boiling water and whisk as hard as I can. It invariably rights itself (though you will be somewhat hot and sweaty).

some quick frying-pan suppers

I have, on many occasions, simply thrown an escalope of pork, lamb (a batted-out piece of fillet), liver and even salmon into a small, shallow pan of foaming butter, flicked it over after a minute or so, then stirred in some lemon juice and cream. Sometimes Marsala, Madeira or vermouth goes in when the meat comes out, in which case I often forget about the cream, thickening the pan juices with some cold butter instead. Sometimes herbs go in, too. Much depends on whether I want something tart and fresh – just lemon juice and capers – or a much creamier affair, in which case I still add the lemon to lighten it but include soft herbs such as tarragon, too. Whatever, this is supper in seconds.

Enough for 2

pork escalopes – 2, about the size of your hand
flour – a little, to coat the escalopes
butter – a thick slice for frying the pork, plus a little more (about 30g), cold from
  the fridge and cut into chunks
booze of some sort – a wine glassful of Madeira, dry Marsala, Noilly Prat or wine
herbs – parsley, tarragon, young thyme leaves or whatever you feel like

Toss your escalopes lightly in flour that you have seasoned with salt and black pepper. I must admit that the flour is not absolutely necessary here but I like the faint crust it gives to the meat. Whatever, waggle it about a bit to shake off any excess. You want a very thin layer of flour left on the meat. Get a shallow pan hot and add a thick slice of butter – you can pour in a drop of oil to discourage it from burning if you wish – then, when it starts to froth and sizzle, lay in the escalopes. The underside will be golden in a matter of a minute or so. Turn them and cook the other side.

Remove the escalopes to a warm place. Tip out most of the butter and pour in your booze. Madeira is so good with pork but any of the others will do nicely, too. Let it bubble and froth while you stir in any good bits from the bottom of the pan. As the wine froths and reduces, add anything else you wish – your herbs, for instance, all chopped up, or capers or lemon juice, and some salt and pepper.

Now add the 30g butter in small chunks, whisking continuously, until you have a glossy sauce. Check the seasoning. Pour the sauce over the meat and eat with hunks of crusty bread to mop it up.

and more

- **lamb with Marsala and, if you like, a dash of balsamic vinegar.** Bat out slices of lamb fillet to make small, oval scallops. They won't be very big, so a whole lamb fillet won't feed more than two or three. There is no need to flour them. Cook them as above, then pour Marsala into the pan and finish with chopped thyme, a dash of balsamic vinegar or a spoonful of grain mustard, and the butter.

- **lamb with anchovies, garlic and rosemary.** Again, bat out your slices of lamb fillet and cook them in the frothing butter. Put them somewhere warm – I suggest on a plate covered with an upturned bowl in a low oven – tip away most of the butter from the pan and stir in two or three finely chopped anchovy fillets, a large clove of garlic, peeled and crushed, and a few finely chopped rosemary leaves. Let them froth in the butter for a minute or two (fabulous smell), then pour in a glass of red wine (something deep and fruity). Once that is bubbling furiously, beat in a large knob of butter and pour the sauce over the warm lamb.

- **pork escalopes with mustard sauce.** Carry on as in the main recipe until you get to the bit about adding the Madeira, then use dry Marsala instead. Let it bubble, then pour in most of a small carton of double cream (you could give the rest to the cat) and stir in a dollop of grain mustard and some salt and pepper. Taste it – you may want more – then let it bubble away until you have a lovely, creamy sauce. Pour the sauce over the pork and eat with some crusty bread to soak up all that mustardy cream.

- **chicken fillets with tarragon sauce.** Fry batted-out chicken fillets as above, deglazing the pan with white vermouth such as Noilly Prat. Add finely chopped tarragon leaves to the bubbling wine, then whisk in either the cold butter or, as it goes so beautifully with both chicken and tarragon, a few glugs of double cream. Letting it simmer for a few minutes while you correct the seasoning will give you a velvety, ivory-coloured sauce.

- **pan-fried liver with capers.** Flour your liver lightly, then lay it in the foaming butter. Turn it after a few seconds and cook the other side – ideally you want the inside to be a deep rose pink. Lift the liver out and keep it warm while you add either Madeira or dry Marsala to the pan. Throw in a few rinsed capers and, if you like, a spoonful of smooth mustard and some chopped parsley. Whisk in a thick slice of butter as above and, when all is shiny, check the seasoning. Spoon the sauce over the liver. Boiled or steamed potatoes would be a dream.

chicken, garlic, herbs; a simple supper

If we are to eat well, we need to know how to exploit every bit of flavour in our food. The idea that follows does exactly that. Meat is cooked slowly on the bone over a low to moderate heat so that as it tenderises it leaves a thin film of goo – the caramelised meat juices – with which we can make a sauce (when I say sauce, I mean something quite thin and meagre in quantity but intensely flavoured rather than a copious creamy blanket).

There is something neat about this recipe, and I am not talking about its frugal use of kitchen equipment, though that is another point in its favour. The shopping list, as always, is short. The method is straightforward, undemanding. The finished meat is suitable for fair weather or foul. Some spinach or courgettes, briefly boiled and tossed with butter and lemon juice, and some French bread for mopping your plate might be good here.

Enough for 4

free-range chicken – either a small bird, jointed by the butcher, or 2 chicken
   pieces per person, skin and bones to remain in place
olive oil
butter – a thick slice
garlic – 6 large, sweet cloves
herbs – a small bunch of parsley, plus tarragon, thyme or chervil
wine – a large wine glass of white wine or dry vermouth

Rub the chicken all over with a little oil and some black pepper. In a large pan – it can be high-sided or shallow but it must have a lid – warm enough olive oil to give a small puddle in the bottom, then add the butter. Once the butter starts to froth, put in the chicken pieces and keep the heat moderately high while they colour. A pale and relatively even gold is what you are after.

Meanwhile, put the whole unpeeled garlic cloves on a board and, with the flat blade of a knife, squash them so that they flatten but remain fairly intact. Throw them in with the chicken. Turn down the heat so that the fat under the chicken is gently fizzing, then add a little sea salt, cover the pan with a lid and leave to cook over a low to moderate heat. The time it takes to cook will depend on the thickness of your chicken joints but you should expect them to need about forty minutes. You will have to turn them during cooking so that they colour on all sides.

While this is happening, pluck the leaves from the herbs and chop them roughly. Transfer the chicken to a serving dish or warm plates, then fish out the garlic (although the garlic has done its work, it may be tender and sweet and is worth adding to the plate, though the skin should be discarded at some point). Tip off most of the fat from the pan – what you are after is the golden, caramelised juice stuck to the bottom – then turn up the heat, pour in the wine and add the herbs and let it bubble. Scrape away at any stuck bits in the pan, encouraging them to dissolve into the wine with a wooden spoon. Let this all bubble away for a minute or two until you have a thin liquor. It should be pale and interesting. Now taste the juice for seasoning – it may need salt, pepper or a squeeze of lemon juice – and spoon it over the chicken.

and more

♦ **a buttery finish.** Once the wine has bubbled down, whisk in a thick slice of butter (about 50g), cut into tiny cubes. Taste and spoon over the chicken.

♦ **or a creamy one.** Once you have removed the chicken from the pan and poured in your wine or vermouth, let it bubble away until you have only half of it left, then add about half as much cream. As it continues to bubble, stir in chopped parsley and slightly less chopped tarragon. Finish with salt, black pepper and a squeeze of lemon juice.

♦ **lamb with garlic and lemon.** What works for a chicken thigh will also work for a lamb chop. Try the original idea but with chump chops and adding parsley and mint. Finish with the squeeze of a lemon.

♦ **pork chops with apple and cream.** Rib chops, with their generous marbling of integral fat (rather than a loin chop with its great wodge of fat running alongside the lean meat), are delectable cooked this way. You should let them colour well before turning down the heat, adding an apple or two, peeled and cut into small cubes, and letting it colour with the pork. When it is time to take out the meat, leave the apple be, then add the wine and let it simmer down a bit before pouring in a small pot of double cream. Stir, taking the sediment from the pan with you and dissolving it into the cream with your wooden spoon. Herbs are not really needed here, though the garlic is. I once crushed a few juniper berries, adding them after the meat and fruit had browned, to great effect.

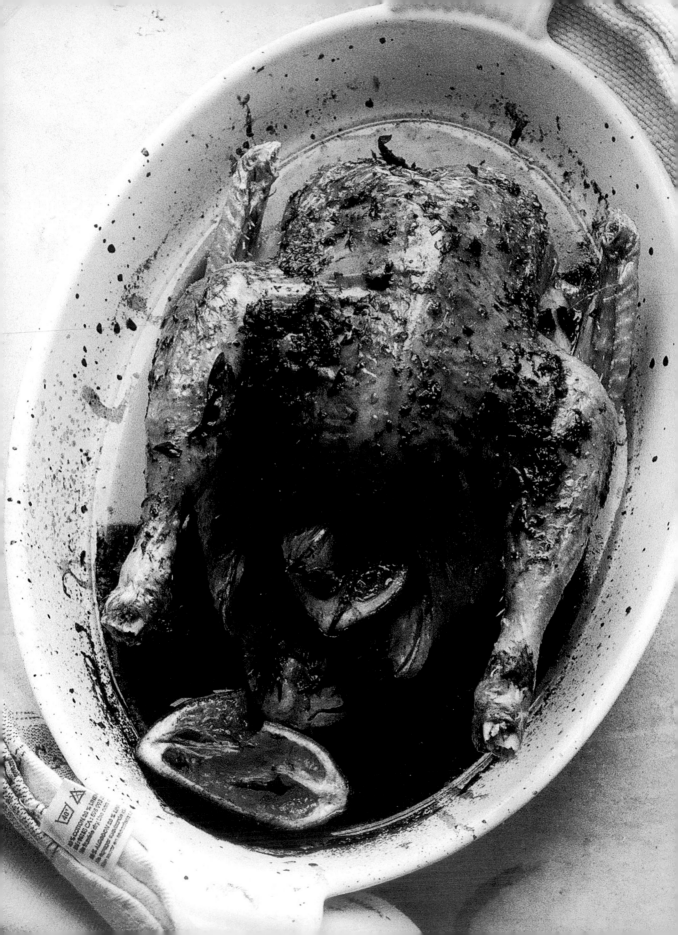

classic, unmucked-about-with roast chicken ... and its pan juices

Don't believe any of the smart-arse recipes you see for roast chicken. This is the one. Basic roast chicken, its skin crisp and buttery, its juices savoury and aromatic – and quite possibly the best meal in the world.

chicken – an organically reared bird
butter
a lemon
garlic – a whole head, cut in half

Set the oven at 200°C/Gas 6. Sit the chicken in a roasting tin or large baking dish. Rub it all over with butter, even putting a walnut-sized knob inside the bird. Season with salt and black pepper. Cut the lemon in two, put one half inside and squeeze the other over the chicken, then throw the shell into the roasting tin with the head of garlic. Roast for twenty minutes per 500g plus an extra half an hour. You can baste it from time to time, though I am not truly convinced of the need for it. When the chicken is ready, by which I mean it is golden-skinned and glossy and its juices run clear when the flesh is deeply pierced with a skewer, remove it from the oven and let it rest for ten minutes.

and more

◆ **about carving.** I tend to cut long, slender slices from the breast first, then hack off the legs. Mine is not an elegant method, but then I am not sure it has to be. Too perfect and considered and it won't be a feast.

◆ **about the gravy.** The juices in the pan will almost certainly be sweet and deeply savoury but there won't be quite enough. I get round this by removing the bird and placing the roasting tin on the stove over a moderate heat. I pour in a glass of white wine or, better still, white vermouth and scrape away at the glossy, caramel-brown stickings in the pan, dissolving them into the wine. As they bubble, I squash the lemon shell and the head of garlic with my spoon to extract the last of the juices and sweetly roasted garlic, then season with salt and pepper. I then spoon this clear, sweet-sharp juice over the sliced chicken, holding the lemon and garlic skins back in the pan.

and more

- **and the potatoes.** I think there have got to be potatoes. They must be the crunchy sort that stick to the roasting tin, their outsides golden and crisp around the edges, their insides fluffy and melting. Scrunchy. You can, and I think should, cook them with the chicken. That way the potatoes caramelise around the edges in the roasting juices. You must peel them. I know this is boring but otherwise they will develop the hide of a rhinoceros. Cut them into large chunks, bring them to the boil in salted water and simmer for ten minutes, then drain thoroughly. Now the important bit. Shake the potatoes around a little in their empty pan, just enough that the edges fluff and bruise. Tip them into the roasting dish with the partially roasted chicken. They will take about an hour to become crisp and frilly around the edges.

- **roast chicken with garlic and herbs.** Mash some chopped tarragon or thyme, a clove or two of garlic and some soft butter together in a small bowl. Smear it all over your chicken, then roast. This one is especially good with a glass of wine tipped into the pan after the chicken has been removed. Let the wine and garlicky, herby juices bubble away a bit, then spoon them over the carved meat.

- **some other birds to roast.** If you can roast a chicken, then it only follows that you can roast a pheasant, a guinea fowl, a turkey even. The principle is the same – keep it moist and leave it alone in the oven to do its stuff. But timings and flavourings vary a little. For a pheasant or guinea fowl you should forget the lemon altogether, keeping the bird moist by wrapping its chest in bacon and still, even then, basting it with butter. Some thyme or sage would be good, stuck inside the bird as well as over it. Roast the bird for about forty minutes at 200°C/Gas 6, till its juices run clear when pierced with a skewer (do this where the leg joins the body as this is the deepest place); if there is no sign of blood it is done. Pull off the bacon for the last ten minutes of roasting to brown the breast. Deglaze the pan by removing the golden bird, pouring off the fat from the pan and tipping in a glass of Madeira. As it bubbles away, stir in the sticky goodies from the pan as above. I often put in a few squashed juniper berries halfway through the roasting time, sieving them out when the gravy is finished. They add a wonderful gin-and-tonic aroma to the gravy.

345

a simple lamb roast for a family lunch

I remember being so nervous about cooking my first roast. Terrified might be a better word. In practice, it turned out to be as easy as cooking gets. You basically rub olive oil, a few chopped herbs and some salt and pepper over the meat, then chuck it in the oven till it smells sweet and tantalising. You do need to keep an eye on the clock so you don't overcook it and at some point you might like to throw together a salad and peel a few spuds, but that really is about as complicated as it gets. Whatever you do, I beg you to ignore any fancy roast recipes you may come across. They are not worth the hassle. Oh, and you don't need to worry about carving – just hack it off in the thinnest slices you can manage with a long-bladed, very sharp knife.

Enough for 6, with salad and potatoes

lamb on the bone – a leg or shoulder, about 2kg in weight
robust herbs – thyme or rosemary, the woodier the better
garlic – a whole head or 2, depending on how much you like it, unpeeled
olive oil – enough to massage the roast

Set the oven at 230°C/Gas 8. Put the lamb in a roasting tin big enough to allow you to get some herbs and garlic around the meat. Strip the thyme or rosemary leaves off their stems – you will need a couple of large sprigs of rosemary or six to eight little sprigs of thyme – and chop or crush the leaves quite finely. Stir enough olive oil into them to make a spreadable slush, then crumble in some salt and crushed black pepper. Massage the seasoned oil all over the meat – you will find there is something quite pleasurable about this – then cut the whole heads of garlic in half and tuck them under the lamb with the stems from the herbs.

Roast in the preheated oven for twenty minutes, then turn the heat down to 200°C/Gas 6 and continue roasting until the fat is golden and crisp and the meat is done as you would like it. Lamb needs about fifteen minutes per 500g of meat, plus the initial twenty minutes, so for a 2kg joint you should start checking after the meat has been in the oven for an hour and twenty minutes. This will give you medium-rare meat, still juicy and quite pink in the middle.

Remove the meat from the oven, discard the garlic and herb twigs (they have served their purpose but do pull out some of the garlic cloves from their skins first) and leave the lamb to rest for ten minutes before carving.

and more

♦ **how to get the timing right.** Everyone has a different idea of perfectly cooked lamb. I know it's fashionable to eat it very rare but in truth I don't really like it that way. I much prefer it to be pink in the middle but darker round the edge. I don't mean well done, when the poor lamb has lost all its juice and therefore its point, but I do like it a bit more well done than is now the tendency. If you like your lamb very rare, then cook it for twelve minutes per 500g.

♦ **on the side.** A salad, perhaps with some dark leaves such as baby spinach and watercress, seems somehow more appropriate than vegetables with a lamb roast. I also like floppy lettuce with mine. If green vegetables it must be, then I suggest some spinach – wash it and, whilst the leaves are still wet, add it to a pan with a tight lid over a high heat. The leaves will cook in seconds in their own steam. Drain and toss with a little melted butter.

♦ **the potatoes.** I am not sure there is any point in a roast without some crunchy-crusted potatoes on the side.

♦ **some juices from the pan.** Thin gravy, more of a juice really, is what I prefer with lamb, though sometimes I admit I hardly bother if the lamb is juicy enough. If you suspect everyone will want gravy of some sort, then do it this way: throw out the herb twigs, pop the garlic flesh from its skin into the roasting tin, and put the tin over a moderate heat. Pour a glass or two – no more – of red wine, Marsala or Madeira (or dry vermouth, white wine, stock or even water) into the tin and bring it to the boil. Scrape at any interesting bits on the pan, stirring them in, at the same time mashing the garlic cloves into the bubbling liquor. Taste and season with salt and black pepper, then strain through a sieve or, as I do, spoon it over the carved lamb, holding any bits back with a draining spoon.

♦ **an onion gravy.** I am not convinced that roast lamb needs any seasoning other than garlic, thyme or rosemary, though I am sure there are those who would disagree. You could make a thicker gravy by adding peeled and roughly chopped onions to the tin so that they roast sweetly. When you get the lamb out to rest, sprinkle a light dusting of flour over the onions, let them sizzle for a few seconds over a high heat, then pour over enough stock, water or wine to make a thin, oniony gravy. Season, but do not sieve; the onions are crucial.

a pork roast

If you are thinking of roasting a piece of pork, you must be after succulent flesh and juicy fat. Both cravings can be fixed by choosing a less than lean cut and by cooking it on the bone. Pork has a sweet, flat quality and so needs seasoning with something particularly aromatic – bay, garlic or mustard – and something hot or sharp – lemons, ginger, vinegar or apples. One of each is enough. So mix a seasoning of lemon and mustard or garlic and ginger, moisten it with oil and spread it over the meat before roasting. Check out the bit about pork on page 126, do your shopping, then proceed as below.

Enough for 4–6, with a frisée or lettuce salad to mop up the juices

belly pork – a piece about 1.8kg, skin on
dried bay leaves – about 8
garlic – 3 or 4 plump, juicy cloves
olive oil
potatoes – about 1kg
white wine, stock or water

If the fat is to crackle, you will need to score and season it. This is how. With an ultra-sharp blade – I use a Stanley knife – score through the skin at finger-thick widths (to give long, pickupable strips of crackling). Go down through the fat under the skin but don't cut into the meat.

Make a seasoning by crumbling the bay leaves with your fingers, peeling the garlic and squashing it with the flat of a knife, then mashing the two together either with a pestle and mortar or in a food processor. Add a good pinch of salt flakes and some black pepper. You are going to spread this seasoning over the meat, so you need to pour in enough oil to make a spreadable mush. Place the pork skin side down and massage the seasoning into it, pushing it into any available crevice or slit. You need to give the seasoning time to do its stuff, so leave the meat in a cool place for an hour or so.

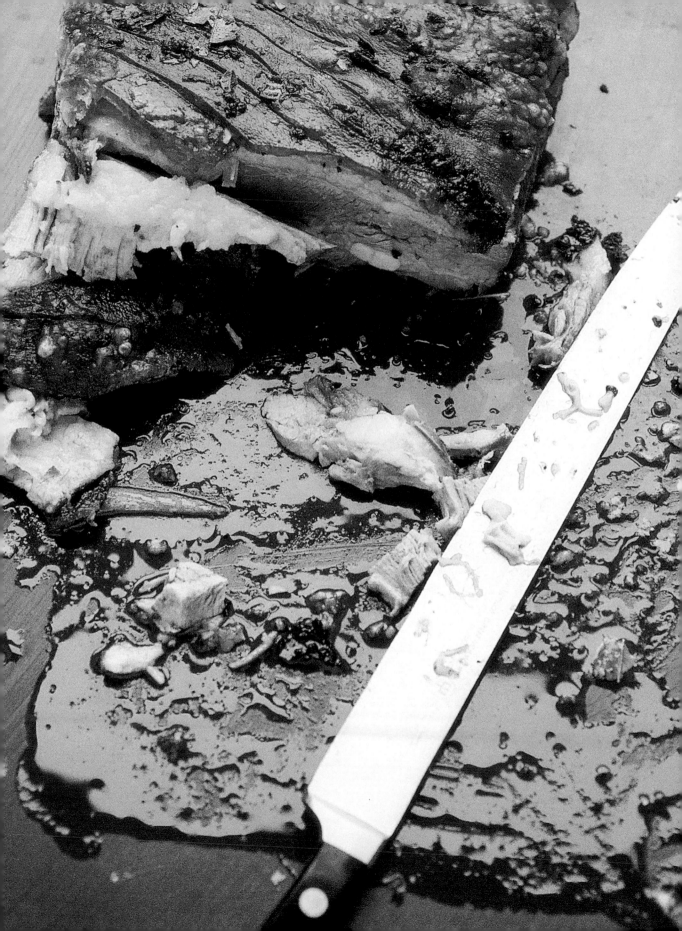

Peel the potatoes, cut them into large chunks (only you know how big you like your roast potatoes) and drop them into boiling salted water. They need to cook until they are just about tender enough to slip the point of a knife into them with hardly any pressure – a matter of ten to fifteen minutes. Drain them, tip them into a roasting tin and shake them about a bit so the edges bruise and fray. That way the potatoes will soak up the seasoned juices from the roast.

Set the oven at 200°C/Gas 6. You are going to cook the pork directly on a shelf above the spuds, so place one oven shelf near the bottom and another two thirds of the way up. When the oven has come up to temperature, pour a little oil over the potatoes, just enough to stop them sticking, add a wine glass of water and shake them about a bit, then put the roasting tin on the lower shelf. Pull the top shelf out and place the pork on it, skin side down, then slide it back. Leave the pork and potatoes for an hour, tossing the potatoes once during cooking, so that they turn over. Presumably you want your pork juicy and barely pink. Cut into it with a sharp knife to check its progress. Any pink in there? Then cook it for a little longer. You should find it will be just right in about an hour and half.

To crisp the crackling, the heat will need to be higher, so turn the oven up to 250°C/Gas 9 and continue cooking until the skin is puffed and crisp. Remove the meat and leave it to rest – it will be juicier that way – then remove the potatoes, which should be sticky and deep brown. It would be a shame not to use the flavour that is left in the pan scrapings, so pour a wine glass of white wine, stock or water into the roasting tin and bring it to the boil on top of the stove, stirring well. The amount you add will depend on how much of the caramelised meat juice there is to dissolve.

Cut the meat into thick chunks rather than slices, following the bones with your carving knife, put some of the potatoes with it, then pour over some of the gravy.

You can, of course, roast a joint of pork in a roasting tin rather than on the bars of the oven.

and more

♦ **a garlic and rosemary roast.** Lay handfuls of wet rosemary in a roasting tin before you add the pork. Tuck whole cloves of garlic, squashed flat, in between the twigs of herbs. The aromatics will gently flavour the meat as it roasts.

♦ **an aniseed pork roast.** Those, like me, who love the marriage of pork and aniseed might like to try adding some fennel seeds to the crushed garlic before spreading it over the pork. Get an even deeper flavour by roasting the pork on fennel twigs instead of the rosemary above. Kitchenware shops, some supermarkets and a few butchers sell them dried, in bundles.

♦ **a Chinese roast.** Instead of the garlic and bay paste in the blueprint above, mix up the crushed garlic with three or four tablespoons of hoisin sauce and one each of rice wine and light soy. Stir in a little vegetable oil and some salt, then massage it all over the pork before roasting. You can forget the potatoes. A dark, subtle Chinese roast, this. Best, I think, with some steamed bok choi and soft, fresh bread. Cold, it makes a good sandwich.

♦ **a barbecue roast.** Mix this for a spicy, sticky roast, one that will make you want to lick your fingers (and probably everyone else's): four tablespoons each of runny honey, muscovado sugar and hoisin sauce, two of rice wine, light soy and dark soy, three crushed cloves of garlic, half a teaspoon of ground black pepper and a teaspoon of salt. Rub it into the pork and leave for a good hour before roasting at 180°C/Gas 4. You will get especially juicy results by adding a finger's depth of water to the roasting tin and sitting the pork on a rack over it, basting it with any leftover marinade once during roasting and then turning up the heat for the last half hour of cooking. Serve with finger bowls and kitchen roll.

a pot-roast bird

Cooking meat, birds or fish in a sealed pot helps keep them singularly moist and succulent. I find this is particularly important when the food itself is short of natural fat – a lean piece of meat, for instance, or a chicken. Anyone who recoils from cooking game birds because of their habit of drying up if even slightly overcooked (and just who can get people to the table on time?) will find the pot-roast method an answer to their prayers. There is also the no small matter that pot-roast food has that laid-back earth-motherly ring to it.

Enough for 4

pheasants – 2, oven ready
olive oil
pancetta or fat bacon – in the piece, about 200g
celery – a short stalk per person
Vin Santo or other sweet wine such as Madeira – a wine glass or two

Get the oven hot; you will need it to be at 220°C/Gas 7. Rub the birds all over with salt, black pepper and olive oil. Cut the pancetta into small dice, scrape it into a casserole and let its fat run slowly over a low heat. If necessary, add a slice of butter or a glug of olive oil to get it going. Once the pancetta is lightly sizzling, add the birds, turn up the heat and let them colour on each side. A pale gold is all we are after. Now chop the celery into small pieces and add it to the pan. Pour in the Vin Santo and bring it to the boil, then cover the casserole with a lid, put it in the oven and roast for a while. A pair of pheasants will usually take about forty-five minutes. They are ready when their juices run clear. The easiest way to check is to pierce the flesh with a skewer at its thickest point, usually where the leg joins the rest of the carcass. If the juices that seep from it are clear and golden, it is ready. If you see a touch of pink, the birds need a bit longer in the oven.

Let the birds rest, still in their pan but out of the oven, for fifteen minutes before you carve them. That way the flesh will be juicier.

and more

♦ **a smaller roast.** You can use partridge instead of pheasant. They will need slightly less time in the oven – about twenty-five minutes.

♦ **a herbal note.** Add some herbs to the pan as you put it in the oven. A few sprigs of the more robust ones would be good. Thyme, rosemary and a couple of bay leaves will work.

♦ **a richer sauce.** You could, I suppose, make an impromptu sauce by adding a little double cream to the juices in the pan once the birds are cooked. Let it thicken and take up the flavours by bringing it to the boil in the pan for a minute or two while the roasted birds are resting somewhere warm.

♦ **more roasting juices.** Fancy more juice? Pour a ladleful of stock in as the birds come out and bring it to the boil for a minute or two.

♦ **a less sweet gravy.** Swap the Vin Santo for dry Marsala or a vermouth such as Noilly Prat.

♦ **something to soak up the juices.** I like my game with thick slices cut from a country loaf and toasted. The bread soaks up the pan juices and provides a modicum of sustenance.

♦ **the perfect accompaniment.** I recommend some boiled potatoes pushed through a ricer. No butter and stuff, just the meagre pan juices.

a rich, meaty braise for hungry friends

When meat cooks slowly on the bone in a moist, aromatic atmosphere it becomes so tender and succulent you can virtually eat it with a spoon. By 'on the bone', I mean the thick, gelatine-rich bones you get in shanks and neck of lamb and in whole, tougher game birds such as pigeon. By 'moist, aromatic atmosphere', I mean in the oven with wine, water, herbs and vegetables, so that the meat partly steams itself to tenderness while picking up flavour from the aromatics. What you get is cheap(ish), unimaginably tender meat that makes its own deeply flavoured sauce.

This is one of those dishes to put on the table when friends come round for winter lunch, when you want the cooking to have all been done by the time they arrive. Some fluffy but not too buttery mash (see page 283), either of chick peas, parsnips or celeriac, is all you need. Oh, and lots of big red wine.

Enough for 6, with some mash

lamb – 6 small shanks, so that people can have a whole one each, or 12 thick
   neck chops
olive oil – just enough to cover the bottom of your roasting tin
flour – a little for dusting
onions – 6 medium-sized red or golden

For the marinade:
a bottle of red wine – Rioja would be appropriate
sherry vinegar – about 4 tablespoons
garlic – 2 whole heads
thyme – a small bunch
bay leaves – 3 or 4
black peppercorns – 9 or 10

Put the lamb in a steel or glass bowl or a roasting tin and add the wine, sherry vinegar, the garlic heads cut in half horizontally, the herbs and their branches and the peppercorns. Set this aside for a few hours, or overnight if that is easier, turning the meat in the aromatic liquor from time to time. Don't miss this step. It imbues the meat with flavour.

360

Set the oven at 200°C/Gas 6. Pour enough oil in a roasting tin to cover the bottom, then set it over two gas burners. Take the shanks out of the marinade, dust them lightly with flour and lay them in the hot oil – you may find it easier doing three at a time. Turn them in the oil so that they colour healthily on all sides, then take them out. If the oil is dark and nutty, chuck it out and add some more but do not remove any sticky lamb debris from the pan; there is much flavour there.

While the lamb is colouring, peel and roughly chop the onions, then, when you have removed all the lamb (and added more oil if necessary), let them soften slowly in the roasting tin, stirring them now and again to stop them burning but not so regularly that they fail to caramelise and soften. After twenty minutes of gentle cooking, they should be deep gold and soft enough to crush between your thumb and finger.

Return the shanks or chops to the pan, pour over the marinade, tucking the herbs in underneath the lamb, then cover with foil and place in the oven. You can happily leave it to cook unattended for a couple of hours, by which time the meat will have shrunk and softened and the wine and onions thickened to a rough sauce (which you should taste for seasoning, adding salt and black pepper as you wish).

and more

363

♦ **a pork braise.** There is no reason why you can't do ths with pork too. Try a knuckle or thick chunks of belly pork on the bone.

♦ **and a beef braise.** This idea will work for oxtail too.

dark, sticky meat for a winter's day

There is a lot to be said for meals that sit quietly in the oven for an hour or two, simmering sweetly and slowly towards tenderness while we do other things. Oxtail, with its gelatine-rich bones and highly flavoured meat, is probably the best contender of all for such treatment, taking a good two hours to submit to the cook. Truth told, it's hardly a battle – you simply chuck it all in the oven and forget it – but what you end up with is big-flavoured, collapsing meat, a few spoonfuls of intensely flavoured juice and some big knobs of bone to suck at.

Enough for 2, with seconds

an oxtail – cut into joints
flour – a little for dusting the oxtail
cayenne pepper
dry mustard powder
butter – a thick slice
carrots – 2 or 3, peeled and roughly chopped
onions – 2 or more, peeled and roughly chopped
celery – a rib or two, chopped
seasonings – garlic and bay leaves, plus one or two from: orange peel, juniper
    berries, thyme
a bottle of ballsy red wine, such as Rioja

Set the oven at 160°C/Gas 3. Trim any particularly large lumps of fat from the meat, then toss each joint in flour that you have seasoned with cayenne, dry mustard and some ground black pepper. Melt the butter in a roasting tin over a moderate heat and seal the meat in it, turning each piece as it colours, then add the carrots, onions, celery and a few cloves of garlic and let them colour a little. By this time the butter will have all but disappeared.

Tuck in the bay leaves (four or five, depending on their size), then pour over the wine and lower in any extra seasonings – a couple of long strips of orange peel, eight or ten juniper berries, or a few bushy thyme sprigs. Bring to the boil, cover with greaseproof paper rubbed with a little oil or butter, then transfer to the oven and leave well alone for an hour, when the meat will be distinctly brown. Turn the meat over and leave for a further hour. What you will now have are lumps of glossy, tender meat and a little sticky sauce. Serve with mashed potato or swede.

and more

♦ **a lamb braise.** If the thing that hangs from the back of a bull seems all too butch, then try the same recipe with lamb. The most suitable cuts are obviously the ones with lots of bone, such as chops cut from the neck, or shanks with their juicy, central bone.

♦ **a beef and tomato braise.** Cooked slowly with red meat, tomatoes often give a deep, sweet-sharp gravy that works particularly well with beef and lamb. Add a can or two of chopped tomatoes to the ingredients above. You will end up with more sauce, though it will be less concentrated, but equally delicious.

♦ **a beef braise with olives.** Add a handful of stoned black olives to the tomato recipe above about half an hour before the end of the cooking time.

♦ **a Chinese oxtail braise.** Replace the red wine with water and add a few spoonfuls of rice wine or dry sherry, 4 or 5 slices of ginger, 2 or 3 star anise, 5 or 6 tablespoons of dark soy sauce and a little brown sugar to the browned vegetables. Orange peel and garlic are fine left in there, too. Cover and cook as before. A succulent, aniseed-scented stew.

♦ **and on the side.** There is not so much gravy here as a few spoonfuls of sticky goo, but you will need something to soak it up nevertheless. Boiled, carefully peeled potatoes or a root vegetable mash of some sort are my suggestions, except with the Chinese version, which begs for rice or noodles.

♦ **and on cooking.** You can take as much care as you like over this, painstakingly browning every slice of vegetable and piece of meat, or you can simply seal everything in the hot butter then throw all the other ingredients in. This is one of those dishes where it seems to make no difference how you approach it. The magic here belongs to the food as it slowly does its stuff in the oven, rather than to the meddling of the cook.

a winter supper to revive and restore

A bowl of food to bring you back from the brink; to restore you to your old self after a cold or flu; to warm you on a cold winter's night when you arrive home chilled to the bone; to rekindle your faith in food after a succession of fancy dinners. I have never found a meal that revives more triumphantly. Soul food, indeed. You will need a knife and fork for the melting, pallid chicken, and a spoon for the broth, which, if this dish is to be allowed to work its magic, must be served so hot that you need to blow on every spoonful of shimmering amber liquor before you put it to your lips.

Enough for 4, at least

pearl barley – a good handful
chicken – a large free-range one, jointed
a little fat – dripping, butter, goose fat or olive oil
carrots – 1 or 2, thoroughly scrubbed
parsnips – 1 or 2, peeled
leeks – a couple of large ones, or one of those enormous, thick winter ones
onions – a large one, or 3 smaller ones, peeled
some herbs – a few bay leaves, 3 or 4 sprigs of thyme and a couple of sage leaves
potatoes – about 4 small to medium ones
parsley – a small bunch, perky and vibrant

You will also need a very large, deep pan with a lid.

Simmer the barley in a pan of salted water until it is tender – a matter of twenty minutes or so but taste it to check – then drain it.

Lightly brown the jointed chicken in the fat in a large, deep ovenproof pan. I do this in a relay, three or four pieces at a time, over a moderately high heat. Transfer the browned chicken to a plate. While the chicken is browning you need to cut the carrot and parsnip into large chunks and the leek, thoroughly scrubbed and freed of grit (it gets between the layers), into short lengths. I think it is important to keep the vegetables in fat juicy chunks for this. Cut the onion in half and then into large segments. Once the chicken is out of the pan, add the vegetables, turn them in the fat and let them soften a little, though don't let them colour. In another pan bring enough water to the boil to cover the bird. Set the oven at 180°C/Gas 4.

Keeping the vegetables in their pan, drain every little bit of oil from the pan, otherwise you will only have to do it later. Now return the chicken to the pan with the pearl barley, then tuck in all the herbs except the parsley and pour over the hot water. Season with salt and some black pepper. Now slice the potatoes the thickness of pound coins – I really think there is no need to peel them – and lay them over the top of the chicken and vegetables. Some will inevitably sink; others will sit on top, the water just lapping at their edges.

Cover with a lid and place in the oven for an hour and a half, by which time the chicken and vegetables will be meltingly tender. Remove the lid, turn up the heat to 200°C/Gas 6 and leave for thirty minutes for the potatoes to colour here and there. Remove very carefully from the oven – the pan will be full and very hot – then scrape off any floating oil from the top. Chop the parsley and sink it into the broth. Taste the broth and adjust the seasoning with a grinding of salt and pepper.

Spoon the chicken, vegetables, barley and plenty of the broth into shallow bowls, scatter with flakes of sea salt and pass round the pepper mill.

and more

◆ **the point of the leeks.** The inclusion of both leeks and onions here is not an oversight. The leeks are tougher and play the part of a vegetable; the onions act as an aromatic, virtually collapsing into the broth.

◆ **a lamb supper.** Do try this soup-stew with lamb instead of chicken. You will get a bit more fat to remove from the broth, of course, but the lamb, falling from its bones, has a truly homely, nannying quality to it. Choose a bony cut, such as neck chops, and ask the butcher to cut them thick, so everyone gets a big wedge of meat.

◆ **and a duck one.** This would be good made with duck, too. If you can bear the endless task of spooning off all the fat, that is.

◆ **a guinea fowl supper.** I sometimes pick up a guinea fowl instead – it's not that I could ever get bored with chicken, it is simply for a change. The broth becomes slightly richer from its gamier flesh, though the preparation is exactly as above.

really juicy, spicy meatballs

Do you ever get an urge for food that is deeply savoury, citrus and fiery? I find the pork, lime leaves and chillies that are so much a part of Thai and Vietnamese cooking will usually do the trick in some form or another. The citrus and chillies turn up in noodle soups, but sometimes the savour I want can only come from meat. You know that point when meat is truly aromatic with red chillies, garlic, lemon grass or lime leaves and is cooked in such a way that its edges caramelise and form a sweet, jammy crust? These meatballs, which I often drop into a savoury chicken broth, may well be what you are after.

smoked bacon or pancetta – a handful or so
minced pork – 500g
groundnut oil – a little for frying

For the seasoning:
onions – either a couple of shallots or 4 small spring onions
chillies – 3 or 4 small, hot red chillies
coriander – a small bunch
lime leaves or lemon grass – 4 lime leaves or 2 thick stalks of lemon grass
garlic – 3 or 4 cloves, peeled and crushed

Chop the shallots or spring onions finely, then chop the chillies even finer, first removing the seeds if you don't like things too hot. I leave them in. Scrub the roots of the coriander and chop them and the leaves finely, discarding the stems. Roll the lime leaves up and shred them finely, then chop them; if you are using lemon grass, remove the coarse outer leaves and discard them, then chop the tender inside leaves very thinly. All of this can be done in a food processor.

Chop the bacon or pancetta and add it, with the seasoning above, to the minced pork. Mix in a good pinch of salt, then cover with clingfilm (otherwise it will taint everything in your fridge) and leave to rest and chill for half an hour or more.

Shape the seasoned pork into small balls. The size is up to you. If you flatten them slightly you will get more of that delectable savoury crust when you fry them. I tend to start with a ball of mince the size of a walnut in its shell, then flatten it slightly.

To cook them you will need to warm a little oil in a heavy frying pan, then lay the meatballs in – without crowding them – and let them colour enticingly on both sides before turning the heat down a bit and letting them cook all the way through. You should find them done after four or five minutes. Test one by breaking it open: the centre should be juicy but not especially pink.

and more

♦ **a European version.** Perhaps you are after something equally savoury but without the chilli rush.

smoked bacon or pancetta – a handful or so
minced pork – 500g
groundnut oil – a little for frying

For the seasoning:
garlic – a couple of plump and juicy cloves, peeled and crushed
fontina – or other easy melting cheese such as Gruyère, roughly diced
lemon – the grated zest of 1 medium-sized unwaxed
thyme – a palmful of leaves, chopped

Make and cook the balls as above.

♦ **meatballs in a hot, refreshing broth.** A hot, herbal, citrus-chilli supper. One of my favourite things to eat involves serving the Thai-inspired meatballs in a hot, herb-scented chicken broth. You will need some good chicken stock – about a large cupful per person and I really think it should be home-made but I suppose bought stuff will do (sometimes it just has to). Bring it to the boil with a smashed stalk of lemon grass or a couple of lime leaves and a couple of chopped red chillies, then let it simmer for a few minutes whilst you fry the meatballs. Drop them into a deep soup bowl, strain over the fragrant, piping hot stock, then stir in some chopped mint leaves and some basil or coriander.

♦ **and in a mild, consoling one.** If you have made the Euro-version with cheese and thyme, you can still turn the meatballs into a substantial soup-supper by using the same chicken broth but flavoured with lots of chopped, vivid green parsley instead of the lemon grass and chillies.

a sausage and mash supper

It is worth pinpointing the heart and soul of a dish, otherwise the whole thing never quite hits the spot and, frankly, you might as well not have bothered. Sausage and mash is one of the great suppers of all time, but the more I cook it the more I have come to realise that the crucial part is neither the sausages nor the potatoes but the accompanying puddle of dark, oniony, mustard-freckled gravy to squash into your mound of mash. What at first appears to be just a bonus is in fact what brings the whole dish together. You can add anything that works naturally with pork to the basic gravy: mustard, juniper berries, chopped thyme or sage leaves, fennel seeds or anything else aniseedy such as Chinese five-spice powder. Best of all, in terms of lusciousness and savour, is to cook the sausages in the gravy.

butter – for mashing the potatoes and for softening the onions in (or use dripping
    for this, if you prefer)
sausages – the herby butcher's type, about 2 or 3 plump ones each
onions – a medium-to-large one per person
seasoning – 1 or 2 only of: juniper berries, thyme leaves, fennel seeds,
    bay leaves
flour – a tablespoon or two for thickening the gravy
booze to enrich the gravy – a wine glass of Marsala
stock – from a cube if you like; about 250ml should be enough to feed 4
Dijon mustard
floury potatoes – 2 or 3 medium ones per person

Melt a little butter in a thick-bottomed roasting tin set over a moderate heat – you need enough butter just to cover the bottom – then add the sausages. The fat that seeps from them should stop the butter burning, but keep the heat quite gentle. Let them colour lightly, turning them over now and again. The laws of nature will ensure that they won't brown evenly on all sides. As they cook, peel the onions, halve them, then cut each half into about six wedges. Now remove the browned sausages from the tin and add the onions. Let them cook slowly in the butter and sausage fat, shoving them round the pan from time to time to stop them burning, until they are soft and deep gold. They should be soft enough to squash between your fingers. Expect this to take about twenty minutes. Set the oven at 180°C/Gas 4.

Now add the seasonings: I suggest eight or ten juniper berries, lightly crushed, or a small palmful of chopped thyme leaves or a teaspoon of fennel seeds. Bay leaves will work with any of them. Turn up the heat so that the onions brown quickly and sprinkle in a little flour. A tablespoon or two should be enough. Let it cook for a minute or so, moving the onions round the pan so they do not burn (though they do need to colour deeply), then pour in the Marsala and stock and let it come to the boil. As you stir, you will see the gravy thicken. Now season it with a little salt, some black pepper (unless the sausages are very peppery) and a tablespoon (or more if you like) of Dijon mustard. Return the sausages to the gravy and place in the oven. They are ready when they are cooked right through, with a little hint of pink, and the gravy is thick, glossy and bubbling. The timing, as always, will depend on the type and thickness of the sausages, the variety of onions (I could go on) but you are looking at about forty minutes.

Meanwhile, peel the potatoes and boil them in salted water until they are tender to the point of a knife. Drain and mash them with a little butter (you need a thick slice or so, but no more), then serve with the sausages and their gravy. The joyous bit comes as you squash the potatoes into the gravy through the tines of your fork.

and more

♦ **sausages with parsnip mash.** Try changing the potato mash for the parsnip one on page 283.

♦ **and with other booze.** Use red wine or Madeira instead of the Marsala, or miss it out altogether.

♦ **and with garlic.** Add crushed or sliced garlic to the onions, allowing one clove per person.

an appetite for
fruit

warm, tender fruit for dessert or breakfast

A bowl of poached fruit is an incredibly useful thing to have around in summer. Glowing in their scented syrup, poached peaches, apricots or plums are an elegant end to a summer dinner and can be finished off for breakfast the following day. Cold from the fridge, they are sweetly refreshing, especially if you go easy on the sugar in the syrup.

The light syrup – which is nothing more than sugar and water – will take on some of the flavour of the fruit, but it can also be flavoured with anything you fancy. I don't see the point of those recipes that include everything in the cupboard – ginger, vanilla, lemon and orange zest, coriander seeds, rose water, honey and cinnamon. One flavouring is quite enough. The apricots and peaches of high summer will benefit from something citrus, while late-summer plums will also take a warmer flavouring such as cinnamon or ginger. Before you use any strong, herbal flavours, it is worth remembering that you may be eating the leftovers for breakfast.

Enough for 4

sugar – about 90g
water
flavourings – either long strips of lemon or orange zest; a vanilla pod;
**   a few coins of ginger root; a few lime leaves; a split and**
**   squashed stalk of lemon grass; or a cinnamon stick**
fruit – about 6 peaches or 12 plums or apricots or 500g damsons

The amount of sugar you put in your poaching syrup is a matter of taste but I suggest put enough sugar into a casserole or sauté pan to cover the bottom, then pour over roughly four times as much water. Let it dissolve over a low heat, then taste a little from a teaspoon, letting it cool before you do so. Too sweet? Add more water. Not sweet enough? Add some more sugar. Once the sugar has dissolved, it is time to introduce the flavourings and the fruit. Put your chosen flavouring into the syrup. I use about six lime leaves but it could be anything from the list above. Bring the syrup to the boil. Slice the peaches, plums or apricots in half, removing the stones if they come easily and leave the damsons whole.

Lower them into the boiling syrup, then turn down the heat so that the syrup is bubbling gently and let the fruit cook until it is tender to the point of a knife – a matter of just fifteen minutes or so. Lift the fruit out into a dish or platter, then turn the heat up under the syrup and let it boil furiously till it starts to thicken slightly. It needs to be thick enough to coat the fruit and form a puddle around it. Serve warm or thoroughly chilled. You need no cream.

and more

♦ **a baked version.** I think you should avoid suggestions to drizzle brandy or vanilla on baked fruit. The heady fragrance of warm, lightly sweetened fruit is all you need.

rhubarb, apricots, peaches, nectarines, figs
sugar

Rinse the fruit and prepare it. In the case of peaches, nectarines and apricots, this will mean stoning them. Rhubarb will need cutting into short lengths. Place the fruit in a baking dish and scatter a little sugar over, the amount depending on the type and ripeness of your fruit. Bake at 220°C/Gas 8 till the fruit is completely tender and plump with juice. The timing will, of course, vary but you should allow about twenty minutes for rhubarb and figs and slightly less for very ripe stone fruits.

♦ **baked rhubarb with orange and lychees.** An unusual-sounding mixture, I know (though not quite so strange when I tell you that rhubarb originated in China), but divinely fragrant. The taste will be pure and clean and you will need nothing in the way of cream. I use twice as much rhubarb as lychees and find that 500g rhubarb is more than enough for four. Trim and cut up the rhubarb, then pile it into a baking dish, sprinkle with sugar (three or four tablespoons per 500g should probably be enough for early-season rhubarb) and tuck in the peeled lychees. Squeeze over the juice of an orange or two and bake at 180°C/Gas 4 for forty minutes or so. Eat warm rather than hot, though it is even better next day, for breakfast.

a fruit and cream dessert for summer

No matter how much care we take over choosing perfect, seasonal fruit with which to finish a summer meal, some people always expect something more. They expect us to have made an effort. This quintessentially English fool never fails to please those who insist on pudding and is hardly what you might call work. I don't go along with the traditional complications of custard or liqueurs. My fools are simply crushed summer fruit and cream. Sometimes the fruit is raw, as in the case of heady, claret-coloured raspberries or lusciously ripe mango. Other times it is cooked with a little sugar – say, when I am using damsons or gooseberries. The richness is up to you and depends on how much cream you add to the crushed fruit.

Enough for 6

fruit – gooseberries, rhubarb, blackcurrants, 500g (for stone fruits
   such as damsons, 1kg)
sugar – the amount depending on the sweetness of your fruit
cream – double or whipping, 300ml

Check the fruit over, removing any leaves or stems, then put it into a stainless steel saucepan (acid fruits react with aluminium), adding as much sugar as you think fit – 500g tart cooking gooseberries usually need about three or four tablespoons or so. Damsons about the same. Let the fruit stew with the sugar over a low heat, slowly coming to the boil. You shouldn't need any water if the heat is low enough to start with. As the fruits warm, they will burst their skins and the sugar will melt, giving probably too much juice. Strain this off through a sieve and use it on your breakfast muesli or over a sponge cake or vanilla ice-cream.

Push the fruit that remains through the sieve with a spoon to give a thick slush. Let this cool and then chill it. Don't try, as I have done more times than I care to remember, to skip the chilling. You will end up with a smoothie.

Pour the cream into a large bowl and whisk until it thickens. It should be thick enough to keep its shape but should not really stand in peaks. Fold the chilled fruit into the cream, slowly, firmly, purposefully. Spoon into glasses – they can be quite pretty for this – and chill thoroughly.

and more

♦ **the cream, its consistency and quantity.** I shall say now that the consistency of the cream in a fool is absolutely crucial. Overwhip it and you have a grainy mess; underwhip and you have fruit soup. What I think you should aim for is cream that is just, and only just, thick enough to hold itself in a soft mound without sliding back to a level pool. The cream should sit rather than being able to stand. It should not be stiff enough to stand in a peak, though if you have taken it that far you will probably get away with it. Think of your bowl of whipped cream as looking like gently rolling hills rather than Annapurna. You will find it much easier to whip it in a cold bowl, so put the bowl, the cream, even the whisk, in the fridge first. Then whisk slowly and firmly till the cream shows signs of thickening – it will feel heavy on the whisk.

There is no correct ratio of cream to fruit. The quantity of cream you will need depends not just on what type of fruit you are using, or even how ripe that fruit may be, but on how creamy you like your fools. I like gooseberry, mango and rhubarb fools to be obscenely creamy, whilst I prefer my damson and raspberry versions to be less so, probably to make the most of the inherent sharpness of the fruit.

♦ **a raspberry fool.** Reckon on roughly equal amounts of fruit to cream, in other words a small bowl of raspberries and a small bowl of cream; 250g raspberries and 250ml cream will feed four. This fool is more beautiful if you only just crush the raspberries so that there is some texture to the finished dessert and the red and white look like an old-fashioned raspberry ripple. I suggest you use a fork rather than a sieve.

♦ **a passion fruit version.** Wonderful in summer but somehow even more welcome when the days are grey. You will need an equal amount of pulp to cream, so tip the cream into a bowl and use the carton as a measure for the passion fruit seeds and juice (sieve out most, though not all, of the seeds, pushing them through a small nylon sieve with the back of a spoon), then fold the thin, intensely flavoured juice into the cream. I reckon on about ten fruits to 300ml cream. Taste as you go, adding a little sugar if you think it needs it.

a summer pudding

People make such a fuss about summer pudding: the quality of the bread, the size to which it is cut and the volume of the dish, not to mention the fist-fights over the ratio of currants to berries. Add a handful of strawberries and you are likely to be lynched. The fact is that summer pudding is simply bread soaked in the sweetened juice of summer fruits. The mix of raspberries, redcurrants and blackcurrants is entirely personal. I like an equal mix of redcurrants and raspberries with a handful of blackcurrants for extra tartness and for their gorgeous colour. I see no reason why we have to make the thing stand on ceremony. Its layers of scarlet, juice-saturated bread and crushed berries are divine whatever their shape, so I make mine in a shallow gratin dish and forget all the pomp. The important thing is simply that there is sufficient juice.

Enough for 6

raspberries, redcurrants and blackcurrants – about 850g
sugar
a white loaf

Finger through the berries and currants, removing any leaves and stalks, then rinse the fruit under running water. Tip it all into a stainless steel saucepan. You will need some sugar to sweeten the currants and to help make the juice. The amount will depend on your taste but it needs to be enough to coat the fruit; I suggest a good 100g. So that there will be plenty of juice you also need to add water – a tumbler full should be enough. Bring the berries to the boil. It is the currants' juice we are after, so let them all burst, giving up a rich, purple-red liquor. This usually takes about three or four minutes.

Meanwhile, cut thin slices from the loaf and pull off the crusts. Layer the bread with the fruit in a shallow dish. The quantity of bread depends on how much juice the berries have given out. It doesn't matter whether you end with bread or fruit. The crucial point is that the bread should be soaked, absolutely saturated, in scarlet juice. Just carry on layering till the juice is used up. The bread will continue to soak up the juice as the dish cools, so make sure there is a pool of juice on top of the last layer.

Leave to chill in the fridge for an hour or so, by which time it will have set a little. Cream, offered in the old-fashioned way in a jug, is essential.

and more

♦ **with frozen fruit.** Summer pudding works perfectly well with frozen fruit, no matter what anyone says.

♦ **an autumn pudding.** When soft fruits are over for the year, use some of the tiny golden mirabelle plums or damsons that follow. Cook them with a little sugar until their juices flow, then continue as above. Remove as many of the niggling little stones as you have patience for.

♦ **as a compote.** Forget the bread and eat the warm fruits and their juice with sponge cake and cream.

a really great trifle

Trifle should, I think, be a soft mound of sponge, cream, custard, alcohol and fruit. Nothing should interfere with its general creaminess, nor would I like anyone to try and temper its indulgence. A trifle is as wantonly extravagant a dessert as you can get and I would never attempt to lessen that. A spoonful of trifle should be a moment of unbridled self-indulgence, and I always make mine with that in mind. I don't like jelly, because it meddles with the voluptuousness of it all. You could make your own sponge (for which you might like to turn to page 431) and your own custard too (page 190), or you could do it the way I most often do it – that is, with a cheap raspberry jam Swiss roll for the cake layer and that ready-made custard you can buy from the chiller cabinets in supermarkets.

Enough for 6

sponge cake – about 200g
sweet wine – Vin Santo, orange muscat
double cream – 300ml
custard – 250ml
raspberries – a couple of good handfuls,
**   plus strawberries, blueberries etc to scatter**

Crumble the sponge cake into rough lumps and put them into a large dish or six smaller ones. Pour over enough sweet wine to soak it thoroughly.

Pour the cream into a cold mixing bowl and whisk it slowly. The consistency is crucial if the trifle is to be perfect. You want it to be thick enough to stand in soft folds, thin enough to almost slide off a spoon unaided. I find this easier when both the cream and the mixing bowl are very cold. Stir half the whipped cream into the custard.

Whiz the berries in a blender or mash them to a purée with a fork. They should be almost at pouring consistency; if not, then add a splash of mineral water. Drizzle most of the purée over the sponge cake. Spoon the custard over the sponge too, letting it fall lazily over the cake to merge somewhat with the puddle of crushed raspberries. Spoon the remaining cream over the top, then scatter over some whole berries and finish with a drizzle of raspberry sauce.

and more

♦ **some other good things.** I once had an anonymous letter from someone berating my suggestion of putting bananas in a trifle (it must surely prove my point about the tyranny of recipes that the writer felt they had to hide their identity in order to disagree). I still put them in my trifle, at least I do sometimes. There is something so nannying about the marriage of bananas and custard. I also have a few other suggestions:

♦ **if you use macaroons or ratafia biscuits instead of cake,** give them a good while to soak up the liquid so that they are soft.

♦ **use blueberries, loganberries, blackberries and golden raspberries** instead of the raspberries.

♦ **try a purée of cooked gooseberries,** sweetened with quite a bit of sugar and thoroughly chilled, in place of the raspberry sauce.

♦ **alternatively, whiz a can of apricots in a blender,** sharpening them with a squeeze of lemon juice.

♦ **sprinkle chopped pistachios or toasted flaked almonds** on top of the finished trifle.

♦ **an orange and lemon trifle.** Soak the sponge cake (which could be one with orange zest in it) in sweet wine mixed with a dash of limoncello or mandarin liqueur (you can buy miniatures of these). Mix half the cream into the custard as before but mix the second half with a few spoonfuls of real lemon curd. Use strawberries or blueberries and perhaps some segments of pink grapefruit and mandarin instead of the raspberries.

♦ **a summer berry trifle.** The raspberry and redcurrant filling for the summer pudding on page 391 will add a thoroughly welcome sharpness to the mixture of sponge, custard and cream. No need to add any extra berries, though some flaked almonds, toasted till golden brown, wouldn't go amiss.

♦ **a coffee and chocolate trifle.** Soak the sponge in sweet Marsala, then pour over a cup or two of sweetened espresso. Mix the cream and custard as above and top with the second layer of softly whipped cream and a thick dusting of cocoa powder.

an appetite for
pastry

a thin, crisp fruit tart

There are, I would venture, fewer more tempting sights than a baking tray of crisp, flaky fruit tarts fresh out of the oven. If you make your own pastry (and why not, if you have the time and the patience?) they will be sublime, but even with shop-bought puff pastry they are pretty fine. The trick is to roll the pastry as thin as you dare and bake them in a very hot oven. To get them at their most pleasurable, eat them warm, with cream or vanilla ice-cream, so you get a mouthful of crisp, hot pastry, luscious fruit and cold ice-cream all at once.

Enough for 6

puff pastry – a 340g pack of defrosted pastry or a 425g pack of ready rolled
apples – 4 fairly tart dessert ones
butter – a thick slice, melted
caster sugar – just a little

Get the oven really hot. I set mine at 230°C/Gas 8. Roll the pastry out as thin as you can without actually being able to see through it. If the tarts are to be really crisp and flaky, the pastry should be no thicker than a pound coin. If you have bought ready-rolled puff pastry, then you need to roll it out just a little more.

Using a large saucer or small side plate as a template, cut out six discs of pastry. Using something smaller – a cup, say – score a slightly smaller circle within each one so that you have a small rim. This will rise and hold in the apples. Slide the pieces of pastry on to a baking sheet, then prick the centre circles of pastry all over with a fork, which will stop them puffing up too much in the oven and throwing the apples off.

Peel the apples, cut them into quarters and carve out their cores, then slice them thinly. Arrange the apple slices on the pastry discs. I like to do this in rather formal overlapping circles but it is up to you. Brush the apples and pastry with melted butter, then dust them with a fine layer of sugar – anything more generous would make the finished tarts too sweet. Bake them until the pastry is golden and is fully crisp underneath, about ten to fifteen minutes. Cool slightly before eating.

and more

♦ **leftover pastry.** Parsimonious cooks will no doubt want to use the scraps of leftover pastry. My suggestion is to brush them with melted butter and dust them with grated Parmesan, then bake as above and eat while still hot and crisp. Frankly, I don't bother. We are only talking about a few scraps of pastry.

♦ **a large apple tart.** There is something rather territorial about having your own individual fruit tart. If you would prefer one large one to put on the table and cut up between your friends, then use one sheet of ready-rolled puff pastry, score a thin border around the edge, prick the centre and lay overlapping slices of apple, as thin as you can cut them, all over. Brush with melted butter, sprinkle with sugar and bake as above.

♦ **a cheese and apple tart.** When you have brushed the tarts above with the butter, scatter a fine layer of finely grated Parmesan over them and bake as above. Neither a starter nor a pudding, this. More of a snack, really.

♦ **pear tarts.** Pears can produce the finest tarts of all, possessing a lusciousness that apples lack. The trick is to cook the fruit slightly beforehand so its flesh is soft and juicy. This is easy. Make up enough sugar syrup to cover the peeled, halved and cored pears (just put the pears in a pan, cover them with water and tip in a cupful of sugar), then simmer them till they are tender to the point of a knife. Lift them out, drain them briefly, then slice thinly and overlap the slices on the pastry. Brush them with some of the sugar syrup, then bake as above.

♦ **a banana tart.** Cut out and prick the tarts as above. Cut six bananas into slices as thick as pound coins, then divide them between the pastries. Brush them, and the pastry edges, with melted butter and sprinkle with sugar. After ten minutes or so in the oven, brush the tarts with melted apricot jam, then return them to the oven for a few minutes more. Eat hot, offering everyone the cream jug or a ball of vanilla ice.

♦ **apricot tarts.** Crisp pastry and juicy fruit. Use tinned apricots, or halve, stone and poach some fresh ones yourself in a little sugar and water. Drain them well, then lay them on the pastry cut side up and bake till the edges are just caught and the pastry is crisp. Since they are so heavy with juice, you may find you need neither ice-cream nor cream here. They are rich enough as it is.

402

a warm and crumbly fruit tart

With friends due for lunch you sometimes need a pudding that will hold good-naturedly in a warm state until you are ready for it. This is that pudding. It will also take a bit of reheating, the edges becoming delectably chewy and the fruit charring enticingly here and there.

Enough for 6–8

fruit – plums, about 10, or apples or pears, about 7 or 8
butter – 75g
sugar – 6 tablespoons

For the pastry:
butter – 120g, cold from the fridge
plain flour – 200g
egg yolks – 1
sugar – either caster or icing, 2 tablespoons

You will need a heavy, solid-bottomed metal pie dish or baking tin for this, around 25cm in diameter. I have used a metal-handled frying pan before now and it worked a treat.

To make the pastry, cut the butter into small chunks and rub it into the flour with your fingertips. Stop when the mixture resembles coarse breadcrumbs. Drop in the egg yolk and sugar and push the ingredients together to form a ball of soft dough. You may sometimes need a little water to achieve this, though it will only be a tablespoon or so. Much will depend on your flour. You can do this whole job in a food processor if you are short of time or have no need of the pleasure that comes from making pastry by hand, in which case it will be done in seconds. Flatten the pastry somewhat, wrap it in greaseproof or clingfilm and put in the fridge. This will allow it to rest.

Heat the oven to 190°C/Gas 5. Peel the apples or pears, cut them into quarters and remove their cores. If you are using plums, simply halve and stone them. Put the metal pie dish, baking tin or frying pan over a low heat and let the butter and sugar melt in it until they form a rich, honey-hued caramel. I think it worth mentioning that the caramel is likely to burn very easily at this point. Turn off the heat and push the fruit, cut side up, into the caramel.

Roll the pastry out so that it fits the top of the tin. I can never find a rolling pin and tend to do this with the nearest wine bottle. Lift the pastry up and place it over the fruit, patching any holes – I find they are inevitable – as you go. Tuck the edges in between the fruit and the tin and place the tart in the oven, where you should leave it until the pastry is deep golden brown and the caramel and fruit juices are bubbling around the edge. This will take the best part of an hour but start checking after forty-five minutes. You want the pastry to be soft and crumbly, the fruit caught here and there with burnt caramel. Let the tart cool for a few minutes before you turn it out.

and more

♦ **getting it out.** Let the tart cool in its tin for fifteen minutes or so. This will give the hot juices time to settle. Place a large plate over the tart and, fully armed with oven gloves, quickly turn the whole thing over, holding the plate and tart firmly. The tart should slip out on to the plate. Beware the hot juices.

♦ **getting the fruit to caramelise.** The whole point of this way of cooking a tart is to caramelise the fruit so that it turns appetisingly black here and there. It is worth remembering that this is easier with apples and pears than it is with fruits that produce a lot of juice, such as plums or rhubarb.

♦ **a rhubarb tart.** This is a good way to use up the dark red stalks at the end of the season. The tart won't brown properly because of the vast amount of juice the fruit produces – and which you will need to watch when you turn it out – but the tart fruit marries beautifully with the sweet, crumbly pastry.

♦ **a version with quinces.** A delicately fragrant alternative and as beautiful as a rose, but you will need to poach the halved and cored fruit in sugar syrup for a good hour first.

♦ **on the side.** Traditionally a pottery bowl of crème fraîche is offered here. While there is nothing wrong with this, I do think a jug of double cream, sweet and yellow, is somehow more appropriate.

a hot fruit pie

I had assumed that making a pie was a complete hassle. Until I tried it. It is simply a question of peeling a few apples, piling them into a dish and covering them with short, buttery pastry – I reckon half an hour's work at the most before it goes in the oven.

Enough for 4, and you will need a jug of cream to pour over

Bramley or other tart apples – 3 large ones
blackberries – a handful or two should be enough, but add more or less as you wish
caster sugar
shortcrust pastry – as in the recipe on page 189
milk – just a little to dampen the pastry

You will need an ovenproof pie dish of some sort. It should have a wide rim and be large enough to hold a litre of water. It can be round or oval; a square one would need a bit more pastry. Set the oven at 200°C/Gas 6.

Peel and quarter the apples, cut out the cores and chop the fruit into large chunks, then put them into the pie dish. Add a double handful of blackberries and toss them with the apples and a sprinkling of sugar. Taste the apples to gauge how much sugar you will need. I add just a dusting because I like the tartness of cooking apples; others may prefer anything up to a tablespoon or two per apple.

Roll the pastry out to fit the top of the pie dish. Wet the rim of the dish with a little milk and lay the pastry over the fruit, pushing the edges down on to the wet rim. Cut a small hole in the middle of the pie so that the pastry does not split as it cooks, then brush the top of the pie with milk and sprinkle some more sugar over it. Bake in the hot oven until the crust is golden and crisp, about forty to forty-five minutes.

and more

♦ **the best of all.** No matter what fancy pâtisserie people come up with, you will never have a more appreciative audience than when you produce a home-made pie. Of course, blackberry and apple is just for starters. I just think it happens to be the best pie of all, probably because of the nostalgia quotient.

♦ **how much sugar?** Whichever fruit you choose, the first thing is to taste it. It is only by doing so – even if you have chosen rhubarb – that you can tell how much sugar you will need. Damsons, gooseberries and rhubarb will need more than sweet, ripe plums for instance. But the plums will vary too. This is why strict instructions are pointless when it comes to sweetening and seasoning. So much depends on the ripeness and variety of the fruit.

♦ **a rhubarb pie.** Rhubarb makes a glorious spring alternative. Fill the pie dish above the top so that the chopped fruit stands in a mound, sprinkle with a handful of sugar and cover. You don't need to cook the fruit first. You will end up with lots of sweet-sour pink juice, too.

♦ **a gooseberry pie.** Come summer, make a gooseberry pie, piling them into the dish, sprinkling unsparingly with sugar, then adding a glug of elderflower cordial or a sprig of elderflowers.

♦ **and a damson one.** Damsons make a staggeringly beautiful pie, the royal purple juice dramatically staining the pastry. You will need to pile them high, unstoned (there's nothing left if you stone a damson), and will probably need quite a bit more sugar than for the apple pie.

♦ **a plum pie.** Plums, greengages and mirabelles have the advantage of producing lots of juice under the crust. Be generous with the sugar here, too. The big question is whether to stone the plums or not. I usually cut one in half, twist it, and if the stone comes out easily, then I do the lot. If the plum just squashes in my hand, then I forget it and just tell everyone they have to spit the stones out. I sometimes think they add more flavour but I could be imagining it.

♦ **a pie all to oneself.** You don't necessarily need a pie dish. I didn't buy one until a couple of years ago. Thick breakfast cups (they need to be ovenproof) can be used instead. They take longer – you have four crusts to seal rather than one – but they look charming, and everyone gets to eat their own little pie.

an appetite for
pudding

Ice-cream

The only thing, with the exception of ice cubes and a bag of peas, I think it is worth having a deep-freeze for. A tub of ice-cream will get you out of all sorts of messes – the children who arrive home unexpectedly with friends; the forgotten dinner-party dessert; the sudden, raging urge for something at midnight; the ultimate bribe for getting children to do what you want; and, of course, the tub that sometimes finds its way into your bedroom.

It is as dessert that ice-cream is at its most indispensable. I have never met anyone who doesn't like it, though I know a few who refuse it because of its effect on their hips, thighs or tummy. Frankly, I am willing to go that extra length in the swimming pool just so I can have a second ball of it. Let's face it, we are talking about a half-litre tub of cream and sugar here.

I regularly bring ice-cream out after dinner without apology. It is not that I can't be bothered to make a pudding, it is simply that, with the exception of home-made pie, there are few things so universally appreciated. There is also the no small matter that such an end to a meal can take some of the pressure off the cook. Sometimes people seem almost relieved that you have gone to so little trouble.

You need a decent ice-cream, of course, and I am sure you know the names as well as I do. Do try some of the British-made organic ones if you haven't yet. Don't be tempted to get flashy, just put the tubs of ice-cream on the table with a scoop and a heap of things to scatter over and let everyone help themselves.

Some good things to offer with vanilla ice-cream:

♦ **crumbled amaretti** in their pretty tissue and a bottle of sweet Marsala to up-end.

♦ **shavings of bitter chocolate** (use a potato peeler).

♦ **strawberries** that you have left to marinate in passion fruit juice and chopped mint.

♦ **a big bowl of Smarties** or broken-up chocolate flakes.

♦ **chopped-up chocolate truffles** (use a warm knife).

♦ **steaming-hot espresso** to pour over.

♦ **melted dark chocolate or hot chocolate sauce.**

♦ **a bottle of rose water,** some dried rose petals and some chopped pistachios (you need barely a teaspoon of each to imbue a heavenly scent of the Middle East).

♦ **or try this hot butterscotch sauce.** Put 50g butter and 100g each of soft brown sugar and golden syrup into a small pan and bring to a rolling boil. Turn it down and let it bubble gently for four or five minutes. Add a few drops of really good vanilla extract, then pour in 150ml double cream. Tip into a cool jug, where it will thicken somewhat as it cools.

♦ **in summer you might like to put a bowl of berries on the table.** When the sun is shining, you may find there is little more welcome than a bowl of ice-cream and summer fruits such as peaches with lemon juice; loganberries or blackberries; or apricots that you have poached in orange juice and a little honey, scented with a drop of orange blossom water and strewn with chopped pistachios.

♦ **a quick home-made ice-cream.** Home-made fruit ices can have a sensational clarity of flavour. Anyone who fancies making their own might like to pick up a copy of my book, *Real Food*, which has a dozen or more recipes (this is not a blatant plug, it is just that there are some seriously good ice-cream recipes in there) or try this particularly easy and refreshing ice:

♦ **a passion fruit cream ice.** Make a syrup by dissolving 125g sugar in 250ml water over heat, then letting it cool thoroughly. No need to boil or simmer, just whip it off the heat once the sugar has dissolved. Cut 20 passion fruit in half and squeeze the seeds and pulp from half of them into a small sieve, pushing the pulp through so all that is left are dry seeds. Discard the seeds and add the juice to the syrup. Squeeze the remaining fruit straight in so you get some of the crunchy seeds in it. Stir in 200ml crème fraîche or thick yoghurt, then tip into a freezer box and freeze until ice crystals form around the edge – about an hour. Stir them into the middle and return to the freezer, stirring every hour until frozen. It should be ready after a further three hours and enough for six.

a rib-sticking pudding for a cold day

Occasionally, and I concede it is only once or twice a year, I get the urge for a rib-sticking, heart-warming suet pudding. Olive oil may now be on everyone's lips but I think the cooking of the cold northern hemisphere is still etched deep in our souls. It will be the depths of winter, of course, and probably when there is someone coming to lunch who is old enough to understand that a handful of suet between six people is not going to bring on instant cardiac arrest.

Suet pastry is the most straightforward of pastries. It takes two minutes flat. As with almost all sweet baking, you will need to use the scales. A truly sweet, sticky, fruit-filled joy, for which you will need a jug of cream.

Enough for 6

apples – Bramleys are probably best, about 1kg
juice of a lemon
mincemeat – about 8 tablespoons

For the suet pastry:
self-raising flour – 200g
grated suet – 100g of ready-shredded beef suet or the vegetable variety
water – a little

You will also need a buttered 1-litre pudding basin, some greaseproof paper, tin foil or muslin and some string.

Peel the apples, core them and cut them into thick wedges. Toss them with the lemon juice. For the pastry, put the flour into a mixing bowl, add a pinch of salt and the suet, then pour in enough water to make a stiff dough. This is usually about 6 tablespoons but the amount will vary somewhat according to the flour you use. Your dough should be soft but not sticky.

Shape the pastry into a short, thick sausage. Cut thin slices from the dough and press them on to the bottom and sides of the buttered pudding basin so that the entire area is covered, leaving enough dough to roll out for a lid.

Mix the apples with the mincemeat, then pile them into the lined pudding basin. Roll or pat out the remaining dough to fit the top of the basin. Wet the edge of the pastry – you can use water but a bit of mincemeat is even more effective – and press the edges together so that the apples are sealed in the pastry.

Cut a piece of greaseproof paper to fit the top of the basin, ample enough for some of it to hang over the edge, and butter one side of it. Fold a pleat into the paper so that it will not tear when the dough expands. Lay the folded paper butter-side down over the top of the pudding, then cover with tin foil or muslin and tie it securely. I use string and a rubber band.

Bring a large, deep pan of water to the boil and lower the pudding gently into it so that the water comes about a third of the way up the pudding basin. Any deeper and it will bubble over the top. Cover tightly with a lid and leave to steam for a good two hours, until well risen, topping up with water if it needs it. You can turn the pudding out if you wish, though it will taste just as good spooned from the basin.

and more

- ♦ **a marmalade pudding.** Marmalade makes a really good substitute for the mincemeat, and I suspect damson or blackcurrant jam would, too.

- ♦ **a pear pudding, or rather not.** Don't bother trying this recipe with pears, they don't fluff up enough during cooking, though you could substitute dessert apples. They will just be less juicy.

- ♦ **dispensing with the laborious bit.** You can buy heatproof plastic pudding basins with clip-on lids if you prefer, dispensing with the need for greaseproof paper, muslin and the elusive ball of string. Clean and easy, yes, but somehow I feel the wonderfully Victorian process of swaddling the pudding in snow-white muslin is part of the satisfaction of making such a pudding.

- ♦ **a vegetarian version.** A lot of people swear by real beef suet for this sort of pastry. To be honest, I have found little difference in the finished pudding whether I have used real suet, ready-prepared suet from a packet or the vegetarian alternative. The choice is yours.

a sponge pudding with its own sauce

I believe passionately in the power of sweet, homely puddings to cure all manner of ills. Warm, nannying, becalming. Tucking into a dairy-rich hot pudding is, I am sure, the adult version of breastfeeding. To have some such pudding recipes to hand can prove endlessly useful, especially the good-natured ones like this, where a few grams either way matters less than is usual with baking. I am not sure you will want anything too sturdy to precede this, unless you are in the depths of winter.

Enough for 6

butter – 100g
caster sugar – 175g
lemon – 1
oranges – 2 medium-sized fruit
eggs – 4
plain flour – 40g
milk – 400ml

Cream the butter and sugar together until they are light and fluffy and the colour of finest double cream. It is easiest to do this is in a food mixer, though you could do it by hand if your butter is soft and you are feeling athletic. Set the oven at 180°C/Gas 4.

Grate the zest from the lemon, making sure that none of the bitter white pith underneath comes with it, then cut the fruit in half and squeeze the juice. Do the same with the oranges.

Separate the eggs and add the yolks to the creamed butter and sugar. The mixture will curdle but I wouldn't let it worry you. Now add the flour and milk alternately, the mixer on slow to medium, so you end up with a soft, cake-like batter. Stir in the orange and lemon zest and then the juice.

Beat the egg whites to stiff peaks with an electric beater, then fold them carefully, so as not to knock out the air, into the batter. Scrape into a heatproof mixing bowl or soufflé dish so that the mixture comes about half way up the sides. Stand the basin in a roasting tin half filled with hot water, then carefully transfer it to the oven. Bake for an hour or so, until the top is puffed and golden – press it with your finger to test; it should feel spongy – cool for five minutes before serving.

and more

♦ **a lemon pudding.** Drop the oranges in favour of another two medium-sized lemons. If they are particularly juicy you may only need one.

♦ **a chocolate pudding.** Into a large bowl put 150g self-raising flour, 2 tablespoons cocoa powder, 200g light soft brown sugar, 100g roughly chopped fine, dark chocolate, 200ml milk, a large knob of butter, melted, and a beaten egg. Mix well, but not overly so. Pour into a buttered pudding basin. Mix together 75g dark soft brown sugar, 75g golden caster sugar and 100g cocoa powder and scatter it on top. Now pour in 400ml of almost boiling water. Put the pudding in a roasting tin of hot water and bake for thirty-five to forty minutes at 180°C/Gas 4.

♦ **a chocolate hazelnut pudding.** Add 50g finely chopped hazelnuts to the ingredients above.

♦ **to serve.** The tartness of the lemon and orange puddings and the obscene richness of the chocolate version are cooled by the addition of double cream. Serve it by the jugful. The idea is that it merges lusciously with the pudding's intense, integral sauce.

an appetite for
cake

a spectacular dessert for a special occasion

The joy of a pavlova is simply the contrast between the crisp meringue, soft cream and sweet-sharp fruit. That is why you need to ensure the meringue has a crisp crust and a deep marshmallow middle and why you really do need a sharp fruit. There is nothing that works as well as passion fruit with its slight acidity and the crunch of its seeds in the deep pile of cream. Avoid the temptation to crown the dessert with every fruit under the sun. To include sweet fruits here is missing the point. I don't hold with the notion that the meringue should be all foam and no crust, although that may be more traditional; I think you need some contrast to the obscenely thick layer of softly whipped cream.

Enough for 8–10

egg whites – 6 large free range
caster sugar – 350g
cornflour – 3 teaspoons
whipping cream – 300ml

Get the oven and baking tin ready before you start beating the egg whites. You will need a non-stick, 25cm diameter cake tin or deep tart tin. I use the mould I make tarte Tatin and most cakes in. Cut a piece of bakewell paper to fit the bottom, then smooth it into place. You don't need to do the sides, you can run a round-bladed knife around those. Set the oven at 180°C/Gas 4.

Separate the eggs, dropping the whites into the bowl of a food mixer, the yolks into a small bowl – you can make mayonnaise with them later. It is important, by the way, that you leave no yellow yolk in amongst the white. The fat in the egg yolk will stop the whites thickening. Beat the egg whites with a metal whisk until they are shiny, thick and well risen. This is best done with an electric mixer with a whisk attachment at moderate speed. You can do it in a mixing bowl with a hand whisk but I never think it comes up quite so well.

When the whites are thick and shiny, add the sugar. This is best done in two lots – just tip it in boldly, letting the whisk continue to turn at a moderate speed. You will hear the mixture start to thicken with the weight of the sugar. Keep whisking for a minute or so until it is thick and glossy. Overwhipping will soften its texture. You want the mixture to be so thick that it takes an age to slide off the whisk as you pull it out. Fold in the cornflour by hand, firmly but gently.

Scoop the meringue into the tin and bake in the preheated oven for an hour. Then turn off the heat, but do not open the oven door: simply leave the meringue alone until it is almost cool.

To fill your pavlova you need to get it out of its tin as best you can. It will crumble here and there but that will only add to its charm. The easiest way is to run a palette knife round the edge of the tin, then gently ease the meringue out. The quantity of cream for filling it may seem scary at first, but it is worth remembering that a little of this pudding goes a long way. You need to whip it into soft, voluptuous folds and pile it on top of the meringue.

and more

♦ **a passion fruit meringue.** The fruity sharpness of passion fruit makes it the perfect choice for topping the deep, snow-like waves of cream and meringue. Its crunchy seeds are a delightful and necessary contrast to the general mountain of softness. The fruits must be ripe, which means they should be heavy for their size, with crinkled, pitted skin. Cut them in half, then squeeze out every seed and bit of juice. Do this straight over the cream so that the juice sits in puddles in the furrows of the cream. You will need about 10–12 passion fruit for the quantity of meringue above.

♦ **a raspberry meringue.** If you cannot get passion fruit, or if the crunchy seeds bother you, I suggest you find some raspberries or, better still, loganberries. Their sharpness is a good second best for this job.

♦ **chocolate meringue.** This sounds like overkill but trust me. Imagine the gooey meringue and thick, soft cream covered with drizzles of crisp, paper-thin, bitter-sweet chocolate. This only works when the chocolate is the dark, suave variety and it sets to a crackling shell over the cream. Melt something dark and fruity, like Valrhona Manjari, in a mixing bowl set over hot water, then drizzle it over the cold cream and meringue. It will set to a crisp coat.

a simple cake to serve with summer fruit

Moist and fragrant, this is one of those endlessly useful cakes that can be eaten at tea or as a dessert. Shallow and pleasingly unfussy, it is perfect with poached fruit – especially pears, greengages, apricots or rhubarb – or with thick yogurt. It is absurdly easy to make and keeps like a dream.

Enough for 12 as a dessert with fruit

butter – 250g
caster sugar – 250g
a lemon – organic or unwaxed
ground almonds – 75g
plain flour – 100g
soft-dried apricots – 100g
eggs – 4 large free range, lightly beaten

You will also need a shallow 23cm cake tin, the base lined with baking parchment or greaseproof paper.

Set the oven at 180°C/Gas 4. Beat the butter and sugar in an electric mixer until white and fluffy. Grate the zest from the lemon and squeeze its juice. Mix the ground almonds and flour together, then whiz the apricots in a food processor until they are very finely chopped. They must be finer than candied peel – almost, but not quite a purée.

Add the eggs to the butter and sugar mixture a little at a time, with the beater on slow. Turn the machine off and add the lemon zest and a third of the almonds and flour, then turn the mixer on slow until the dry ingredients are incorporated. Add the second and then the third lot of almonds and flour, switching the machine off each time. If you do this too quickly you will end up with a heavy cake.

Lastly, with the machine still on slow, mix in the lemon juice and the apricots. Transfer the mixture to the lined cake tin with a rubber spatula, gently smoothing the top as you go, then bake until the cake is firm to the touch – about thirty-five minutes. Test the cake by inserting a thin metal skewer into the centre; if it comes out clean, without any wet cake mixture attached, then the cake is ready. If there is sticky batter on the skewer, bake a while longer.

After you take it from the oven, run a palette knife around the edge of the tin and turn the cake out on to sugared greaseproof paper. Peel off the lining paper, then flip the cake back again on to a plate. It is lovely served just slightly warm from the oven.

and more

- ♦ **making changes.** Despite being easy to follow, cake recipes do not take kindly to being tweaked and altered at the whim of the cook. Changes in the ratio of eggs to sugar to flour and so on will have a major effect, not just on the texture and flavour of the cake but also on its behaviour in the oven. Yet having said that, there is no reason why you cannot alter the flavourings of the blueprint cake recipe above to suit what you have around. Just leave the basic egg, sugar, flour quantities be.

- ♦ **a hazelnut cake.** Make this a more autumnal cake by swapping the almonds for ground hazelnuts, then serving it with pears poached in red wine.

- ♦ **an orange cake.** Use grated orange zest and juice instead of lemon to make the cake into something more suitable for serving with strawberries or raspberries.

- ♦ **a deeply citrus version.** If you want to make the cake more luscious, dredge it quite heavily with caster sugar, pouring over the juice of two oranges spiked with that of half a lemon.

- ♦ **a more fragrant version.** Add a teaspoon or two of orange-flower water to the juice, or mix a tablespoon of it into the cake mixture before you bake. The extra liquid will make little difference to the texture of the finished cake but will impart a faint, magical whiff of orange trees in flower.

- ♦ **an iced cake.** Make a few spoonfuls of thin white icing with icing sugar and a very little lemon and orange juice and leave it to run carelessly over the cake. A single candle would make this a charming, hand-made alternative to the Big Birthday Cake.

a big fruit cake

Of course, there are some wonderfully moist and deeply old-fashioned fruit cakes in the shops, so why, you may ask, should anyone want to make their own? My answer is simply that there is almost nothing that gives me more pleasure than offering someone a piece of cake I have made myself. Call it egotistical, or just plain showing off, but even though I am normally at my happiest cooking hot, spicy, savoury food, I really get a buzz from making a cake – a proper one, that is, none of that posh pâtisserie stuff. Ignore the unusually long ingredients list here and the mega baking time; you basically just mix all the ingredients together and chuck it in the oven. This is one of those absurdly useful cakes that you can turn to, trustingly, at Christmas, birthdays and any time you need a big fruit cake.

butter – 350g, at room temperature
soft dark brown sugar – 350g
dried fruits – ready-to-eat figs, prunes, apricots, candied peel, glacé cherries,
    1kg in total
eggs – 5 large free range
ground almonds – 100g
shelled hazelnuts – 150g
vine fruits – raisins, sultanas, currants, 500g in total
brandy – 5 tablespoons
the zest and juice of an orange and a lemon
baking powder – ½ teaspoon
plain flour – 350g

You will also need a 24cm cake tin with a removable base. Line it with buttered greaseproof paper, which should come 5cm above the top of the tin.

Set the oven to 160°C/Gas 3. Beat the butter and sugar till pale and fluffy. I needn't tell you that this is much easier in an electric mixer but I have occasionally done it by hand. Don't forget to push the mixture down the sides of the bowl from time to time with a spatula. While the butter and sugar are beating to a cappuccino-coloured fluff, cut the dried fruits into small pieces, removing the hard stalks from the figs. Add the eggs to the mixture one at a time – it will curdle but don't worry – then slowly mix in the ground almonds, hazelnuts, all the dried fruit, the brandy and the citrus zest and juice.

Now mix the baking powder and flour together and fold them lightly into the mix. Scrape the mixture into the prepared tin, smoothing the top gently, and put it in the oven. Leave it for an hour, then, without opening the oven door, turn down the heat to 150°C/Gas 2 and continue baking for two hours.

Check whether the cake is done by inserting a skewer – a knitting needle will do – into the centre. It should come out with just a few crumbs attached but no trace of raw cake mixture. Take the cake out of the oven and leave to cool before removing from the tin.

and more

◆ **a cranberry or cherry version.** The fruit content of the cake is something we can change at whim. So, if you don't like candied peel, for example, leave it out and bolster the mixture with an equal quantity of something else. Dried cranberries, perhaps, or simply more sultanas or cherries. The only rule is to keep the weight of fruit the same – what that fruit comprises, and the ratio of one fruit to another, is very much up to us.

◆ **a tropical fruit cake.** Although vine fruits are traditional in a rich fruit cake you could reasonably swap them for some of the dried tropical fruits around nowadays, such as papaya, banana and mango. They are less juicy than raisins or cherries, though, so it might be a good idea to soak them in brandy or orange juice for a few hours before you stir them into the cake.

◆ **a particularly juicy cake.** When you are changing ingredients it is worth remembering that cherries and dried apricots make a cake particularly juicy.

◆ **a boozy Christmas cake.** I like to make my Christmas cake a couple of weeks in advance and then ply it with alcohol to keep it moist and boozy. Brandy is the spirit I use, because I think its flavour works well with the fruit, but whisky would work, too. To get the booze into the cake, pierce the underside deeply with a knitting needle or skewer, then pour a little brandy into the holes. Wrap the cake tightly in greaseproof paper and then in foil or clingfilm and lower it into a tin. Covered, it will be fine for several weeks. I have had moist, flavoursome, but not too brandy-soaked results by feeding the cake every three or four days for a fortnight.

a great chocolate cake for family, friends, dessert, tea, birthdays…

If ever there was a recipe that embodied the spirit of this book it is this one. Appropriately it is the last. It started life as Tamasin Day-Lewis's wholewheat chocolate cake, which, incidentally, she had adapted from one of her cousin's. I had made it several times before (yes, it was that good) but I decided I wanted a coffee and chocolate cake, so one day I swapped the milk in her recipe for very strong coffee, and then put in some coarsely ground hazelnuts. I used plain flour instead of her wholemeal and as I had none of the muscovado sugar she suggested I used demerara instead. The result was quite different – in terms of texture, appearance and flavour – but I felt there was still a connection with her lovely recipe. Yet I had made something that was mine, something that fitted what I had an appetite for that day. And you can do that with almost any recipe and rarely come to grief. It is simply a question of having a little bit of confidence to put your own taste, ideas and appetite into practice.

Enough for 12

butter – 250g
demerara sugar – 250g
eggs – 4 large free range
espresso coffee – a small one, or about 3 tablespoons
plain flour – 250g
baking powder – 2 gently heaped teaspoons
skinned hazelnuts – 200g, coarsely ground
fine, dark chocolate – 250g, coarsely chopped (it should look like gravel)

You will also need a 23cm cake tin with a loose bottom and preferably with spring-clip sides. This is simply to make it easier getting the cake out of the tin. Line the base with greaseproof paper or baking parchment; I suggest you do this even if the cake tin is non-stick.

Set the oven at 180°C/Gas 4. Beat the butter and sugar till they are fluffy and pale. The easiest way to do this is with an electric beater of some sort. I have, in the past, done it by hand but it is seriously hard work, even with the butter at room temperature. Add the eggs one at a time, beating lightly between each addition. You may find the mixture curdles a little but don't worry, it will come good in the end. Stir in the coffee.

Sift in the flour and baking powder and fold them in, then fold in most of the hazelnuts and the chopped chocolate, keeping a little back for the top of the cake. The mixture should be quite firm; you may have to slide it off the spoon with your finger. Put it into the lined cake tin and gently smooth the top, scattering over the last of the chocolate and nuts.

Bake for an hour and twenty minutes or until the cake is springy, testing for doneness by spearing the centre with a skewer. It should come out without any raw cake mixture on it. Leave for half an hour or so before cutting. It is at its best slightly warm.

and more

♦ **some variations.** You can make a few changes to this recipe without coming unstuck. Walnuts and almonds, the latter lightly toasted, could be used instead of the hazelnuts. You could add the finely grated zest of a small orange or even some finely chopped fruit such as dried apricots (they work well with chocolate) or some stoned ready-to-eat prunes.

441

the art of washing up

Dinner is gone and there is the contented murmur of a full dishwasher from somewhere behind you in the kitchen. Everyone is fed. You have put the leftovers in the fridge to pick at much later, silently, secretly, when everyone else has gone to bed. (No matter how beautiful a laid table looks, there is much solace to be had eating in the dark, the room lit only by the light from the open fridge.) This is when I curl up in a squashy chair, my feet tucked under me, to finish off the wine and to read or watch something unchallenging, trashy. I would honestly rather part with my television, my stereo, possibly even the odd relative, than lose my dishwasher.

I have met those who tell me they enjoy washing up by hand. I can see the appeal of dipping your hands in hot, soapy water. I don't, after all, put everything in the dishwasher. I do see how it could be faintly relaxing, especially if you have got the water to the perfect temperature and were to take your time over it, rather than rush at it just to get it done. As much as I adore the warm stainless steel of a hot dishwasher, I do like the paraphernalia of washing up: the old-fashioned wooden brushes that a friend's mother sends down from her shop in Carlisle; the French string pot-scrubbers that I buy from the most beautiful kitchen shop in London; the old, soft, honey-coloured linen tea-towels that have done years of service, not to mention the froth of bubbles of the same brand of washing-up liquid my mother always used.

There is much satisfaction in getting things clean, in basking in the moment when everyone is quiet and the dishes are shining in their cupboard (am I alone in loving my dishwasher but hating, absolutely loathing, emptying it when it's finished?). The great thing about having done the washing up is the feeling of calm and quiet accomplishment that goes with it. You have made yourself and others something nice to eat. You can close down, check out, sign off ... until breakfast.

442

so what do you want to eat today?